Quantitative Models
for Project Planning,
Scheduling, and Control

Quantitative Models for Project Planning, Scheduling, and Control

Adedeji Bodunde Badiru

Q

Quorum Books
Westport, Connecticut • London

Library of Congress Cataloging-in-Publication Data

Badiru, Adedeji Bodunde, 1952-
   Quantitative models for project planning, scheduling, and control /
Adedeji Bodunde Badiru.
      p.   cm.
   Includes bibliographical references and index.
   ISBN 0-89930-730-2 (alk. paper)
   1. Industrial project management—Planning—Mathematical models.
I. Title.
   HD69.P75B33   1993
   658.4′04—dc20   92-34377

British Library Cataloguing in Publication Data is available.

Library of Congress Catalog Card Number: 92-34377
ISBN: 0-89930-730-2

First published in 1993

Quorum Books, 88 Post Road West, Westport, CT 06881
An imprint of Greenwood Publishing Group, Inc.

Printed in the United States of America

The paper used in this book complies with the
Permanent Paper Standard issued by the National
Information Standards Organization (Z39.48-1984).

10 9 8 7 6 5 4 3 2 1

To Dr. Sid G. Gilbreath and Dr. Gary E. Whitehouse,
whose guiding lights continue to shine on me

CONTENTS

ACKNOWLEDGMENTS

I gratefully acknowledge the help and support of all my colleagues in the School of Industrial Engineering at the University of Oklahoma. I thank Eric Valentine, the publisher of Quorum Books, for his expeditious handling of the publication of the book. I also thank the entire staff of Greenwood Publishing Group for their excellent job throughout the production process. Special thanks go to the copy editor, Bayard VanHecke, and the production editor, William Neenan. I thank all members of my family for their continuing understanding and support throughout the many nights I spent with my computer in the preparation of the manuscript.

PREFACE

The tools for project management can be classified into three major categories:

1. Qualitative Tools
2. Computer Tools
3. Quantitative Tools

Numerous books exist on the qualitative aspects of managing projects. The computer tools for project management have also received extensive coverage in the literature. Unfortunately, very few books have been published specifically on the quantitative tools for project management. Quantitative tools are just as important as other tools for project planning, scheduling, and control.

Quantitative models suitable for project management applications are scattered in diverse publications that do not necessarily focus on project management. Thus, readers who need quantitative techniques for project management have to refer to several publications to assemble the desired materials. The materials thus assembled often present disjointed views, since their original focus is not project management. Consequently, the teaching of advanced topics in project management typically suffers from a lack of suitable textbooks.

At the undergraduate level, project management is normally covered as a brief section in another course (e.g., operations research). Even then, the treatment is limited to the basic CPM and PERT network analysis. Many graduate schools now offer project management degree programs. Many schools that don't offer degree programs do offer dedicated graduate level project management courses. These project management programs and courses can benefit from a quantitatively oriented project management textbook. Traditionally, the life cycle of a project covers the following items:

Need Analysis
Problem Definition
Specification of Project Requirements
Proposal Development/Evaluation
Bid Analysis and Vendor Selection
Cost Analysis
Project Approval
Contract Development
Organization of Project Team
Design Specification and Approval
Project Initiation
Project Scheduling, Monitoring, and Control
Transfer to End User
Project Phase-out
Post-Project Support and Maintenance

All the elements above require quantitative analysis. This book presents a unified collection of quantitative techniques for project management. The primary targets for the book are graduate level courses related to project planning, scheduling, and control. It should also appeal to project management professionals, managers, R&D engineers, consultants, and researchers interested in advanced topics in project management. Students will find that the book provides a concise, unified treatment of quantitative tools available for project management.

Topics covered include PERT/CPM/PDM and extensions, mathematical project scheduling, heuristic project scheduling, project economics, statistical data analysis for project planning, computer simulation, assignment and transportation problems, and learning curve analysis.

Chapter 1 gives a brief overview of project management. Chapter 2 covers CPM, PERT, and PDM network techniques. Chapter 3 covers project scheduling subject to resource constraints. Chapter 4 covers project optimization. Chapter 5 discusses economic analysis for project planning and control. Chapter 6 covers learning curve analysis. Chapter 7 covers statistical data analysis for project planning and control. Chapter 8 presents techniques for project analysis and selection. Numerous tables and figures are used throughout the book to enhance the effectiveness of the discussions. An extensive bibliography is presented at the end of the book for the reader's further reference.

Adedeji B. Badiru
Norman, Oklahoma

Quantitative Models for Project Planning, Scheduling, and Control

CHAPTER 1

INTRODUCTION TO
PROJECT MANAGEMENT

Project management is the process of managing, allocating, and timing resources to achieve a given goal in an efficient and expedient manner. The objectives that constitute the specified goal may be in terms of time, costs, or technical results. A project can be quite simple or very complex. An example of a simple project is painting a small, vacant room. An example of a complex project is launching a space shuttle.

Project management techniques are used widely in many enterprises, including construction, banking, manufacturing, marketing, health care services, transportation, R&D, public services, and so on. The standard hierarchy of the elements of project consists of system, program, project, task, and activity.

System: A project system consists of interrelated elements organized for the purpose of achieving a common goal. The elements are expected to work synergistically together to generate a unified output that is greater than the sum of the individual outputs of the components.

Program: A program is a very large and prolonged undertaking. Typically, such project endeavors span several years. Programs are usually associated with particular systems, for example, a space exploration program within a national defense system.

Project: A project is a time-phased effort of much smaller scope and duration than a program. Programs are sometimes viewed as consisting of a set of projects, but practitioners often refer to both without distinction. Government projects are often called *programs* because of their broad and comprehensive nature. The industrial sector, on the other hand, tends to use the term *project* because of the short-term and focused nature of most industrial efforts.

Task: A task is a functional element of a project. A project is normally composed of contiguous arrays of tasks that all contribute to the overall project goal.

Activity: An activity can be defined as a single element of a project. Activities are generally smaller in scope than tasks. In a detailed analysis of a project, an activity may be viewed as the smallest, practically indivisible work element of the project. For example, we can regard a manufacturing plant as a system. A plant-wide endeavor to improve productivity can be viewed as a program. The installation of a flexible manufacturing system is a project within the productivity improvement program. The process of identifying and selecting equipment vendors is a task, and the actual process of placing an order with a preferred vendor is an activity. Figure 1-1 presents the functional and hierarchical relationships between the components of a project.

Figure 1-1. Hierarchy of Project Components

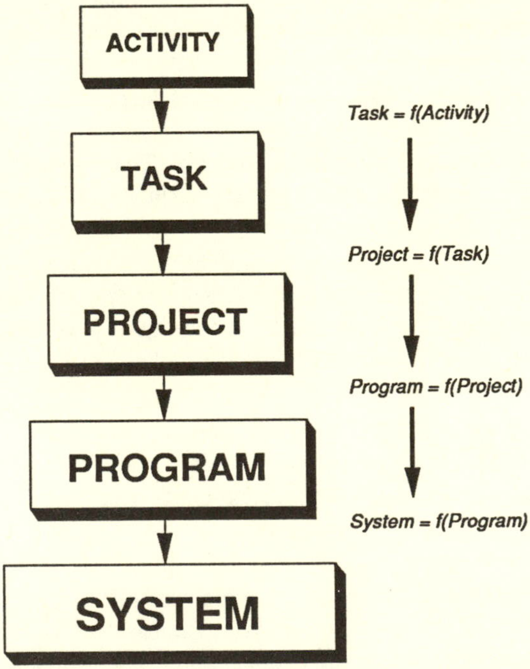

The techniques of project management can help achieve goals relating to better product quality, improved resource utilization, better customer relations, higher productivity, and fulfillment of due dates. These can generally be expressed in terms of the following project constraints:

- *Performance Specifications*
- *Schedule Requirements*
- *Cost Limitations*

STEPS OF PROJECT MANAGEMENT

Figure 1-2 presents the major steps in project management. The life cycle of a project typically consists of several steps going from problem identification, definition, planning (specifications and project formulation), organizing, resource allocation, scheduling, tracking and reporting, and control to project termination. The steps are typically performed strategically in accordance with the specified project goal. These steps are discussed briefly below; some are discussed in further detail in subsequent sections.

Figure 1-2. Steps of Project Planning, Scheduling, and Control

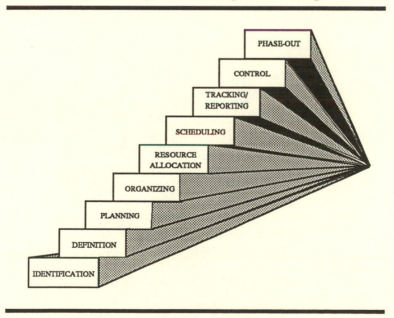

Problem Identification

This is the stage where a need for a proposed project is identified, defined, and justified. A project may be concerned with the development of new products, implementation of new processes, or improvement of existing facilities.

Project Definition

This is the phase at which the purpose of the project is clarified. A *mission statement* is the major output of this stage. For example, a prevailing low level of productivity may trigger a need for a new CIM technology. In general, the definition should specify how project management may be used to avoid missed deadlines, poor scheduling, inadequate resource allocation, lack of coordination, poor quality, and conflicting priorities.

Project Planning

Project planning determines how to initiate a project and execute its objectives. Because of its need for extensive coverage, project planning is discussed in detail in a subsequent section of this chapter.

Project Organizing

Project organization specifies how to integrate the functions of the personnel involved in a project. Organizing is normally done concurrently with project planning. Directing is an important aspect of project organization. Directing involves guiding and supervising the project personnel. It is a crucial aspect of the management function. Directing requires skillful managers who can interact with subordinates effectively through good communication and motivation techniques. A successful manager improves the performance of his subordinates by directing them, through proper task assignments, toward the project goal. Workers perform better when there are clearly defined expectations. They need to know how their job functions contribute to the overall goals of the project. Workers should be given some flexibility for self-direction in performing their functions. Individual worker needs and limitations should be recognized by the manager when directing project functions. Project directing consists of the following elements:

Approach: Development of a method of approach (communication or otherwise) to subordinates at various levels and in different situations.

Supervising: Monitoring, guiding, and reviewing of the day-to-day activities of subordinates with respect to the project goal.

Delegating: Assignment of responsibility or secondary authority to subordinates for the execution of certain functions so as to enhance the utilization of manpower resources.

Motivating: Boosting the morale and interest of subordinates in performing their jobs. This requires understanding the needs, motives, and feelings of subordinates and an appreciation for the nature of their responses to certain directives.

Resource Allocation

Project goals and objectives are accomplished by applying resources to functional requirements. Resources, in the context of project management, are generally made up of people and equipment, which are typically in short supply. The people needed for a particular task may be committed to other ongoing projects. A crucial piece of equipment may be under the control of a competitor.

Project Scheduling

Scheduling is often recognized as the major function in project management. The main purpose of scheduling is to allocate resources so that the overall project objectives are achieved within a reasonable time span. In general, scheduling involves the assignment of time periods to specific tasks within the work schedule. Resource availability, time limitations, urgency level, required performance level, precedence requirements, work priorities, technical constraints, and other factors complicate the scheduling process. Thus, the assignment of a time slot to a task does not necessarily ensure that the task will be performed satisfactorily in accordance with the schedule. Consequently, careful control must be developed and maintained throughout the project scheduling process. A separate section of this chapter is devoted to further discussion of project scheduling. Many of the quantitative models presented in this book relate to achieving better project schedules.

Project Tracking and Reporting

This phase involves the process of checking whether or not project results conform to plans and specifications. Tracking and reporting are prerequisites for project control. A properly organized report of the project status will quickly identify the deficiencies in the progress of the project and help pinpoint necessary corrective actions.

Project Control

In this function, necessary actions are taken to correct unacceptable deviations from expected performance. Control is effected by measurement, evaluation, and corrective action. Measurement is the process of measuring the relationship between planned performance and actual performance with respect to project objectives. The variables to be measured, the measurement scales, and the measuring approaches should be clearly specified during the planning stage.

Project Phase Out

This is the last stage of a project. The phase out is as important as the initiation. The termination of a project should be implemented expeditiously. A project should not be allowed to drag on after the expected completion time. A terminal activity should be defined for a project during the planning phase. An example of a terminal activity may be the submission of a final report, the "power-on" of new equipment, or the signing of a release order. The conclusion of such an activity should be viewed as the completion of the project. To prevent a project from dragging on needlessly, strict directives should be issued about when it will end. However, provisions should be made for follow-up activities that may improve the results of the project. These follow-up or spin-off projects should be managed as totally separate projects but with proper input-output relationships within the sequence of projects. If a project is not terminated when appropriate, the motivation for it will wane and subsequent activities may become counterproductive. This is particularly true for technology-based projects where the "fear of the unknown" and "resistance to change" are already major obstacles.

PROJECT ORGANIZATION STRUCTURES

Project organization structures may be selected on the basis of functional specializations, departmental proximity, standard management boundaries, organizational policies, operational relationships, or product requirements.

Formal and Informal Organization

A formal organization is an officially sanctioned structure within an organization. An informal organization develops when people organize in an unofficial way to accomplish an objective that is in line with the overall project goal. Such an informal organization is often very subtle in that not everyone in the general organization is aware of its existence. Even some of those who are aware of its existence may not be welcome to participate in it. Friends and close associates often organize informally to pursue project goals. Both formal and informal modes of organization are practiced in any organization, even those that have strict hierarchical structures, such as the military.

Functional Organization

Projects that are organized along functional lines are normally found in some departmental area of specialization. That is, the project is located in a specific department. For example, projects that involve manufacturing operations may be under the direction of the vice-president of manufacturing, while a project involving new technology may be assigned to the technology development department. Functional organization is the most common type of formal organization. The advantages of functional organization are:

- Flexibility in manpower utilization
- Improved productivity of specially skilled personnel
- Enhanced comradeship of technical staff
- Potential for staff advancement along functional lines
- Improved accountability
- Clear lines of control

The disadvantages of functional organization are:

- Conflict between project objectives and regular functions
- Overlap in project responsibilities, for example, conduct of similar quality control projects by different departments
- Potential for unreceptive attitude toward the project by the participating departments
- Multiple layers of management between the project personnel and the beneficiaries of the project

- Lack of concentrated effort (divided attention between project tasks and regular tasks)

Product Organization

Another approach to organizing a project is to use the end product or goal of the project as the determining factor for the organization structure. This is often referred to as the product organization. The project is set up as a unique entity within the parent organization. It has its own dedicated technical staff and administration. It is linked to the rest of the organization through progress reports, organizational policies, procedures, and funding. The interface between product organized projects and other elements of the organization may be strict or liberal depending on the organization.

Product organization is common in large project-driven organizations. Unlike the other organization structures, product organization decentralizes functions. It creates a group consisting of specialized skills around a given task. The project group is sometimes referred to as a team or a task force. Product organization is also common in public and research organizations where specially organized and designated groups are assigned specific functions. A major advantage of product organization is that it gives the project members a feeling of dedication to and identification with a particular project goal. A possible shortcoming is the requirement that the project group be sufficiently funded to be able to operate independently without sharing resources or personnel with other functional groups or programs. At the conclusion of a project, the project team may be reassigned to other projects. Product organization can facilitate the most diverse and flexible grouping of project participants and permits highly dedicated attention to the project at hand. The advantages of product organization are:

- Full control by the project manager
- Direct responsibility of the project members to the project manager (one boss)
- Condensation of communication lines
- Skill development due to project specialization
- Improved motivation, commitment, and concentration
- Quicker decisions due to centralized authority
- Improved morale resulting from belonging to a given project
- Simplicity of structure
- Unity of project purpose

The disadvantages of product organization are:

- Duplication of effort on different but similar projects
- Monopoly of organizational resources
- Mutually exclusive allocation of resources (one person to one project)
- Narrow view of project personnel (as opposed to global organization view)
- Reduced skill diversification
- Concern about new job assignment after the project
- Need for a consistent source of project funding

Matrix Organization

Matrix organization represents a mixture of project organization and functional organization. It permits both vertical and horizontal flows of information. The matrix model is sometimes called a multiple-boss organization. It is a model that is becoming increasingly popular as the need for resource sharing increases. Engineering projects, for example, require the integration of specialized skills from different functional areas. Under matrix organization, projects are permitted to share physical resources as well as managerial assets.

A matrix organization is suitable where there is multiple managerial accountability and responsibility for a job function. There are usually two chains of command, horizontal and vertical, dealing with functional and project lines. The project line in the matrix is usually of a temporary nature, while the functional line is more permanent. The matrix organization is quite dynamic, with its actual structure being determined by the prevailing project scenarios. The matrix organization has several advantages and some disadvantages. The advantages are:

- Consolidation of objectives: The objectives of the task at hand are jointly shared and pursued by multiple departments.
- Efficient utilization of resources: The allocation of company resources is more streamlined. Manpower and equipment can be allocated at the most suitable usage level jointly among departments working toward a common goal.
- Free flow of information: Since departments are cooperating rather than competing, there is an unhindered flow of common information both vertically and horizontally in the matrix structure.

- Interpersonal contacts: The joint responsibility for projects creates an atmosphere of functional compatibility. Good working relationships that develop under one matrix structure become useful in other projects.
- High morale: The success achieved on one project effort motivates workers to cooperate on other projects.
- Lateral functional interactions: The multiple responsibility for projects allows workers to be exposed to other functional activities and, thereby, permits smooth transition to other departments should that become necessary.
- Post-project interactions: The matrix structure allows continuity of functions after project conclusion. The functional departments simply redirect their efforts to other responsibilities. Unlike a project organization structure, where project shutdown could necessitate layoffs, the matrix structure makes a provision for returning to regular responsibilities.

The disadvantages of the matrix organization are:

- Multiple bosses: A major disadvantage of the matrix structure is the fact that workers report to two bosses on a given project. Playing one boss against another is a potential problem in a matrix structure.
- Power struggle: A power struggle between the bosses may adversely affect the performance of the project personnel.
- Complexity of structure: The number of managers and personnel involved in a given project can easily be confusing. Difficulties can arise with respect to monitoring and controlling personnel activities. Other potential problems are obstruction of information, slow response time, difficulty in resolving conflicts, unclear channels for supervision, and incompatibility of policies and procedures.
- Overhead cost: By doubling up the chain of command, the matrix structure leads to higher interdepartmental and intradepartmental overhead costs. However, as productivity gains are realized, the overhead costs may become negligible.
- Conflicting priorities: Since multiple responsibilities is a major characteristic of a matrix organization, it is sometimes difficult to determine which responsibility has higher priority. Each functional manager may view his own direct responsibilities as having higher priority than other project responsibilities.

Despite its disadvantages, the matrix organization is widely used. Its numerous advantages tend to outweigh the disadvantages. Besides, the disadvantages can be overcome with proper planning and coordination. This can be achieved through the Triple C model, discussed later in this chapter.

Mixed Organization

Another possibility for organizing a project is to adopt some combined implementation of functional, product, and matrix models. This permits a combination of the advantages of the various organization structures. The mixed model facilitates flexibility in meeting special problem situations. The structure can adapt to the prevailing needs of the project or the organization. However, a disadvantage is the difficulty in identifying lines of responsibility within a given project.

Selecting The Project Manager

A *project manager* is needed to direct the functional groups within the project organizational structure. The project manager has the overall responsibility for supervising the project planning, scheduling, and control functions. He or she must be very versatile with a broad range of knowledge covering analytical as well as managerial skills. The project manager must have both the power and authority to effectively pursue project goals within the confines of the prevailing project organizational structure. When selecting a project manager, several desirable characteristics and factors must be considered. These characteristics and factors include:

- Analytical and technical background
- Communication skills
- Leadership and managerial skills
- Availability, accessibility, and attentiveness
- Rapport with subordinates, peers, and top management
- Inquisitiveness
- Ability to be a motivator and a facilitator
- Familiarity with company operations

- Overall personality
- Perseverance
- Technical and administrative credibility

WORK BREAKDOWN STRUCTURE

Project decomposition and work simplification are important for enhancing project planning, scheduling, and control. A graphical tool for decomposing complex projects into a manageable structure is the work breakdown structure (WBS). A work breakdown structure is a hierarchical organization of the work elements contained in a project. Tasks that are contained in the WBS collectively describe the overall project. The WBS serves to describe the link between the end objective and the intermediate tasks. It shows work elements in a conceptual framework for planning, scheduling, and control. The objective of developing a WBS is to study the elemental components of a project in detail. It permits the implementation of the "divide and conquer" concepts. Overall project planning and control are substantially improved by using WBS. A large project may be broken down into smaller subprojects which may, in turn, be decomposed into task groups.

Individual components in a WBS are referred to as WBS elements, and the hierarchy of each is designated by a level identifier. Elements at the same level of subdivision are said to be of the same WBS level. Descending levels provide increasingly detailed definition of project tasks. The complexity of a project and the degree of control desired will determine the number of levels in the WBS. The graphical structure of a WBS is similar to an organization chart, with different levels associated with different levels of detail about a project. The basic approach to developing a WBS is presented below:

Level 1: Level 1 contains only the final project purpose.

Level 2: Level 2 contains the major phases or subsections of the project. These phases are usually identified by their contiguous location or by their related purpose.

Level 3: Level 3 contains definable components of the level 2 phases.

Subsequent levels are constructed in more specific detail depending on the level of control desired. If a complete WBS is very large, separate WBS diagrams may be drawn for the level 2 components. A specification of work (SOW) or WBS summary should accompany the WBS. A statement of work is a narrative of the work to be done. It should include the objectives of the work, its nature, resource requirements, and tentative schedule. Each WBS element is assigned a code that is used for its identification throughout the project life cycle. Alphanumeric codes may be used to indicate element level as well as task group. The U.S. Department of Energy (DOE, 1981) published a detailed guide for the preparation of a work breakdown structure. Interested readers should consult the reference for further details. The various management phases of a project can be condensed into three major functions of *planning, scheduling,* and *control.* In this book, various quantitative models are presented for project planning, scheduling, and control.

PROJECT PLANNING

Project planning determines the nature of actions and responsibilities needed to achieve the project goal. It entails the development of alternate courses of action and the selection of the best action to achieve the objectives making up the goal. Planning determines what needs to be done, by whom, for whom, and when. Whether it is done for long-range (strategic) purposes or short-range (operational) purposes, planning should address the following components:

1. Project goal and objectives. This involves the specification of what must be accomplished at each stage of the project.

2. Technical and managerial approach. This involves the determination of the technical and managerial strategies to be employed in pursuing the project goal.

3. Resource availability. This requires the allocation of resources for carrying out the actions needed to achieve the project goal.

4. Project schedule. This involves a logical and time-based organization of the tasks and milestones contained in the project. The schedule is typically influenced by resource limitations.

5. Contingency plan and replanning. This involves the identification of auxiliary actions to be taken in case of unexpected developments in the project.

6. Project policy. This involves specifying the general guidelines for carrying out tasks within the project.

7. Project procedure. This involves specifying the detailed method for implementing a given policy relative to the tasks needed to achieve the project goal.

8. Performance standard. This involves the establishment of a minimum acceptable level of quality for the products of the project.

9. Tracking, reporting, and auditing. These involve keeping track of the project plans, evaluating tasks, and scrutinizing the records of the project.

Strategic Levels of Planning

Badiru (1991a) outlined the strategic levels of planning. Decisions involving strategic planning lay the foundation for successful implementation of projects. Planning forms the basis for all actions. Strategic decisions may be divided into three strategy levels of *supra level planning, macro level planning,* and *micro level planning:*

Supra Level Planning: Planning at this level deals with the big picture of how the project fits the overall and long-range organizational goals. Questions faced at this level concern potential contributions of the project to the welfare of the organization, effect on the depletion of company resources, required interfaces with other projects within and outside the organization, risk exposure, management support for the project, concurrent projects, company culture, market share, shareholder expectations, and financial stability.

Macro Level Planning: Planning decisions at this level address the overall planning within the project boundary. The scope of the project and its operational interfaces should be addressed at this level. Questions faced at the macro level include goal definition, project scope, availability of qualified personnel, resource availability, project policies, communication interfaces, budget requirements, goal interactions, deadline, and conflict resolution strategies.

Micro Level Planning: This deals with detailed operational plans at the task levels of the project. Definite and explicit tactics for accomplishing specific project objectives are developed at the micro level. The concept of MBO (management by objective) may be particularly effective at this level. MBO permits each project member to plan his or own work at the micro level. Factors to be considered at the micro level of project decisions include scheduled time, training requirement, tools required, task procedures, reporting requirements, and quality requirements.

Project decisions at the three levels defined above will involve numerous personnel within the organization with various types and levels of expertise. In addition to the conventional roles of the project manager, specialized roles may be developed within the project scope. Such roles include the following:

1. *Technical specialist*: This person will have responsibility for addressing specific technical requirements of the project. In a large project, there will typically be several technical specialists working together to solve project problems.

2. *Operations integrator*: This person will be responsible for making sure that all operational components of the project interface correctly to satisfy project goals. This person should have good technical awareness and excellent interpersonal skills.

3. *Project specialist*: This person has specific expertise related to the specific goals and requirements of the project. Even though a technical specialist may also serve as a project specialist, the two roles should be distinguished. A general electrical engineer may be a technical specialist on the electronic design components of a project. However, if the specific setting of the electronics project is in the medical field, then an electrical engineer with expertise in medical operations may be needed to serve as the project specialist.

Project organization is a crucial component of project planning. Organizing a project involves determining the interfaces needed among personnel in order to assure a dedicated pursuit of the project goal. It involves the determination of what activities should be performed in what functional areas and under what supervisory hierarchy. Staffing is a component of organizing. Staffing is the process of defining the required personnel and the assignment of the personnel to appropriate functions with respect to the project goal. The staffing process may include hiring new people, reassignment of existing personnel, training or retraining, and realignment of responsibilities.

The Triple C model presented by Badiru (1987) is particularly useful for organizing a project. The model states that project management can be enhanced by implementing it within the integrated functions of:

- Communication
- Cooperation
- Coordination

The model facilitates a systematic approach to project planning, organizing, scheduling, and control. The Triple C principle is different from the 3C approach commonly used in the military. The military approach emphasizes personnel management in the hierarchy of command, control, and communication. This makes communication the last function. The Triple C, by contrast, suggests communication as the first and foremost function.

Communication

The communication function of project management involves making all those concerned aware of project requirements and progress. Those who will be affected by the project directly or indirectly, as participants or as recipients, should be informed as appropriate regarding the following:

- What is the project?
- Why is the project needed?
- Who is in charge of the project?
- What alternatives are available?
- What is the expected cost of the project?
- What penalties are associated with the project?
- Who will be affected by the failure of the project?
- What are the possible negative impacts of the project?
- What are the potential direct and indirect benefits?
- What precedents are available for the project?
- Who else already knows about the project?
- What personnel contribution is needed?
- When will the project be implemented?
- How will the project be organized?
- What is the project scope?

The communication channel must be kept open throughout the project life cycle. In addition to in-house communication, external sources should also be consulted as appropriate. The project manager must:

- Exude commitment to the project
- Develop a communication responsibility matrix
- Facilitate multichannel communication interfaces
- Identify internal and external communication needs
- Resolve organizational and communication hierarchies
- Endorse both formal and informal communication links

Cooperation

The cooperation of the project personnel must be explicitly elicited. Merely signing off on or giving a nod to a project is not enough assurance of full cooperation. The participants in and customers of the project must be convinced of the merits of the project. Some of the factors that influence cooperation in a project environment include manpower requirements, resource requirements, budget limitations, past experiences, conflicting priorities, and lack of uniform organizational support. A structured approach to seeking cooperation should clarify the following:

- The rewards of cooperation
- What cooperative efforts are needed
- The implications of lack of cooperation
- The criticality of cooperation to the project
- What time frame is involved for the project
- The organizational impact of cooperation
- The precedents for future projects

A documentation of the prevailing level of cooperation is useful for winning further support for a project. Clarification of project priorities will facilitate personnel cooperation. Relative priorities of multiple projects should be specified so that a project that is of high priority to the organization is also of high priority to all groups within the organization.

Coordination

After successfully initiating the communication and cooperation functions, the efforts of the project personnel must be coordinated. Coordination facilitates harmonious organization of project efforts. The development of a responsibility chart can be very helpful at this stage. A responsibility chart is a matrix consisting of columns of individual or functional departments and rows of required actions. Cells within the matrix are filled with relationship codes that indicate who is responsible for what. The responsibility chart helps to avoid neglecting crucial communication requirements and obligations. It can help resolve questions such as:

- Who is to do what?
- Who is to inform whom of what?
- Whose approval is needed for what?
- Who is responsible for which results?
- What personnel interfaces are involved?
- What support is needed from whom and when?

Management By Objective

Management by objective (MBO) is the management concept whereby the worker is allowed to take responsibility for the design and performance of a task under general guidelines. It is a planning tool that gives each worker a chance to set his own objectives in achieving project goals. The worker can monitor his own progress and take corrective actions when needed without explicit management intervention. Self-motivated workers seem to be best suited for the application of the MBO concept.   The advantages of MBO include:

1. It encourages the worker to find better ways of performing the assigned tasks.
2. It avoids over-supervision of self-motivated workers.
3. It raises the awareness of the worker about organizational goals and expectations.
4. It permits timely feedback on worker performance.

However, MBO does have some disadvantages, which include possible abuse of the freedom to self-direct and possible disruption of overall project coordination.

Management By Exception

Management by exception (MBE) is an after-the-fact management approach to control. Contingency plans are not made and there is no strict monitoring of performance. Deviations from expectations are considered exceptions to the rule. When unacceptable deviations from plans occur, they are investigated, and only then is an action taken. The concept is also often referred to as management by crisis or crisis management. The irony of MBE is that managers that operate under crisis management are often recognized as superstars because they solve problems whenever they develop. On the other hand, managers that prevent problems may be viewed as inactive because they are rarely seen solving problems. The major advantage of MBE is that it lessens the management workload. However, it is a risky concept to follow. Management should work toward avoiding problems rather than exposing the organization to potentially expensive crisis management actions. A manager who operates under the notion of "if it is not broken, don't fix it" will never have the opportunity to improve the managerial process.

PROJECT SCHEDULING

Project scheduling is a major function in project management. The project schedule shows the timing of the efforts and resources committed to the project. A master schedule for the overall project is often developed for general overview of a project. In addition, detailed work schedules are developed for specific segments or phases of the project. The detailed schedules serve as operating guides for the project personnel.

Project scheduling should be distinguished from sequencing and scheduling in production management even though the same principles and procedures are applicable to both. Production sequencing involves ordering of operations on each machine (resource) so as to satisfy the sequence of operations required by a job. A sequence of operations on a job may require that the same type of operation be performed on the same job (or product) at different times while the job is in production. This may necessitate repeated routing of the job to the same machine (or resource center) at different times. Production scheduling provides a basis for determining when a job is routed from machine to machine for specific operations. This establishes the starting and finishing times of each operation. Production sequencing and scheduling involve developing relative priorities of operations at each machine in order to meet scheduled due dates of individual jobs. The method of prioritizing jobs is often referred to as the *dispatching rule* for sending jobs to resource centers. In production management, sequencing and scheduling are performed as complementary functions.

By contrast, project scheduling deals strictly with the timing of tasks that must be performed in a project. This does not require a machine sequencing process. Even when a task requires multiple performance of the same action, each occurrence of the action is viewed as an activity that must be scheduled separately. Thus, project scheduling is a simplied form of the production scheduling problem. Project scheduling can be carried out as the specific means through which the tasks involved in production management are scheduled and accomplished. Project scheduling involves the following functions.

- Time and Resource Estimation: Estimates are made of the time and resources required to perform each of the network activities.

- Basic Scheduling: The basic scheduling computations are performed on a project network by using forward pass and backward pass computational procedures. These computations give the earliest and latest start and finish times for each activity. Schedule management often involves performing time-cost trade-off analysis. The scheduling procedure makes use of tools such as CPM (Critical Path Method), PERT (Program Evaluation and Review Technique), and Gantt charts. These are discussed in detail in chapter 2.

- Time-Cost Trade-offs: In this function, the time-cost trade-off analysis of activity performance times is conducted to determine the cost of reducing the project duration.

- Resource Allocation: Constrained resource allocation refers to the process of allocating limited resources to competing activities in a project. Scheduling heuristics or mathematical allocation models are used in allocating the limited resources during the scheduling phase. A data base of resource availability (see chapter 3) should be developed for each project prior to starting the scheduling process.

- Resource Loading and Leveling: Resource loading develops the profile of the resource units allocated over time. Resource leveling refers to the process of shifting activities to reduce the period-to-period fluctuations in resource requirements.

- Schedule Control: When the network plan and schedule have been satisfactorily developed, they are disseminated in final form for operational use. The schedule is tracked and controlled by comparing actual status to expected status at selected review times. Schedule tracking facilitates frequent review and revision of the project plan.

PROJECT CONTROL

Time, cost, and performance form the basis for the operating characteristics of a project. These factors help to determine the basis for project control. Project control is the process of reducing the deviation between actual performance and planned performance. To control a project, we must be able to measure performance. Measurements are taken on each of the three project constraints of time, performance, and cost as shown in Figure 1-3.

Figure 1-3. Components of Project Control

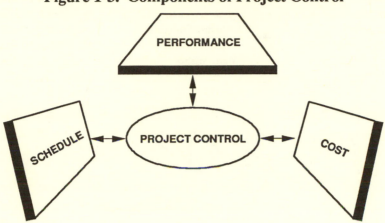

Performance may be expressed in terms of quality, productivity, or any other measure of interest. Cost may be expressed in terms of resource expenditure or budget requirements. Schedule is typically expressed in terms of the timing of activities and the expected project duration. It is impossible to achieve an optimal simultaneous satisfaction of all three project constraints. Consequently, it becomes necessary to compromise one constraint in favor of another. Figure 1-4 presents a model of the trade-offs between performance, time, and resource (cost).

Better performance can be achieved if more time and resources are available for a project. If lower costs and tighter schedules are desired, then performance may have to be compromised and vice versa. From the point of view of the project manager, the project should be at the highest point along the performance axis. Of course, this represents an extreme case of getting something for nothing. From the point of view of the project personnel, the project should be at the point indicating highest performance, longest time, and most resources. This, of course, may be an unrealistic expectation since time and resources are typically in short supply. Thus, a feasible trade-off strategy must be developed. Even though the trade-off boundary is represented by a box in Figure 1-4, it is obvious that the surface of the box will not be flat. If a multifactor mathematical model is developed for the three factors, the nature of the response surface will vary depending on the specific interactions of the factors for any given project. A hypothetical response surface is presented in Figure 1-5.

Figure 1-4. Performance-Time-Resource Trade-off Boundary

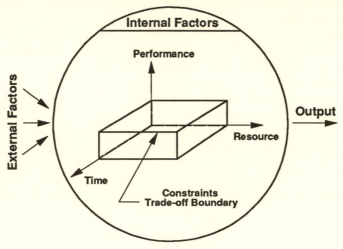

Figure 1-5. Performance-Time-Cost Response Surface

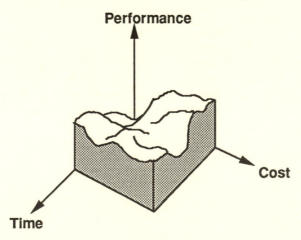

If we consider only two of the three constraints at a time, we can better study their respective relationships. Figure 1-6 shows some potential two-factor relationships. In plot (a), performance is modeled as the dependent variable, while cost is the independent variable. Performance increases as cost increases up to a point where performance levels off. If cost is allowed to continue to increase, performance eventually starts to drop. In plot (b), performance is modeled as being dependent on time. The more the time that is allowed for a project, the higher the expected performance up to a point where performance levels off. In plot (c), cost depends on time. As project duration increases, cost increases. The increases in cost may be composed of labor cost, raw material cost, and/or cost associated with decreasing productivity. Note that there may be a fixed cost associated with a project even when a time schedule is not in effect.

Figure 1-6. Potential Trade-off Relationships

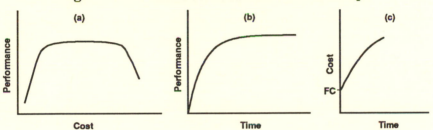

Figure 1-7 shows an alternate time-cost trade-off relationship. In this case, the shorter the desired project duration, the higher the cost of the project. If more time is available for the project, then cost can be reduced. However, there is a limit to the possible reduction in cost. After some time, the cost function turns upward due to the increasing cost of keeping manpower and resources tied up on the project for a long period of time. The optimal duration of the project corresponds to the point where the lowest cost is realized.

Figure 1-7. Time-Cost Trade-off Example

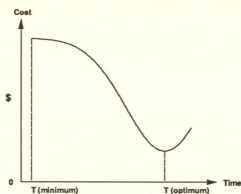

Some of the causes of control problems in project scheduling, performance, and cost are summarized below:

Schedule Problems	*Performance Problems*	*Cost Problems*
Bad time estimates	Poor quality	High labor cost
Technical problems	Poor mobility	Inadequate budget
Change of due dates	Lack of training	Poor cost reporting
Precedence structure	Poor functionality	Effects of inflation
Unreliable time estimates	Maintenance problems	High overhead cost
Delay of critical activities	Lack of clear objectives	Increase in scope of work

Schedule Control

The Gantt charts developed in the scheduling phase of a project can serve as the yardstick for measuring project progress. Project status should be monitored frequently. A record should be maintained of the difference between the expected progress of an activity and its actual progress. This information should be conveyed to the appropriate personnel. The more milestones or control points there are in the project, the better the monitoring function. The larger number allows for more frequent and distinct avenues for monitoring the schedule. Thus, problems can be identified and controlled before they accumulate into a bigger problem. Some corrective actions that may be taken for schedule problems include:

- Crashing tasks
- Redesigning tasks
- Revising milestones
- Adjusting time estimates
- Changing the scope of work
- Combining related activities
- Introduction of new technology
- Eliminating unnecessary activities

Performance Control

Most project performance problems will not surface until after the project is completed. This makes performance control very difficult. However, every effort should be made to measure all the intermediate factors affecting the project. After-the-fact measurements generally do not facilitate good control. Some of the performance problems may be indicated by time and cost deviations. So, when schedule and cost problems exist, an analysis of how the problems may affect performance should be made. Since project performance requirements usually relate to the performance of the end products, controlling performance problems may necessitate the following:

- Modifying policies and procedures
- Introducing improved technology
- Adjusting project specifications
- Improving management control
- Reviewing project priorities
- Changing quality standards
- Allocating more resources
- Improving work ethics

Cost Control

Cost control has received extensive coverage in the literature. Numerous accounting and reporting systems have been developed over the years for project cost monitoring and control. Some of the strategies suitable for controlling project cost include:

- Reducing labor costs
- Using competitive bidding
- Modification of work process
- Adjusting work breakdown structure
- Improving coordination of project functions
- Improving cost estimation procedures
- Using less expensive raw materials
- Controlling inflationary trends
- Cutting overhead costs

The Triple C model presented earlier can be implemented for project control purposes. In Figure 1-8, the model shows the important interfaces between communication, cooperation, coordination, performance, cost, and schedule control.

Figure 1-8. Implementation of Triple C Model for Control

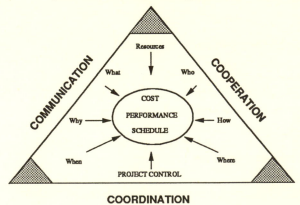

PROJECT DECISION MODEL

Badiru (1991a) presents decision steps for project management. The steps facilitate a proper consideration of the essential elements of decisions in a project environment. These essential elements include problem statement, information, performance measure, decision model, and an implementation of the decision. The steps recommended by Badiru for project decisions are outlined below.

Step 1. Problem Statement

A problem involves choosing between competing, and probably conflicting, alternatives. The components of problem solving in project management include:

- Describing the problem
- Defining a model to represent the problem
- Solving the model
- Testing the solution
- Implementing and maintaining the solution

Problem definition is very crucial. In many cases, *symptoms* of a problem are recognized more readily than its *cause* and *location*. Even after the problem is accurately identified and defined, a benefit/cost analysis may be needed to determine if the cost of solving the problem is justified.

Step 2. Data and Information Requirements

Information is the driving force for the project decision process. Information clarifies the relative states of past, present, and future events. The collection, storage, retrieval, organization, and processing of raw data are important components for generating information. Without data, there can be no information. Without good information, there cannot be a valid decision. The essential requirements for generating information are:

- Ensure that an effective data collection procedure is followed.
- Determine the type and the appropriate amount of data to collect.
- Evaluate the data collected with respect to information potential.
- Evaluate the cost of collecting the required data.

For example: Suppose a manager is presented with a recorded fact that says, *"sales for the last quarter are 10,000 units."* This constitutes ordinary data.   There are many ways of using this data to make a decision depending on the manager's value system.   An analyst, however, can ensure the proper use of the data by transforming it into information, such as, *"sales of 10,000 units for last quarter are low."* This type of information is more useful to the manager for decision making.

Step 3. Performance Measure

A performance measure for the competing alternatives should be specified. The decision maker assigns a perceived worth or value to the available alternatives. Setting a measure of performance is crucial to the process of defining and selecting alternatives.

Step 4. Decision Model

A decision model provides the basis for the analysis and synthesis of information, and is the mechanism by which competing alternatives are compared. To be effective, a decision model must be based on a systematic and logical framework for guiding project decisions.   A decision model can be a verbal, graphical, or mathematical representation of the ideas in the decision-making process.   A project decision model should have the following characteristics:

- Simplified representation of the actual situation
- Explanation and prediction of the actual situation
- Validity and appropriateness
- Applicability to similar problems

The formulation of a decision model involves three essential components:
Abstraction: Determining the relevant factors
Construction: Combining the factors into a logical model
Validation: Assuring that the model adequately represents the problem

The basic types of decision models for project management are:

Descriptive models: These are directed at describing a decision scenario and identifying the associated problem.   For example, a project analyst might use a CPM network model to identify bottleneck tasks in a project.

Prescriptive models: These furnish procedural guidelines for implementing actions. The Triple C approach, for example, is a model that prescribes the procedures for achieving communication, cooperation, and coordination in a project environment.

Predictive models: These models are used to predict future events in a problem environment. They are typically based on historical data about the problem situation. For example, a regression model based on past data may be used to predict future productivity gains associated with expected levels of resource allocation.

Satisficing models: These are models that provide trade-off strategies for achieving a satisfactory solution to a problem within given constraints. Goal programming and other multi-criteria techniques provide good satisficing solutions. For example, these models are helpful in cases where time limitation, resource shortage, and performance requirements constrain the implementation of a project.

Optimizing models: These models are designed to find the best available solution to a problem subject to a certain set of constraints. For example, a linear programming model can be used to determine the optinum product mix in a production environment.

In many situations, two or more of the above models may be involved in the solution of a problem. For example, a descriptive model might provide insights into the nature of the problem; an optimization model might provide the optimal set of actions to take in solving the problem; a satisficing model might temper the optimal solution with reality; a prescriptive model might suggest the procedures for implementing the selected solution; and a predictive model might predict the expected outcome of implementing the solution.

Step 5. Making the Decision

Using the available data, information, and the decision model, the decision maker will determine the real-world actions that are needed to solve the stated problem. A sensitivity analysis may be useful for determining what changes in parameter values might cause a change in the decision.

Step 6. Implementing the Decision

A decision represents the selection of an alternative that satisfies the objective stated in the problem statement. A good decision is useless until it is implemented.

An important aspect of a decision is to specify how it is to be implemented. Selling the decision and the project to management requires a well-organized persuasive presentation. The way a decision is presented can directly influence whether or not it is adopted.   The presentation of a decision should include at least the following: an executive summary, technical aspects of the decision, managerial aspects of the decision, resources required to implement the decision, cost of the decision, and the time frame for implementing the decision.

PROJECT IMPLEMENTATION MODEL

It is helpful to have a model that can be adopted for project implementation purposes. Presented below is a comprehensive model for the essential tasks in project planning, scheduling, and control.

1: Planning

I.   Specify Project Background
    A. Define Current Situation and Process
        1. Understand the Process
        2. Identify Important Variables
        3. Quantify Variables
    B. Identify Areas for Improvement
        1. List and Explain the Areas
        2. Study Potential Strategy for Solution
II.   Define Unique Terminologies Relevant to the Project
        1. Industry-specific Terminologies
        2. Company-specific Terminologies
        3. Project-specific Terminologies
III. Define Project Goal and Objectives
    A. Write Mission Statement
    B. Solicit Inputs and Ideas from Personnel
IV. Establish Performance Standards
    A. Schedule
    B. Performance
    C. Cost
V.   Conduct Formal Project Feasibility Study
    A. Determine Impact on Cost
    B. Determine on Organization
    C. Determine Project Deliverables
VI. Secure Management Support

2: Organizing

I. Identify Project Management Team
    A. Specify Project Organization Structure
        1. Matrix Structure
        2. Formal and Informal Structures
        3. Justify Structure
    B. Specify Departments Involved and Key Personnel
        1. Purchasing
        2. Materials Management
        3. Engineering, Design, Manufacturing, etc.
    C. Define Project Management Responsibilities
        1. Select Project Manager
        2. Write Project Charter
        3. Establish Project Policies and Procedures
II. Implement Triple C Model
    A. *Communication*
        1. Determine Communication Interfaces
        2. Develop Communication Matrix
    B. *Cooperation*
        1. Outline Cooperation Requirements
    C. *Coordination*
        1. Develop Work Breakdown Structure
        2. Assign Task Responsibilities
        3. Develop Responsibility Chart

3: Scheduling and Resource Allocation

I. Develop Master Schedule
    A. Estimate Task Duration
    B. Identify Task Precedence Requirements
        1. Technical Precedence
        2. Resource-imposed Precedence
        3. Procedural Precedence
    C. Use Analytical Models
        1. CPM
        2. PERT
        3. Gantt Chart
        4. Optimization Models

4: Tracking, Reporting, and Control

I.   Establish Guidelines for Tracking, Reporting, and Control
    A. Define Data Requirements
        1. Data Categories
        2. Data Characterization
        3. Measurement Scales
    B. Develop Data Documentation
        1. Data Update Requirements
        2. Data Quality Control
        3. Establish Data Security Measures
II. Categorize Control Points
    A. Schedule Audit
        1. Activity Network and Gantt Charts
        2. Milestones
        3. Delivery Schedule
    B. Performance Audit
        1. Employee Performance
        2. Product Quality
    C. Cost Audit
        1. Cost Containment Measures
        2. Percent Completion versus Budget Depletion
III. Identify Implementation Process
IV. Phase out the Project
    A. Performance Review
    B. Strategy for Follow-up Projects
    C. Personnel Retention and Releases
V.   Document Project and Submit Final Report

The model above gives a general guideline for project planning, scheduling, and control. The skeleton of the model can be adapted for implementation as required for specific projects. Not all projects will be amenable to all the contents of the model. Customization will always be necessary when implementing the model.

SELLING THE PROJECT PLAN

The project plan must be sold throughout the organization. Different levels of detail will be needed when presenting the project to various groups in the organization. The higher the level of management, the lower the level of detail. Top management will be more interested in the global aspects of the project. For example, when presenting the project to management, it is necessary to specify how the overall organization will be affected by the project. When presenting the project to the supervisory level staff, the most important aspect of the project will be the operational level of detail. At the worker or operator level, the individual will be more concerned about how his or her job will be affected by the project. The project manager or analyst must be able to accommodate these various levels of detail when presenting the plan to both participants in and customers of the project. Regardless of the group being addressed, the project presentation should cover the essential elements below at the appropriate levels of detail:

Introduction
Project Description
    Goals and Objectives
    Expected Outcome
Performance Measure
Conclusion

IMPORTANCE OF QUANTITATIVE PROJECT ANALYSIS

The tools for project management can be classified into three major categories as outlined by Badiru (1991a):

1. Qualitative Models
2. Computer Models
3. Quantitative Models

While numerous books exist on the qualitative aspects of managing projects, very few books focus on the quantitative tools for project management. It is no longer effective to manage projects on the basis of technical expertise or managerial skills alone. Various skills and tools must be integrated for more effective project planning, scheduling, and control. Numerous publications treat qualitative project management. For example, Meredith and Mantel (1989) present a managerial approach to project management. Computerized project management has also received extensive coverage in the literature (Assad and Wasil, 1986; Badiru and Whitehouse, 1989; Drigani, 1989; East and Kirby, 1989; Levine, 1986; Samaras and Yensuang, 1979).

Several publications on quantitative models are available for general management applications. Examples are: Buffa and Dyer (1977), Dallenback and George (1978), Eck (1976), Gordon and Pressman (1978), Johnson and Winn (1976), Kim (1976), Lapin (1976), Levin and Kirkpatrick (1978), D. Smith (1977), Thierauf (1978), and Verma and Gross (1978). But, very few books have been published specifically on the quantitative tools for project management.

Quantitative tools are just as important as other tools for project planning, scheduling, and control. In practice, it is essential to have a balanced mix of qualitative, computer, and quantitative tools in project analysis. Many of the components of the life cycle of a project can benefit from quantitative analysis. Although the scheduling and resource allocation functions are the most suitable for the application of quantitative models, the broad spectrum of project planning, scheduling, and control should be considered for the application of the quantitative models presented in this book.

This chapter has presented an overview of the various functions involved in project planning, scheduling, and control. The managerial aspects of project management were discussed briefly. The next chapter presents project network scheduling techniques with particular emphasis on CPM and PERT. Subsequent chapters present specific quantitative techniques suitable for application to various project management functions.

EXERCISES

1-1. Following the examples in Figures 1-6 and 1-7, plot potential relationships for the following: cost versus performance, time versus performance, time versus cost.

1-2. Sketch a Venn diagram that will illustrate the relationships between system, program, project, task, and activity in a project environment.

1-3. Refer to the hypothetical performance-time-cost response surface presented in this chapter. Discuss the rationale behind the appearance of the surface. Can you modify the sketch to convey your own impression of what the surface should look like? Explain.

1-4. Considering the three constraints of performance, time, and cost, which one will be the easiest to compromise? Which one will be the most difficult to compromise? Discuss.

1-5. Define the functions of project planning, scheduling, and control in your own words.

1-6. Compare the advantages and disadvantages of qualitative and quantitative tools for project management.

1-7. What project parameters or variables may be important for defining qualitative responsibility for project planning, scheduling, and control?

1-8. What project parameters or variables may be important for defining quantitative accountability for project planning, scheduling, and control?

1-9. Give examples to illustrate the differences between a *project specialist* and a *technical specialist*.

1-10. How can quantitative analysis be used to develop a project implementation strategy?

CHAPTER 2

CPM, PERT, AND PDM NETWORKS

The network of activities contained in a project provide the basis for scheduling the project. The critical path method (CPM) and the program evaluation and review technique (PERT) are the two most popular techniques for project network analysis. The precedence diagramming method (PDM) has gained in popularity in recent years because of the move toward concurrent engineering in manufacturing operations. A project network is the graphical representation of the contents and objectives of the project. The basic project network analysis is typically implemented in three phases: Network Planning Phase, Network Scheduling Phase, and Network Control Phase.

Network planning is sometimes referred to as activity planning. This involves the identification of the relevant activities for the project. The required activities and their precedence relationships are determined. Precedence requirements may be determined on the basis of technological, procedural, or imposed constraints. The activities are then represented in the form of a network diagram. The two popular models for network drawing are the activity-on-arrow (AOA) and the activity-on-node (AON) conventions. In the AOA approach, arrows are used to represent activities, while nodes represent starting and ending points of activities. In the AON approach, nodes represent activities, while arrows represent precedence relationships. Time, cost, and resource requirement estimates are developed for each activity during the network planning phase. The estimates may be based on historical records, time standards, forecasting, regression functions, or other quantitative models.

Network scheduling is performed by using forward pass and backward pass computational procedures. These computations give the earliest and latest starting and finishing times for each activity. The amount of slack or float associated with each activity is determined. The activity path with the minimum slack in the network is used to determine the critical activities. This path also determines the duration of the project. Resource allocation, and time-cost trade-offs are other functions performed during network scheduling.

Network control involves tracking the progress of a project on the basis of the network schedule and taking corrective actions when needed. An evaluation of actual performance versus expected performance determines deficiencies in the project progress. The advantages of project network analysis are presented below:

- Advantages for communication
    It clarifies project objectives.
    It establishes the specifications for project performance.
    It provides a starting point for more detailed task analysis.
    It presents a documentation of the project plan.
    It serves as a visual communication tool.

- Advantages for control
    It presents a measure for evaluating project performance.
    It helps determine what corrective actions are needed.
    It gives a clear message of what is expected.
    It encourages team interactions.

- Advantages for team interaction
    It offers a mechanism for a quick introduction to the project.
    It specifies functional interfaces on the project.
    It facilitates ease of application.

CRITICAL PATH METHOD

Precedence relationships in a CPM network fall into the three major categories listed below:

1. Technical precedence
2. Procedural precedence
3. Imposed precedence

Technical precedence requirements are caused by the technical relationships among activities in a project. For example, in conventional construction, walls must be erected before the roof can be installed. Procedural precedence requirements are determined by policies and procedures. Such policies and procedures are often subjective, with no concrete justification. Imposed precedence requirements can be classified as resource-imposed, state-imposed, or environment-imposed. For example, resource shortages may require that one task be before another. The current status of a project (e.g., percent completion) may determine that one activity be performed before another. The environment of a project, for example, weather changes or the effects of concurrent projects, may determine the precedence relationships of the activities in a project.

The primary goal of a CPM analysis of a project is the determination of the "critical path." The critical path determines the minimum completion time for a project. The computational analysis involves forward pass and backward pass procedures. The forward pass determines the earliest start time and the earliest completion time for each activity in the network. The backward pass determines the latest start time and the latest completion time for each activity. Figure 2-1 shows an example of an activity network using the activity-on-node convention. Conventional network logic is always drawn from left to right. If this convention is followed, there is no need to use arrows to indicate the directional flow in the activity network. The notations used for activity A in the network are explained below:

A: Activity Identification
ES: Earliest starting time
EC: Earliest completion time
LS: Latest starting time
LC: Latest completion time
t: Activity Duration

Figure 2-1. Example of Activity Network

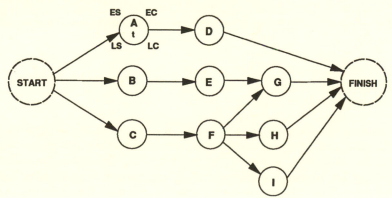

During the forward pass analysis of the network, it is assumed that each activity will begin at its earliest starting time. An activity can begin as soon as the last of its predecessors is finished. The completion of the forward pass determines the earliest completion time of the project. The backward pass analysis is a reverse of the forward pass. It begins at the latest project completion time and ends at the latest starting time of the first activity in the project network. The rules for implementing the forward pass and backward pass analyses in CPM are presented below. These rules are implemented iteratively until the ES, EC, LS, and LC have been calculated for all nodes in the activity network.

Rule 1:   Unless otherwise stated, the starting time of a project is set equal to time zero. That is, the first node in the network diagram has an earliest start time of zero. Thus,
ES of first activity = 0.
If a desired starting time is specified, then
ES of first activity = Specified starting time.

Rule 2:   The earliest start time (ES) for any activity is equal to the maximum of the earliest completion times (EC) of the immediate predecessors of the activity. That is,
ES = Maximum {Immediately Preceding ECs}.

Rule 3:   The earliest completion time (EC) of an activity is the activity's earliest start time plus its estimated time. That is,
EC = ES + (Activity Time).

Rule 4:   The earliest completion time of a project is equal to the earliest completion time of the very last node in the project network. That is,
EC of Project = EC of last activity.

Rule 5:   Unless the latest completion time (LC) of a project is explicitly specified, it is set equal to the earliest completion time of the project. This is called the *zero project slack convention.* That is,
LC of Project = EC of Project.

Rule 6:   If a desired deadline is specified for the project, then
LC of Project = Specified Deadline.
It should be noted that a latest completion time or deadline may sometimes be specified for a project on the basis of contractual agreements.

Rule 7:   The latest completion time (LC) for an activity is the smallest of the latest start times of the activity's immediate successors. That is,
LC = Minimum {Immediately Succeeding LS's}.

Rule 8:   The latest start time for an activity is the latest completion time minus the activity time. That is,
LS = LC - (Activity Time).

CPM Example

Table 2-1 presents the data for a simple project network. This network and extensions of it will be used for computational examples in this chapter and subsequent chapters. The AON network for the example is given in Figure 2-2. Dummy activities are included in the network to designate single starting and ending points for the network.

Table 2-1. Data for Sample Project for CPM Analysis

Activity	Predecessor	Duration (Days)
A	-	2
B	-	6
C	-	4
D	A	3
E	C	5
F	A	4
G	B, D, E	2

Figure 2-2. Example of Activity Network

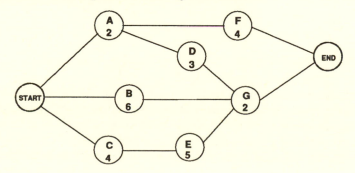

Forward Pass

The forward pass calculations are shown in Figure 2-3. Zero is entered as the ES for the initial node. Since the initial node for the example is a dummy node, its duration is zero. Thus, EC for the starting node is equal to its ES. The ES values for the immediate successors of the starting node are set equal to the EC of the START node and the resulting EC values are computed. Each node is treated as the "start" node for its successor or successors. However, if an activity has more than one predecessor, the maximum of the ECS of the preceding activities is used as the activity's starting time. This happens in the case of activity G, whose ES is determined as Max {6, 5, 9} = 9. The earliest project completion time for the example is 11 days. Note that this is the maximum of the immediately preceding earliest completion times: Max {6, 11} = 11. Since the dummy ending node has no duration, its earliest completion time is set equal to its earliest start time of 11 days.

Figure 2-3. Forward Pass Analysis for CPM Example

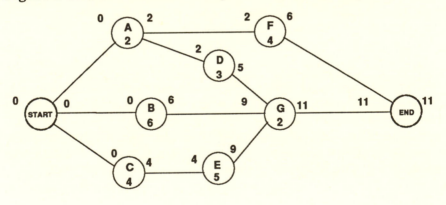

Backward Pass

The backward pass computations establish the latest start time (LS) and latest completion time (LC) for each node in the network. The results of the backward pass computations are shown in Figure 2-4. Since no deadline is specified, the latest completion time of the project is set equal to the earliest completion time. By back tracking and using the network analysis rules presented earlier, the latest completion and latest start times are determined for each node. Note that in the case of activity A with two successors, the latest completion time is determined as the minimum of the immediately succeeding latest start times. That is, Min {6, 7} = 6.   A similar situation occurs for the dummy starting node.   In that case, the latest completion time of the dummy start node is Min {0, 3, 4} = 0.   Since this dummy node has no duration, the latest starting time of the project is set equal to the node's latest completion time.   Thus, the project starts at time 0 and is expected to be completed by time 11.

Figure 2-4. Backward Pass Analysis for CPM Example

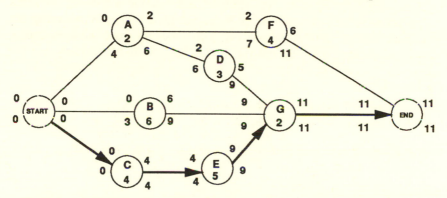

Within a project network, there are usually several possible paths and a number of activities that must be performed sequentially and some activities that may be performed concurrently.   If an activity has ES and EC times that are not equal, then the actual start and completion times of that activity may be flexible.   The amount of flexibility an activity possesses is called a slack time.   The slack time is used to determine the critical activities in the network as discussed below.

Determination of Critical Activities

The critical path is defined as the path with the least slack in the network diagram.   All the activities on the critical path are said to be critical activities. These activities can create bottlenecks in the network if they are delayed.   The critical path is also the longest path in the network diagram.   In some networks, particularly large ones, it is possible to have multiple critical paths.   If there is a large number of paths in the network, it may be very difficult to visually identify all the critical paths.   The slack time of an activity is also referred to as its *float*. There are four basic types of activity slack.   They are described below.

- Total Slack (TS)

Total slack is defined as the amount of time an activity may be delayed from its earliest starting time without delaying the latest completion time of the project. The total slack of an activity is the difference between the latest completion time and the earliest completion time of the activity, or the difference between the latest starting time and the earliest starting time of the activity.

TS = LC - EC or TS = LS - ES.

Total slack is the measure that is used to determine the critical activities in a project network. The critical activities are identified as those having the minimum total slack in the network diagram. If there is only one critical path in the network, then all the critical activities will be on that one path.

- Free Slack (FS)

Free slack is the amount of time an activity may be delayed from its earliest starting time without delaying the starting time of any of its immediate successors. Activity free slack is calculated as the difference between the minimum earliest starting time of the activity's successors and the earliest completion time of the activity.

FS = Min {Succeeding ES's} - EC.

- Interfering Slack (IS)

Interfering slack or interfering float is the amount of time by which an activity interferes with (or obstructs) its successors when its total slack is fully used. This is rarely used in practice. The interfering float is computed as the difference between the total slack and the free slack.

IS = TS - FS.

- Independent Float (IF)

Independent float or independent slack is the amount of float that an activity will always have regardless of the completion times of its predecessors or the starting times of its successors. Independent float is computed as:

Independent Float = Max $\{0, (ES_j - LC_i - t)\}$,

where ES_j is the earliest starting time of the preceding activity, LC_i is the latest completion time of the succeeding activity, and t is the duration of the activity whose independent float is being calculated. Independent float takes a pessimistic view of the situation of an activity. It evaluates the situation whereby the activity is pressured from either side. That is, when its predecessors are delayed as late as possible while its successors are to be started as early as possible. Independent float is useful for conservative planning purposes, but it is not used much in practice. Despite its low level of use, independent float does have practical implications for better project management. Activities can be buffered with independent floats as a way to handle contingencies.

In Figure 2-4 the total slack and the free slack for activity A are calculated, respectively, as:

TS = 6 - 2 = 4 days
FS = Min {2, 2} - 2 = 2 - 2 = 0.

Similarly, the total slack and the free slack for activity F are:

TS = 11 - 6 = 5 days
FS = Min {11} - 6 = 11 - 6 = 5 days.

Table 2-2 presents a tabulation of the results of the CPM example. The table contains the earliest and latest times for each activity as well as the total and free slacks. The results indicate that the minimum total slack in the network is zero. Thus, activities C, E, and G are identified as the critical activities. The critical path is highlighted in Figure 2-4 and consists of the following sequence of activities:

START ---> C ---> E ---> G ---> END.

Table 2-2. Result of CPM Analysis for Sample Project

Activity	Duration	ES	EC	LS	LC	TS	FS	Critical
A	2	0	2	4	6	4	0	-
B	6	0	6	3	9	3	3	-
C	4	0	4	0	4	0	0	Critical
D	3	2	5	6	9	4	4	-
E	5	4	9	4	9	0	0	Critical
F	4	2	6	7	11	5	5	-
G	2	9	11	9	11	0	0	Critical

The total slack for the overall project itself is equal to the total slack observed on the critical path. The minimum slack in most networks will be zero since the ending LC is set equal to the ending EC. If a deadline is specified for a project, then we would set the project's latest completion time to the specified deadline. In that case, the minimum total slack in the network would be given by:

TS_{Min} = (Project Deadline) - EC of the last node.

This minimum total slack will then appear as the total slack for each activity on the critical path. If a specified deadline is lower than the EC at the finish node, then the project will start out with a negative slack. That means that it will be behind schedule before it even starts. It may then become necessary to expedite some activities (i.e., crashing) in order to overcome the negative slack. Figure 2-5 shows an example with a specified project deadline. In this case, the deadline of 18 days comes after the earliest completion time of the last node in the network.

Figure 2-5. CPM Network with Deadline

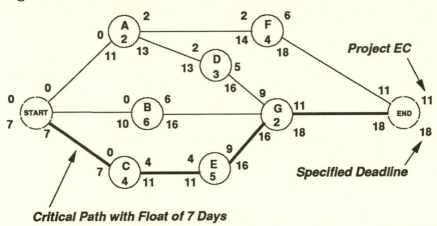

Critical Path with Float of 7 Days

Using Forward Pass to Determine the Critical Path

The critical path in CPM analysis can be determined from the forward pass only. This can be helpful in cases where it is desired to quickly identify the critical activities without performing all the other calculations needed to obtain the latest starting times, the latest completion times, and total slacks. The steps for determining the critical path from the forward pass only are:

1. Complete the forward pass in the usual manner.

2. Identify the last node in the network as a critical activity.

3. Work backward from the last node. Whenever a merge node occurs, the critical path will be along the path where the earliest completion time (EC) is equal to the earliest start time (ES).

4.   Continue the backtracking from each critical activity until the project starting node is reached. Note that if there is a single starting node or a single ending node in the network, then that node will always be on the critical path.

Subcritical Paths

In a large project network, there may be paths that are near critical. Such paths require almost as much attention as the critical path since they have a high potential of becoming critical when changes occur in the network. Analysis of subcritical paths may help in the classification of tasks into ABC categories on the basis of Pareto analysis. Pareto analysis separates the "vital" few activities from the "trivial" many activities. This permits a more efficient allocation of resources. The principle of Pareto analysis originated from the work of Italian economist Vilfredo Pareto (1848-1923). In his studies, Pareto discovered that most of the wealth in his country was held by a few individuals.

For project control purposes, the Pareto principle states that 80% of the bottlenecks are caused by only 20% of the tasks. This principle is applicable to many management processes. For example, in cost analysis, one can infer that 80% of the total cost is associated with only 20% of the cost items. Similarly, 20% of an automobile's parts cause 80% of the maintenance problems. In personnel management, about 20% of employees account for about 80% of the absenteeism. For critical path analysis, 20% of the network activities will take up 80% of our control efforts. The ABC classification based on Pareto analysis divides items into three priority categories: A (most important), B (moderately important), and C (least important). Appropriate percentages (e.g., 20%, 25%, 55%) are assigned to the categories.

With Pareto analysis, attention can be shifted from focusing only on the critical path to managing critical and near-critical tasks. The level of criticality of each path may be assessed by the procedure presented below:

Step 1:   Sort activities in increasing order of total slack.

Step 2:   Partition the sorted activities into groups based on the magnitudes of their total slacks.

Step 3:   Sort the activities within each group in increasing order of their earliest starting times.

Step 4:   Assign the highest level of criticality to the first group of activities (e.g., 100%). This first group represents the usual critical path.

Step 5:   Calculate the relative criticality indices for the other groups in decreasing order of criticality.

Define the following variables:

α_1 = the minimum total slack in the network

α_2 = the maximum total slack in the network

β = total slack for the path whose criticality is to be calculated.
Compute the path's criticality as:

$$\lambda = \frac{\alpha_2 - \beta}{\alpha_2 - \alpha_1}(100\%).$$

The above procedure yields relative criticality levels between 0% and 100%. Table 2-3 presents an hypothetical example of path criticality indices. The criticality level may be converted to a scale between 1 (least critical) and 10 (most critical) by the expression below:

$$\lambda' = 1 + 0.09\lambda.$$

Table 2-3. Analysis of Subcritical Paths

Path No.	Activities on Path	Total Slack	λ	λ'
1	A, C, G, H	0	100%	10
2	B, D, E	1	97.56%	9.78
3	F, I	5	87.81%	8.90
4	J, K, L	9	78.05%	8.03
5	O, P, Q, R	10	75.61%	7.81
6	M, S, T	25	39.02%	4.51
7	N, AA, BB, U	30	26.83%	3.42
8	V, W, X	32	21.95%	2.98
9	Y, CC, EE	35	17.14%	2.54
10	DD, Z, FF	41	0%	1.00

GANTT CHARTS

When the results of a CPM analysis are fitted to a calendar time, the project plan becomes a schedule. The Gantt chart is one of the most widely used tools for presenting a project schedule. A Gantt chart can show planned and actual progress of activities. The time scale is indicated along the horizontal axis, while horizontal bars or lines representing activities are ordered along the vertical axis. As a project progresses, markers are made on the activity bars to indicate actual work accomplished. Gantt charts must be updated periodically to indicate project status. Figure 2-6 presents the Gantt chart for our illustrative example using the earliest starting (ES) times from Table 2-2. Figure 2-7 presents the Gantt chart for the example based on the latest starting (LS) times. Critical activities are indicated by the shaded bars.

Figure 2-6. Gantt Chart Based on Earliest Starting Times

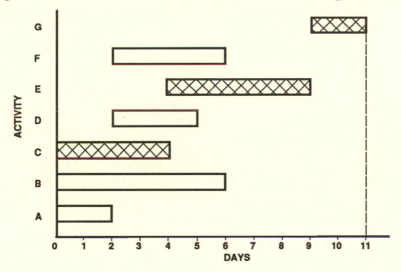

Figure 2-6 shows that the starting time of activity F can be delayed from day two until day seven (i.e., TS=5) without delaying the overall project. Likewise, A, D, or both may be delayed by a combined total of four days (TS=4) without delaying the overall project. If all the four days of slack are used up by A, then D cannot be delayed. If A is delayed by one day, then D can be delayed by up to three days without causing a delay of G, which determines project completion. The Gantt chart also indicates that activity B may be delayed by up to three days without affecting the project completion time.

Figure 2-7. Gantt Chart Based on Latest Starting Times

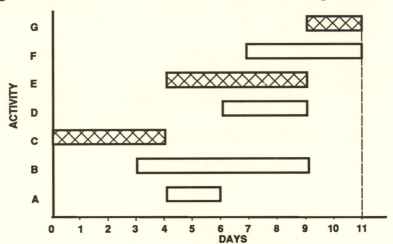

In Figure 2-7, the activities are scheduled by their latest completion times. This represents the extreme case where activity slack times are fully used. No activity in this schedule can be delayed without delaying the project. In Figure 2-7, only one activity is scheduled over the first three days. This may be compared to the schedule in Figure 2-6, which has three starting activities. The schedule in Figure 2-7 may be useful if there is a situation that permits only a few activities to be scheduled in the early stages of the project. Such situations may involve shortage of project personnel, lack of initial budget, time for project initiation, time for personnel training, allowance for learning period, or general resource constraints. Scheduling of activities based on ES times indicates an optimistic view. Scheduling on the basis of LS times represents a pessimistic approach.

Gantt Chart Variations

The basic Gantt chart does not show the precedence relationships among activities. The chart can be modified to show these relationships by linking appropriate bars, as shown in Figure 2-8. However, the linked bars become cluttered and confusing for large networks. Figure 2-9 shows a Gantt chart which presents a comparison of planned and actual schedules. Note that two tasks are in progress at the current time indicated in the figure. One of the ongoing tasks is an unplanned task. Figure 2-10 shows a Gantt chart on which important milestones have been indicated. Figure 2-11 shows a Gantt chart in which bars represent a combination of related tasks. Tasks may be combined for scheduling purposes or for conveying functional relationships required on a project. Figure 2-12 presents a Gantt chart of project phases. Each phase is further divided into parts. Figure 2-13 shows a multiple projects Gantt chart. Multiple projects charts are useful for evaluating resource allocation strategies. Resource loading over multiple projects may be needed for capital budgeting and cash flow analysis decisions. Figure 2-14 shows a project slippage chart that is useful for project tracking and control. Other variations of the basic Gantt chart may be developed for specific needs.

Figure 2-8. Linked Bars in Gantt Chart

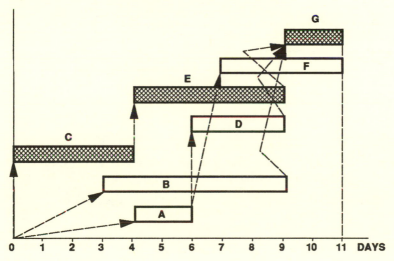

Figure 2-9. Progress Monitoring Gantt Chart

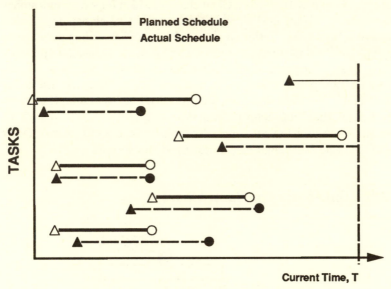

Figure 2-10. Milestone Gantt Chart

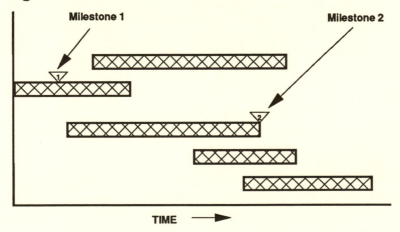

Figure 2-11. Task Combination Gantt Chart

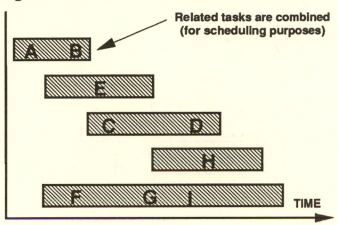

Related tasks are combined
(for scheduling purposes)

Figure 2-12. Phase-Based Gantt Chart

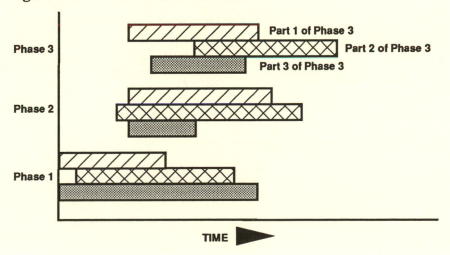

Figure 2-13. Multiple Projects Gantt Chart

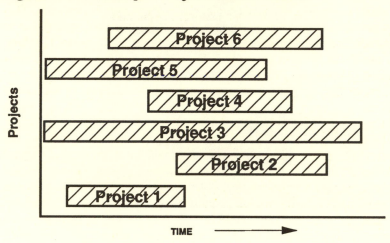

Figure 2-14. Project Slippage Tracking Gantt Chart

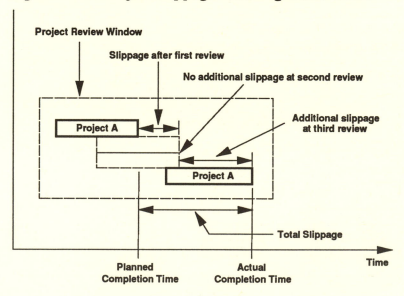

Activity Crashing and Schedule Compression

Schedule compression refers to reducing the length of a project network. This is often accomplished by crashing activities. Crashing, sometimes referred to as expediting, reduces activity durations, thereby reducing project duration. Crashing is done as a trade-off between shorter task duration and higher task cost. It must be determined whether the total cost savings realized from reducing the project duration is enough to justify the higher costs associated with reducing individual task durations. If there is a delay penalty associated with a project, it may be possible to reduce the total project cost even though individual task costs are increased by crashing. If the cost savings on delay penalty is higher than the incremental cost of reducing the project duration, then crashing is justified. Under conventional crashing, the further the duration of a project is compressed, the higher the total cost of the project. The objective is to determine at what point to terminate further crashing in a network. *Normal task duration* refers to the time required to perform a task under normal circumstances. *Crash task duration* refers to the reduced time required to perform a task when additional resources are allocated to it.

If each activity is assigned a range of time and cost estimates, then several combinations of time and cost values will be associated with the overall project. Iterative procedures are used to determine the best time or cost combination for a project. Time-cost trade-off analysis may be conducted, for example, to determine the marginal cost of reducing the duration of the project by one time unit. Table 2-4 presents an extension of the data for the example problem to include normal and crash times as well as normal and crash costs for each activity. The normal duration of the project is 11 days, as seen earlier, and the normal cost is $2,775.

Table 2-4. Normal and Crash Time and Cost Data

Activity	Normal Duration	Normal Cost	Crash Duration	Crash Cost	Crashing Ratio
A	2	$210	2	$210	0
B	6	400	4	600	100
C	4	500	3	750	250
D	3	540	2	600	60
E	5	750	3	950	100
F	4	275	3	310	35
G	2	100	1	125	25
		$2,775		$3,545	

If all the activities are reduced to their respective crash durations, the total crash cost of the project will be $3,545. In that case, the crash time is found by CPM analysis to be seven days. The CPM network for the fully crashed project is shown in Figure 2-15. Note that activities C, E, and G remain critical. Sometimes, the crashing of activities may result in a new critical path. The Gantt chart in Figure 2-16 shows a schedule of the crashed project using the ES times. In practice, one would not crash all activities in a network. Rather, some heuristic would be used to determine which activity should be crashed and by how much. One approach is to crash only the critical activities or those activities with the best ratios of incremental cost versus time reduction. The last column in Table 2-4 presents the respective ratios for the activities in our example. The crashing ratios are computed as:

$$r = \frac{Crash \quad Cost \quad - \quad Normal \quad Cost}{Normal \quad Duration \quad - \quad Crash \quad Duration}$$

This method of computing the crashing ratio gives crashing priority to the activity with the lowest cost slope. It is a commonly used approach to expediting in CPM networks.

Figure 2-15. Example of Fully Crashed CPM Network

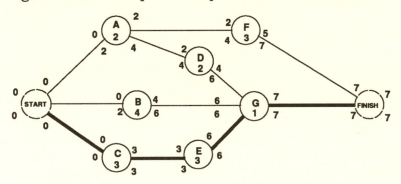

Activity G offers the lowest cost per unit time reduction of $25. If our approach is to crash only one activity at a time, we may decide to crash activity G first and evaluate the increase in project cost versus the reduction in project duration. The process can then be repeated for the next best candidate for crashing, which is activity F in this case. After F has been crashed, activity D can then be crashed.

Figure 2-16. Gantt Chart of Fully Crashed CPM Network

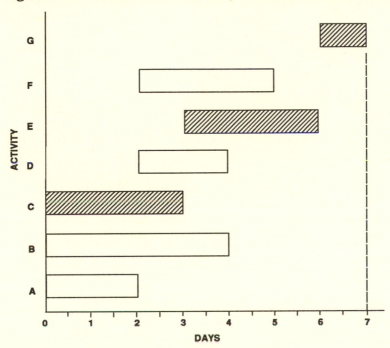

This approach is repeated iteratively in order of activity preference until no further reduction in project duration can be achieved or until the total project cost exceeds a specified limit.

A more comprehensive analysis is to evaluate all possible combinations of the activities that can be crashed. However, such a complete enumeration would be prohibitive, since there would be a total of 2^c crashed networks to evaluate, where c is the number of activities that can be crashed out of the n activities in the network ($c<=n$). For our example, only 6 out of the 7 activities in the network can be crashed. Thus, a complete enumeration will involve $2^6 = 64$ alternate networks. Table 2-5 shows 7 of the 64 crashing options. Activity G, which offers the best crashing ratio, reduces the project duration by only one day. Even though activities F, D, and B are crashed by a total of four days at an incremental cost of $295, they do not generate any reduction in project duration. Activity E is crashed by two days and it generates a reduction of two days in project duration. Activity

C, which is crashed by one day, generates a further reduction of one day in the project duration. It should be noted that the activities which generate reductions in project duration are the ones that were identified earlier as the critical activities.

Figure 2-17 shows the crashed project duration versus the crashing options, while Figure 2-18 shows a plot of the total project cost after crashing versus the selected crashing options. As more activities are crashed, the project duration decreases while the total project cost increases. If full enumeration were performed, Figure 2-17 would contain additional points between the minimum possible project duration of 7 days (fully crashed) and the normal project duration of 11 days (no crashing). Similarly, the plot for total project cost (Figure 2-18) would contain additional points between the normal cost of $2,775 and the crash cost of $3,545.

Table 2-5. Selected Crashing Options for CPM Example

Option No.	Activities Crashed	Network Duration	Time Reduction	Incremental Cost	Total Cost
1.	None	11	-	-	2775
2.	G	10	1	25	2800
3.	G, F	10	0	35	2835
4.	G, F, D	10	0	60	2895
5.	G, F, D, B	10	0	200	3095
6.	G, F, D, B, E	8	2	200	3295
7.	G, F, D, B, E, C	7	1	250	3545

Figure 2-17. Duration as a Function of Crashing Options

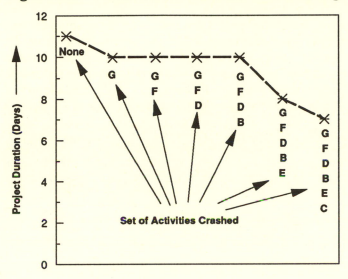

Figure 2-18. Project Cost as a Function of Crashing Options

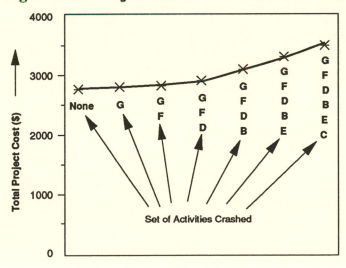

Several other approaches exist for determining which activities to crash in a project network. Two alternate approaches are presented below for computing the crashing ratio, *r*:

$$r = Criticality \quad Index$$

$$r = \frac{Crash \quad Cost \quad - \quad Normal \quad Cost}{(Normal \quad Duration \quad - \quad Crash \quad Duration)(Criticality \quad Index)}.$$

The first approach gives crashing priority to the activity with the highest probability of being on the critical path. In deterministic networks, this refers to the critical activities. In stochastic networks, an activity is expected to fall on the critical path only a percentage of the time. The second approach is a combination of the approach used for the illustrative example and the criticality index approach. It reflects the process of selecting the least-cost expected value. The denominator of the expression represents the expected number of days by which the critical path can be shortened. For different project networks, different crashing approaches should be considered, and the one that best fits the nature of the network should be selected.

PERT NETWORK ANALYSIS

Program Evaluation Review Technique (PERT) is an extension of CPM which incorporates variabilities in activity durations into project network analysis. PERT has been used extensively and successfully in practice.

In real life, activities are often prone to uncertainties which determine the actual durations of the activities. In CPM, activity durations are assumed to be deterministic. In PERT, the potential uncertainties in activity durations are accounted for by using three time estimates for each activity. The three time estimates represent the spread of the estimated activity duration. The greater the uncertainty of an activity, the wider the range of the estimates.

PERT Estimates and Formulas

PERT uses the three time estimates and the simple equations to compute the expected duration and variance for each activity. The PERT formulas are based on a simplification of the expressions for the mean and variance of a beta distribution. The approximation formula for the mean is a simple weighted average of the three time estimates, with the end points assumed to be equally likely and the mode four times as likely. The approximation formula for PERT is based on the recognition that most of the observations from a distribution will lie within plus or minus three standard deviations, or a spread of six standard deviations. This leads to the simple method of setting the PERT formula for standard deviation equal to one sixth of the estimated duration range. While there is no theoretical validation for these approximation approaches, the PERT formulas do facilitate ease of use. The formulas are presented below:

$$t_e = \frac{a + 4m + b}{6}$$

$$s^2 = \frac{(b - a)^2}{36} \, ,$$

where
a = optimistic time estimate
m = most likely time estimate
b = pessimistic time estimate $(a < m < b)$
t_e = expected time for the activity
s^2 = variance of the duration of the activity.

After obtaining the estimate of the duration for each activity, the network analysis is carried out in the same manner previously illustrated for the CPM approach. The major steps in PERT analysis are summarized below:

1. Obtain three time estimates a, m, and b for each activity.

2. Compute the expected duration for each activity by using the formula for t_e.

3. Compute the variance of the duration of each activity from the formula for s^2. It should be noted that CPM analysis cannot calculate variance of activity duration, since it uses a single time estimate for each activity.

4. Compute the expected project duration, T_e. As in the case of CPM, the duration of a project in PERT analysis is the sum of the durations of the activities on the critical path.

5. Compute the variance of the project duration as the sum of the variances of the activities on the critical path. The variance of the project duration is denoted by S^2. It should be recalled that CPM cannot compute the variance of the project duration, since variances of activity durations are not computed.

6. If there are two or more critical paths in the network, choose the one with the largest variance to determine the project duration and the variance of the project duration. Thus, PERT is pessimistic with respect to the variance of project duration when there are multiple critical paths in the project network.

For some networks, it may be necessary to perform a mean-variance analysis to determine the relative importance of the multiple paths by plotting the expected project duration versus the path duration variance.

7.   If desired, compute the probability of completing the project within a specified time period. This is not possible under CPM.

In practice, a question often arises as to how to obtain good estimates of *a*, *m*, and *b*. Several approaches can be used in obtaining the required time estimates for PERT. Some of the approaches are:

*   Estimates furnished by an experienced person

*   Estimates extracted from standard time data

*   Estimates obtained from historical data

*   Estimates obtained from simple regression and/or forecasting

*   Estimates generated by simulation

*   Estimates derived from heuristic assumptions

*   Estimates dictated by customer requirements

Several researchers including Golenko-Ginzburg (1988, 1989a, 1989b), Donaldson (1965), Johnson and Schou (1990), Littlefield and Randolph (1987), Sasieni (1986), Troutt (1989), Farnum and Stanton (1987), Gallagher (1987), Grubbs (1962), MacCrimmon and Ryavec (1964), McBride and McClelland (1967), and Welsh (1965) have addressed the deficiencies in the PERT estimation procedure.

The pitfall of using estimates furnished by an individual is that they may be inconsistent, since they are limited by the experience and personal bias of the person providing them. Individuals responsible for furnishing time estimates are usually not experts in estimation, and they generally have difficulty in providing accurate PERT time estimates. There is often a tendency to select values of *a*, *m*, and *b* that are optimistically skewed. This is because a conservatively large value is typically assigned to *b* by inexperienced individuals.

The use of time standards, on the other hand, may not reflect the changes occurring in the current operating environment due to new technology, work simplification, new personnel, and so on. The use of historical data and forecasting is very popular because estimates can be verified and validated by actual records. In the case of regression and forecasting, there is the danger of extrapolation beyond the data range used for fitting the regression and forecasting models. If the sample size in a historical data set is sufficient and the data can be assumed to reasonably represent prevailing operating conditions, the three PERT estimates can be computed as follows:

$$\hat{a} = \bar{t} - kR$$

$$\hat{m} = \bar{t}$$

$$\hat{b} = \bar{t} + kR,$$

where

R = range of the sample data

$\bar{t}$ = arithmetic average of the sample data

k = $3/d_2$

d_2 = an adjustment factor for estimating the standard deviation of a population

If $kR > \bar{t}$, then set $a=0$ and $b=2\bar{t}$. The factor d_2 is widely tabulated in the quality control literature as a function of the number of sample points, n. Selected values of d_2 are presented below.

n	5	10	15	20	25	30	40	50	75	100
d_2	2.326	3.078	3.472	3.735	3.931	4.086	4.322	4.498	4.806	5.015

In practice, probability distributions of activity times can be determined from historical data. The procedure involves three steps:

1. Appropriate organization of the historical data into histograms.

2. Determination of a distribution that reasonably fits the shape of the histogram.

3. Testing of the goodness-of-fit of the hypothesized distribution by using an appropriate statistical model. The chi-square Test and the Kolmogrov-Smirnov (K-S) test are two popular methods for testing goodness-of-fit. Most statistical texts present the details of how to carry out goodness-of-fit tests.

The Beta Distribution

PERT analysis assumes that the probabilistic properties of activity duration can be modeled by the beta probability density function. The beta distribution is defined by two end points and two shape parameters. The beta distribution was chosen by the original developers of PERT as a reasonable distribution to model activity times because it has finite end points and can assume a variety of shapes based on different shape parameters. While the true distribution of activity time will rarely ever be known, the beta distribution serves as an acceptable model. Figure 2-19 shows examples of alternate shapes of the standard beta distribution between zero and one. The uniform distribution between 0 and 1 is a special case of the beta distribution with, both shape parameters equal to one.

Figure 2-19. Alternate Shapes of the Beta Distribution

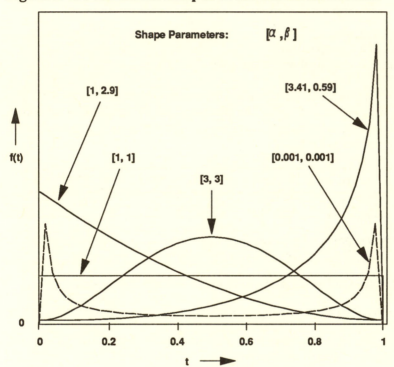

Many analytical studies of the beta distribution and the PERT approach have been presented in the literature. Interested readers should consult MacCrimmon and Ryavec (1964), Grubbs (1962), McBride and McClelland (1967), Van Slyke (1963), Sasieni (1986), Welsh (1965), Farnum and Stanton (1987), Troutt (1989), Gallagher (1987), Golenko-Ginzburg (1988), and Golenko-Ginzburg (1989a).

The standard beta distribution is defined over the interval 0 to 1, while the general beta distribution is defined over any interval *a* to *b*. The general beta probability density function is given by:

$$f(t) = \frac{\Gamma(\alpha+\beta)}{\Gamma(\alpha)\Gamma(\beta)} \cdot \frac{1}{(b-a)^{\alpha+\beta-1}} \cdot (t-a)^{\alpha-1}(b-t)^{\beta-1};$$

for $a \le t \le b$ and $\alpha > 0$, $\beta > 0$.

where:
a = lower end point of the distribution
b = upper end point of the distribution
α, β are the shape parameters for the distribution.

The mean, variance, and mode of the general beta distribution are defined as:

$$\mu = a + (b-a)\frac{\alpha}{\alpha+\beta}$$

$$\sigma^2 = (b-a)^2\frac{\alpha\beta}{(\alpha+\beta+1)(\alpha+\beta)^2}$$

$$m = \frac{a(\beta-1)+b(\alpha-1)}{\alpha+\beta-2}.$$

The general beta distribution can be transformed into a standardized distribution by changing its domain from $[a,b]$ to the unit interval, $[0,1]$. This is accomplished by using the relationship $t_g = a + (b-a)t_s$, where t_s is the standard beta random variable between 0 and 1. This yields the standardized beta distribution, given by:

$$f(t) = \frac{\Gamma(\alpha+\beta)}{\Gamma(\alpha)\Gamma(\beta)}t^{\alpha-1}(1-t)^{\beta-1}; \quad 0 < t < 1; \quad \alpha, \beta > 0$$

$$= 0; \quad \text{elsewhere},$$

with mean, variance, and mode defined as:

$$\mu = \frac{\alpha}{\alpha+\beta}$$

$$\sigma^2 = \frac{\alpha\beta}{(\alpha+\beta+1)(\alpha+\beta)^2}$$

$$m = \frac{a(\beta-1)+b(\alpha-1)}{\alpha+\beta-2}.$$

Triangular Distribution

The triangular probability density function has been used as an alternative to the beta distribution for modeling activity times. The triangular density has three essential parameters: a minimum value, a mode, and a maximum. The triangular density function is defined mathematically as:

$$f(t) = \frac{2(t - a)}{(m - a)(b - a)}; \quad a \leq t \leq m$$

$$= \frac{2(b - t)}{(b - m)(b - a)}; \quad m \leq t \leq b,$$

with mean and variance defined, respectively, as:

$$\mu = \frac{a + m + b}{3}$$

$$\sigma^2 = \frac{a(a - m) + b(b - a) + m(m - b)}{18}.$$

Figure 2-20 presents a graphical representation of the triangular density function. The three time estimates of PERT can be inserted into the expression for the mean of the triangular distribution to obtain an estimate of the expected activity duration. Note that in the conventional PERT formula, the mode (m) is assumed to carry four times as much weight as either a or b when calculating the expected activity duration. By contrast, under the triangular distribution, the three time estimates are assumed to carry equal weights.

Figure 2-20. Triangular Probability Density Function

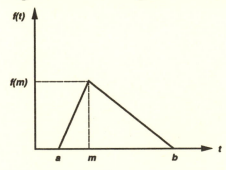

Uniform Distribution

For cases where only two time estimates instead of three are to be used for network analysis, the uniform density function may be assumed for the activity times. This is acceptable for situations where the extreme limits of an activity duration can be estimated and it can be assumed that the intermediate values are equally likely to occur. The uniform distribution is defined mathematically as:

$$f(t) = \frac{1}{b - a}; \qquad a \leq t \leq b$$

$$= 0; \qquad \text{otherwise},$$

with mean and variance defined, respectively, as:

$$\mu = \frac{a + b}{2}$$

$$\sigma^2 = \frac{(b - a)^2}{12}.$$

Figure 2-21 presents a graphical representation of the uniform distribution. In the case of the uniform distribution, the expected activity duration is computed as the average of the upper and lower limits of the distribution. The appeal of using only two time estimates a and b is that the estimation error due to subjectivity can be reduced and the estimation task simplified. Even when a uniform distribution is not assumed, other statistical distributions can be modeled over the range of a to b.

Figure 2-21. Uniform Probability Density Function

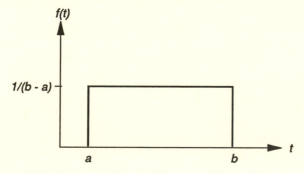

Other distributions that have been explored for activity time modeling include the normal distribution, lognormal distribution, truncated exponential distribution, and Weibull distribution. Once the expected activity durations have been computed, the analysis of the activity network is carried out just as in the case of single-estimate CPM network analysis.

Distribution of Project Duration

Regardless of the distribution assumed for activity durations, the *central limit theorem* suggests that the distribution of the project duration will be approximately normally distributed. The theorem says that the distribution of averages obtained from any probability density function will be approximately normally distributed if the sample size is large and the averages are independent. In mathematical terms, the theorem is stated as given below.

Central limit Theorem:
Let $X_1, X_2, ..., X_N$ be independent and identically distributed random variables. Then the sum of the random variables is normally distributed for large values of N. The sum is defined as:

$$T = X_1 + X_2 + ... + X_N.$$

In activity network analysis, T represents the total project length as determined by the sum of the durations of the activities on the critical path. The mean and variance of T are expressed as:

$$\mu = \sum_{i=1}^{N} E[X_i]$$

$$\sigma^2 = \sum_{i=1}^{N} V[X_i],$$

where
$E[X_i]$ = expected value of random variable X_i
$V[X_i]$ = variance of random variable X_i.

When applying the central limit theorem to activity networks, one should note that the assumption of independent activity times may not always be satisfied. Because of precedence relationships and other interdependencies of activities, some activity durations may not be independent.

Probability Calculation

If the project duration T_e can be assumed to be approximately normally distributed based on the central limit theorem, then the probability of meeting a specified deadline T_d can be computed by finding the area under the standard normal curve to the left of T_d. Figure 2-22 shows an example of a normal distribution describing the project duration.

Figure 2-22. Area under the Normal Curve

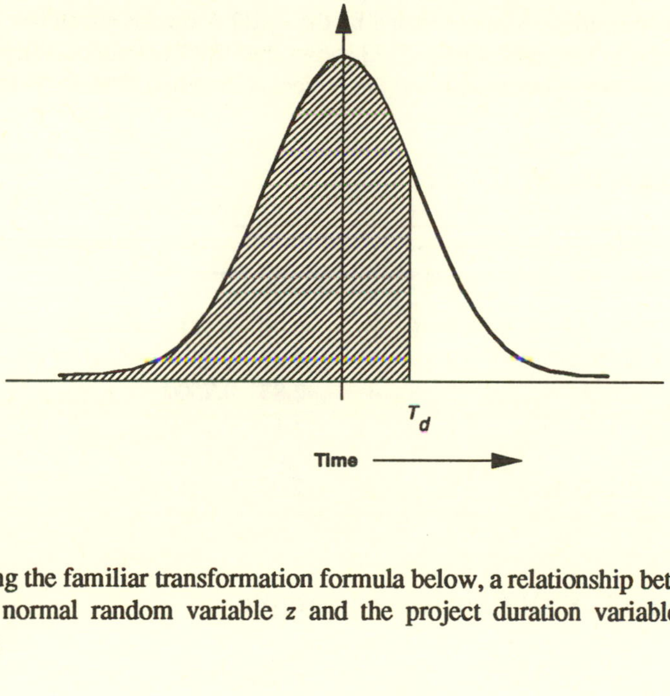

Using the familiar transformation formula below, a relationship between the standard normal random variable z and the project duration variable can be obtained:

$$z = \frac{T_d - T_e}{S},$$

where
T_d = specified deadline
T_e = expected project duration based on network analysis
S = standard deviation of the project duration.

The probability of completing a project by the deadline T_d is then computed as:

$$P(T \leq T_d) = P\left(z \leq \frac{T_d - T_e}{S}\right).$$

The probability is obtained from the standard normal table presented in the Appendix. Examples presented below illustrate the procedure for probability calculations in PERT.

PERT Network Example

Suppose we have the project data presented in Table 2-6. The expected activity durations and variances as calculated by the PERT formulas are shown in the last two columns of the table. Figure 2-23 shows the PERT network. Activities C, E, and G are shown to be critical, and the project completion time is 11 time units.

Table 2-6. PERT Project Data

Activity	Predecessors	a	m	b	t_e	s^2
A	-	1	2	4	2.17	0.2500
B	-	5	6	7	6.00	0.1111
C	-	2	4	5	3.83	0.2500
D	A	1	3	4	2.83	0.2500
E	C	4	5	7	5.17	0.2500
F	A	3	4	5	4.00	0.1111
G	B, D, E	1	2	3	2.00	0.1111

Figure 2-23. PERT Network Example

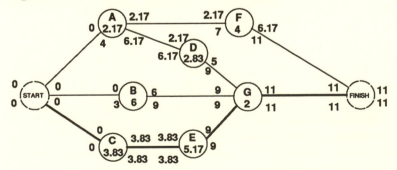

The probability of completing the project on or before a deadline of 10 time units (i.e., $T_d = 10$) is calculated as shown below:

$$T_e \; = \; 11$$

$$S^2 \; = \; V[C] \; + \; V[E] \; + \; V[G]$$

$$= \; 0.25 \; + \; 0.25 \; + \; 0.1111$$

$$= \; 0.6111$$

$$S \; = \; \sqrt{0.6111}$$

$$= \; .7817$$

$$P(T \leq T_d) \; = \; P(T \leq 10)$$

$$= \; P\left(z \; \leq \; \frac{10 - T_e}{S}\right)$$

$$= \; P\left(z \; \leq \; \frac{10 - 11}{0.7817}\right)$$

$$= \; P(z \; \leq \; -1.2793)$$

$$= \; 1 \; - \; P(z \; \leq \; 1.2793)$$

$$= \; 1 \; - \; 0.8997$$

$$= \; 0.1003 \; .$$

Thus, there is just over 10% probability of finishing the project within 10 days. By contrast, the probability of finishing the project in 13 days is calculated as:

$$P(T \leq 13) \; = \; P\left(z \; \leq \; \frac{13 - 11}{0.7817}\right)$$

$$= \; P(z \; \leq \; 2.5585)$$

$$= \; 0.9948 \; .$$

This implies that there is over 99% probability of finishing the project within 13 days. Note that the probability of finishing the project in exactly 13 days will be zero. An exercise at the end of this chapter requires the reader to show that $P(T = T_d) = 0$. If we desire the probability that the project can be completed within a certain lower limit (T_L) and a certain upper limit (T_U), the computation will proceed as follows: Let $T_L = 9$ and $T_U = 11.5$. Then,

$$P(T_L \leq T \leq T_U) = P(9 \leq T \leq 11.5)$$

$$= P(T \leq 11.5) - P(T \leq 9)$$

$$= P\left(z \leq \frac{11.5 - 11}{0.7817}\right) - P\left(z \leq \frac{9 - 11}{0.7817}\right)$$

$$= P(z \leq 0.6396) - P(z \leq -2.5585)$$

$$= P(z \leq 0.6396) - [1 - P(z \leq 2.5585)]$$

$$= 0.7389 - [1 - 0.9948]$$

$$= 0.7389 - 0.0052$$

$$= 0.7337.$$

PRECEDENCE DIAGRAMMING METHOD

The precedence diagramming method (PDM) was developed in the early 1960s as an extension of the basic PERT/CPM network analysis (Crandall, 1973; Wiest, 1981; Moder et al., 1983; Harhalakis, 1990). PDM permits mutually dependent activities to be performed partially in parallel instead of serially. The usual finish-to-start dependencies between activities are relaxed to allow activities to be overlapped. This facilitates schedule compression. An example is the requirement that concrete should be allowed to dry for a number of days before drilling holes for handrails. That is, drilling cannot start until so many days after the completion of concrete work. This is a finish-to-start constraint. The time between the finishing time of the first activity and the starting time of the second activity is called the *lead-lag* requirement between the two activities. Figure 2-24 shows the graphical representation of the basic lead-lag relationships between activity A and activity B. The terminology presented in Figure 2-24 is explained as follows.

SS_{AB} (Start-to-Start) lead: This specifies that activity B cannot start until activity A has been in progress for at least SS time units.

FF_{AB} (Finish-to-Finish) lead: This specifies that activity B cannot finish until at least FF time units after the completion of activity A.

FS_{AB} (Finish-to-Start) lead: This specifies that activity B cannot start until at least FS time units after the completion of activity A. Note that PERT/CPM approaches use $FS_{AB} = 0$ for network analysis.

SF$_{AB}$ (Start-to-Finish) lead: This specifies that there must be at least SF time units between the start of activity A and the completion of activity B.

Figure 2-24. Lead-Lag Relationships in PDM

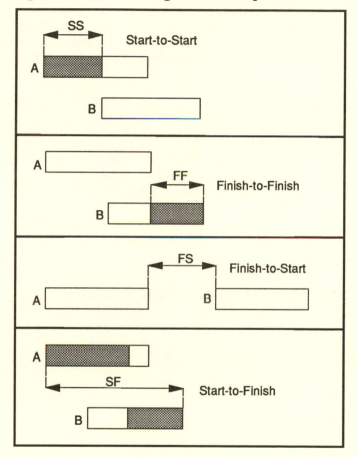

The leads or lags may, alternately, be expressed in percentages rather than time units. For example, we may specify that 25 percent of the work content of activity A must be completed before activity B can start. If percentage of work completed is used for determining lead-lag constraints, then a reliable procedure must be used for estimating the percent completion. If the project work is broken up properly using work breakdown structure (WBS), it will be much easier to estimate percent completion by evaluating the work completed at the elementary task levels. The lead-lag relationships may also be specified in terms of *at most* relationships instead of *at least* relationships. For example, we may have at most FF lag requirement between the finishing time of one activity and the finishing time of another activity. Splitting of activities often simplifies the implementation of PDM, as will be shown later with some examples. Some of the factors that will determine whether or not an activity can be split are technical limitations affecting splitting of a task, morale of the person working on the split task, setup times required to recommence split tasks, difficulty involved in managing resources for split tasks, loss of consistency of work, and management policy about splitting jobs.

Figure 2-25 presents a simple CPM network consisting of three activities. The activities are to be performed serially and each has an expected duration of 10 days. The conventional CPM network analysis indicates that the duration of the network is 30 days. The earliest times and the latest times are as shown in the figure.

Figure 2-25. Serial Activities in CPM Network

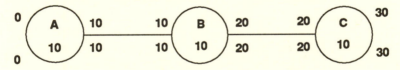

The Gantt chart for the example is shown in Figure 2-26. For a comparison, Figure 2-27 shows the same network but with some lead-lag constraints. For example, there is an SS constraint of 2 days and an FF constraint of 2 days between activities A and B. Thus, activity B can start as early as 2 days after activity A starts, but it cannot finish until 2 days after the completion of A. In order words, *at least* 2 days must be between the starting times of A and B. Likewise, *at least* 2 days must separate the finishing time of A and the finishing time of B. A similar precedence relationship exists between activity B and activity C. The earliest and latest times obtained by considering the lag constraints are indicated in Figure 2-27.

Figure 2-26. Gantt Chart of Serial Activities in CPM Example

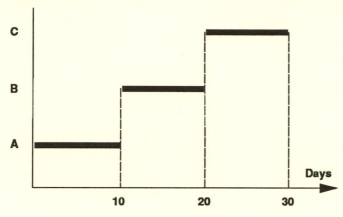

Figure 2-27. PDM Network Example

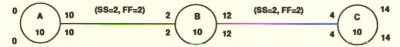

The calculations show that if B is started just 2 days after A is started, it can be completed as early as 12 days as opposed to the 20 days obtained in the case of conventional CPM. Similarly, activity C is completed at time 14, which is considerably less than the 30 days calculated by conventional CPM. The lead-lag constraints allow us to compress or overlap activities. Depending on the nature of the tasks involved, an activity does not have to wait until its predecessor finishes before it can start. Figure 2-28 shows the Gantt chart for the example incorporating the lead-lag constraints. It should be noted that a portion of a succeeding activity can be performed simultaneously with a portion of the preceding activity.

A portion of an activity that overlaps with a portion of another activity may be viewed as a distinct portion of the required work. Thus, partial completion of an activity may be evaluated. Figure 2-29 shows how each of the three activities is partitioned into contiguous parts. Even though there is no physical break or termination of work in any activity, the distinct parts (beginning and ending) can still be identified. This means that there is no physical splitting of the work content

Figure 2-28. Gantt Chart for PDM Example

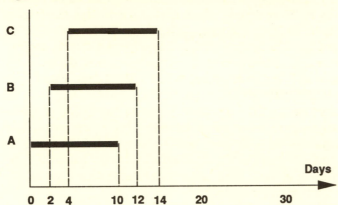

of any activity.   The distinct parts are determined on the basis of the amount of work that must be completed before or after another activity, as dictated by the lead-lag relationships. In Figure 2-29, activity A is partitioned into the parts A_1 and A_2. The duration of A_1 is 2 days because there is an SS=2 relationship between activity A and activity B. Since the original duration of A is 10 days, the duration of A_2 is then calculated to be 10 - 2 = 8 days.

Figure 2-29. Partitioning of Activities in PDM Example

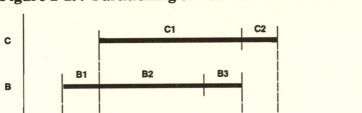

Likewise, activity B is partitioned into the parts B_1, B_2, and B_3. The duration of B_1 is 2 days because there is an SS=2 relationship between activity B and activity C. The duration of B_3 is also 2 days because there is an FF=2 relationship between activity A and acitivity B. Since the original duration of B is 10 days, the duration of B_2 is calculated to be 10-(2+2) = 6 days. In a similar fashion, activity C is partitioned into C_1 and C_2. The duration of C_2 is 2 days because there is an FF=2 relationship between activity B and activity C. Since the original duration of C is 10 days, the duration of C_1 is then calculated to be 10 - 2 = 8 days. Figure 2-30 shows a conventional CPM network drawn for the three activities after they are partitioned into distinct parts. The conventional forward and backward passes reveal that all the activity parts are on the critical path. This makes sense, since the original three activities are performed serially and no physical splitting of activities has been performed. Note that there are three critical paths in Figure 2-30, each with a length of 14 days. It should also be noted that the distinct parts of each activity are performed contiguously.

Figure 2-30. CPM Network of Partitioned Activities

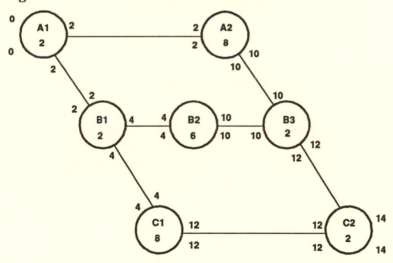

Figure 2-31 shows an alternate example of three serial activities. The conventional CPM analysis shows that the duration of the network is 30 days. When lead-lag constraints are introduced into the network as shown in Figure 2-32, the network duration is compressed to 18 days.

Figure 2-31. Another CPM Example of Serial Activities

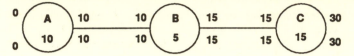

Figure 2-32. Compressed PDM Network

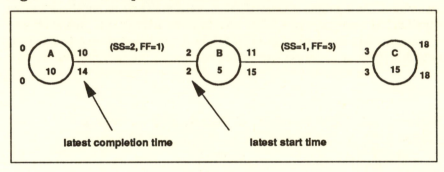

In the forward pass computations in Figure 2-32, note that the earliest completion time of B is time 11, because there is an FF=1 restriction between activity A and activity B. Since A finishes at time 10, B cannot finish until at least time 11. Even though the earliest starting time of B is time 2 and its duration is 5 days, its earliest completion time cannot be earlier than time 11. Also note that C can start as early as time 3 because there an SS=1 relationship between B and C. Thus, given a duration of 15 days for C, the earliest completion time of the network is 3 + 15 = 18 days. The difference between the earliest completion time of C and the earliest completion time of B is 18 - 11 = 7 days, which satisfies the FF=3 relationship between B and C.

In the backward pass, the latest completion time of B is 15 (i.e., 18 - 3 = 15), since there is an FF=3 relationship between activity B and activity C. The latest start time for B is time 2 (i.e., 3 - 1 = 2), since there is an SS=1 relationship between activity B and activity C. If we are not careful, we may erroneously set the latest start time of B to 10 (i.e., 15 - 5 = 10). But that would violate the SS=1 restriction between B and C. The latest completion time of A is found to be 14 (i.e., 15 - 1 = 14), since there is an FF=1 relationship between A and B. All the earliest times and latest times at each node must be evaluated to ensure that they conform to all the lead-lag constraints. When computing earliest start or earliest completion times, the smallest possible value that satisfies the lead-lag constraints should be used. By the same reasoning, when computing the latest start or latest completion times, the largest possible value that satisfies the lead-lag constraints should be used.

Manual evaluations of the lead-lag precedence network analysis can become very tedious for large networks. A computer program may be used to simplify the implementation of PDM. If manual analysis must be done for PDM computations, it is suggested that the network be partitioned into more manageable segments. The segments may then be linked after the computations are completed. The expanded CPM network in Figure 2-33 was developed on the basis of the precedence network in Figure 2-32. It is seen that activity A is partitioned into two parts, activity B is partitioned into three parts, and activity C is partitioned into two parts. The forward and backward passes show that only the first parts of activities A and B are on the critical path. Both parts of activity C are on the critical path.

Figure 2-33. CPM Expansion of Second PDM Example

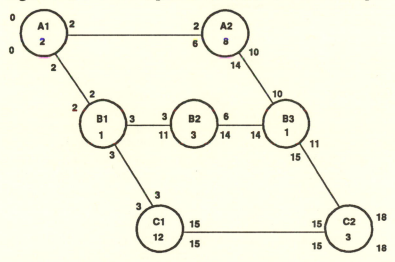

Figure 2-34 shows the corresponding earliest-start Gantt chart for the expanded network. Looking at the earliest start times, one can see that activity B is physically split at the boundary of B_2 and B_3 in such a way that B_3 is separated from B_2 by 4 days. This implies that work on activity B is temporarily stopped at time 6 after B_2 is finished and is not started again until time 10. Note that despite the 4-day delay in starting B_3, the entire project is not delayed. This is because B_3, the last part of activity B, is not on the critical path. In fact, B_3 has a total slack of 4 days. In a situation like this, the duration of activity B can actually be increased from 5 days to 9 days without any adverse effect on the project duration. It should be recognized, however, that increasing the duration of an activity may have negative implications for project cost and personnel productivity.

Figure 2-34. Compressed PDM Schedule Based on ES Times

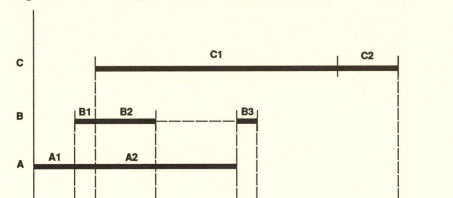

If physical splitting of activities is not permitted, then the best option available in Figure 2-34 is to stretch the duration of B_2 so as to fill up the gap from time 6 to time 10. An alternative is to delay the starting time of B_1 until time 4 so as to use up the 4-day slack right at the beginning of activity B. Unfortunately, delaying the starting time of B_1 by 4 days will delay the overall project by 4 days, since B_1 is on the critical path as shown in Figure 2-33. The project analyst will need to evaluate the appropriate trade-offs between splitting of activities, delaying activities, increasing activity durations, and incurring higher project costs. The prevailing project scenario should be considered when making such trade-off decisions. Figure 2-35 shows the Gantt chart for the compressed PDM schedule based on latest start times. In this case, it will be necessary to split both activities A and B even though the total project duration remains the same at 18 days. If activity splitting is to be avoided, then we can increase the duration of activity A from 10 to 14 days and the duration of B from 5 to 13 days without adversely affecting the entire project duration. The important benefit of precedence diagramming is that the ability to overlap activities facilitates some flexibilities in manipulating individual activity times and compressing the project duration.

Figure 2-35. Compressed PDM Schedule Based on LS Times

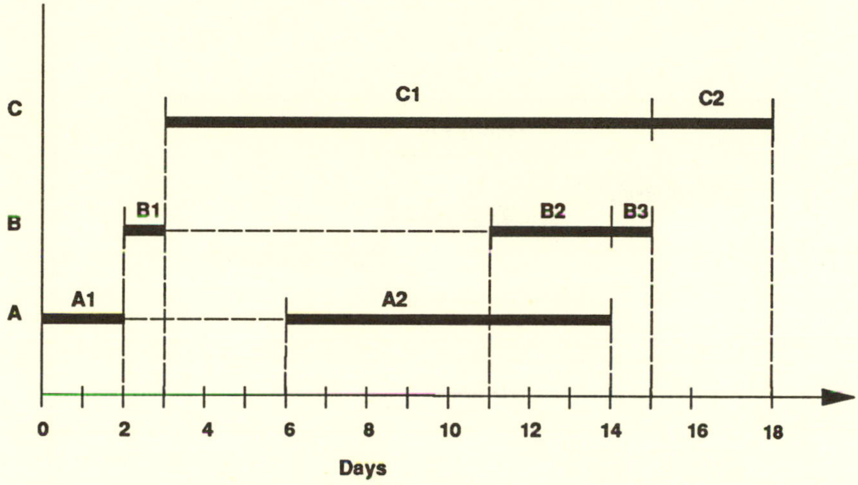

Anomalies In PDM Networks
Care must be exercised when working with PDM networks because of the potential for misuse or misinterpretation. Because of the lead and lag requirements, activities that do not have any slacks may appear to have generous slacks. Also, "reverse critical" activities may occur in PDM. Reverse critical activities are activities that can cause a decrease in project duration when their durations are increased. This may happen when the critical path enters the completion of an activity through a finish lead-lag constraint. Also, if a "finish-to-finish" dependency and a "start-to-start" dependency are connected to a reverse critical task, a reduction in the duration of the task may actually lead to an increase in the project duration. Figure 2-36 illustrates this anomalous situation. The finish-to-finish constraint between A and B requires that B should finish no earlier than 20 days. If the duration of task B is reduced from 10 days to 5 days, the start-to-start constraint between B and C forces the starting time of C to be shifted forward by 5 days, thereby resulting in a 5-day increase in the project duration.

Figure 2-36. Reverse Critical Activity in PDM Network

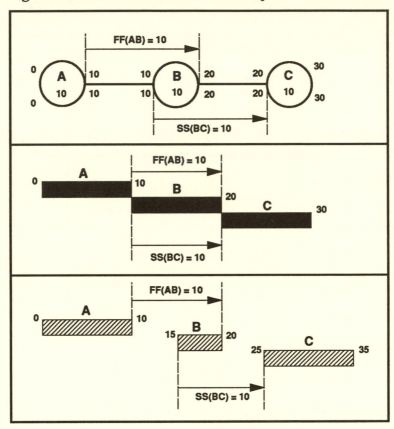

The preceding anomalies can occur without being noticed in large PDM networks. One safeguard against their adverse effects is to make only one activity change at a time and document the resulting effect on the network structure and length. Wiest (1981) suggests using the following categorizations for the unusual characteristics of activities in PDM networks:

Normal Critical (NC): This refers to an activity for which the project duration shifts in the same direction as the shift in the duration of the activity.

Reverse Critical (RC): This refers to an activity for which the project duration shifts in the reverse direction to the shift in the duration of the activity.

Bi-Critical (BC): This refers to an activity for which the project duration increases as a result of any shift in the duration of the activity.

Start Critical (SC): This refers to an activity for which the project duration shifts in the direction of the shift in the start time of the activity, but is unaffected (neutral) by a shift in the overall duration of the activity.

Finish Critical (FC): This refers to an activity for which the project duration shifts in the direction of the shift in the finish time of the activity, but is unaffected (neutral) by a shift in the overall duration of the activity.

Mid Normal Critical (MNC): This refers to an activity whose mid portion is normal critical.

Mid Reverse Critical (MRC): This refers to an activity whose mid portion is reverse critical.

Mid Bi-Critical (MBC): This refers to an activity whose mid portion is bi-critical.

An expert system can facilitate the integration and consistent usage of all the relevant information in a complex scheduling environment (Badiru 1992). Task precedence relaxation assessment and resource-constrained heuristic scheduling constitute an example of a problem suitable for expert system implementation. The applicable expert system rules may be expressed in the general forms presented below:

IF: *Logistical conditions are satisfied*
THEN: *Perform the selected scheduling action*

IF   condition A is satisfied and
       condition B is false and
       evidence C is present or
       observation D is available
THEN   precedence belongs in class X

IF   *if precedence belongs to class X*
THEN   *activate heuristic scheduling procedure Y*

The function of the expert system model will be to aid a decision maker in developing a task sequence that fits the needs of concurrent scheduling. Based on user input, the model will determine the type of task precedence, establish precedence relaxation strategy, implement task scheduling heuristic, match the schedule to resource availability, and present a recommended task sequence to the user. The user can perform "what-if" analysis by making changes in the input data and conducting sensitivity analysis. The expert system implementation can be achieved in an interactive environment as shown in Figure 2-37. The user will provide task definitions and resource availabilities with appropriate precedence requirements. At each stage, the user is prompted to consider potential points for precedence relaxation. Wherever schedule options exist, they will be presented to the user for consideration and approval. The need for task splitting will be assessed implicitly by the expert system. The user will have the opportunity to make final decisions about task sequence.

Figure 2-37. Decision Support Model for PDM

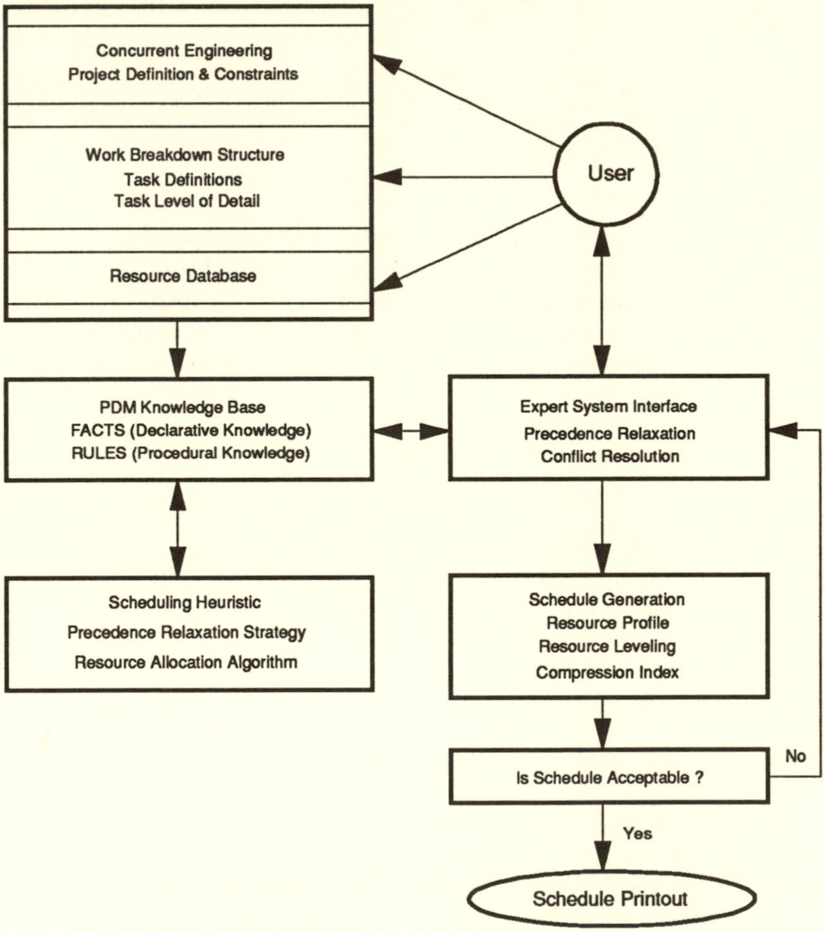

QUESTIONS AND EXERCISES

2-1.   Suppose the following historical data has been compiled for the time (days) it takes to perform a certain task:

11, 18, 25, 30, 8, 42, 25, 30, 13, 21, 26, 35, 15, 23, 29, 36, 17, 25, 30, 21.

Based on the above data, suggest reasonable values for the PERT estimates *a*, *m*, and *b* for the task. Justify your answer.

2-2.   Show that for any PERT project network, the probability of finishing the project in *exactly* x time units is zero.

2-3.   Repeat the crashing exercise presented in Table 2-5 by crashing only the three critical activities, C, E, and G. What is the new project duration? What is the new total project cost?

2-4.   For the PERT project data below, answer the questions that follow:

		Duration (Days)
Activity	Predecessor	*a, m, b*
A	-	7, 9, 11
B	-	7, 8, 10
C	A	2, 4, 6
D	A	1, 3, 7
E	B	1, 3, 7
F	B	2, 4, 6

a)   Draw the AON CPM network for the project, perform the forward and backward computations, and determine the project duration.

b)   Draw the Gantt chart using the earliest start times.

c)   Draw the Gantt chart using the latest start times.

d)   Compare and discuss the relative differences/advantages/disadvantages of the two Gantt charts in parts (b) and (c) above.

2-5.   The CPM network below is subject to the following two simultaneous restrictions:

a) The project cannot start until 5 days from time 0 (i.e., ES of the Start node = 5).

b) There is a deadline of 35 days (i.e., LC of the finish node = 35). Perform the forward and backward CPM computations and show ES, LS, EC, LC, TS, and FS for each activity. What is the TS for each activity on the critical path?

Activity	Predecessor	Duration (days)
A	-	2
B	A	4
C	B	6
D	A	3
E	B	2
F	E	1
G	C, D	2
H	G	3
I	H	4

2-6. Using the mathematical expressions for the free slack (FS) and total slack (TS), show that FS cannot be larger than TS.

2-7. Show that even if TS > 0, FS may or may not be greater than zero.

2-8. Suppose five activities are on a CPM critical path and each activity has TS = 2. Determine the overall effect on the critical path length if 2 of the critical activities are delayed by two time units each. Discuss.

2-9. Give practical examples of SS, SF, FF, and FS precedence constraints.

2-10. Suppose two serial activities A and B are the only activities in a precedence diagramming network. Activity A precedes activity B. There is an SS restriction of 4 time units and an FF restriction of 3 time units between A and B.

a) Determine the mathematical relationship between the duration of A (t_A) and the duration of B (t_B).

b) Verify your response to part (a) above by considering the following alternate cases:
Case 1: $t_A = 0$
Case 2: $0 < t_A <= 1$

Case 3: $1 < t_A < 4$
Case 4: $t_A = 4$
Case 5: $t_A > 4$

2-11. Perform a PERT analysis of the project given below and find the probability of finishing the project between 16 and 20 days inclusive:

Activity	Predecessors	Duration Estimates (Days) (a, m, b)
1	-	1, 4, 5
2	-	2, 3, 4
3	1	6, 10, 13
4	1	6, 6, 7
5	2	2, 2, 2
6	3	1, 2, 3
7	4, 5	5, 8, 9
8	2	12, 16, 19

2-12. Given the project data below, answer the questions that follow.

Project Phase	Preceding Phase	Normal Time	Normal Cost	Crash Time	Crash Cost	Variance of Duration
A	-	40	$9,000	30	$12,000	10
B	A	53	15,000	50	15,300	9
C	A	60	7,500	30	6,000*	600
D	A	35	20,000	30	22,000	25
E	C, D	28	12,000	20	15,000	40
F	B, E	30	6,000	27	7,000	30

* *Crashing of this activity results in significant savings in direct labor cost.*

a) There is a penalty of $3,000 per day beyond the normal PERT duration. Perform a crashing analysis to compare total normal cost to total crash cost. First crash only the critical activities, then crash all activities.

b) Find the probability that the total lateness penalty will be less than $3,000.

c) Find the probability that the total lateness penalty will be $3,000 or less.

d) Find the probability that the total lateness penalty will be more than $3,000.

e) Find the probability that the total lateness penalty will be less than $9,000.

2-13. Suppose it is known that the duration of a project has a triangular distribution with a lower limit of 24 months, an upper limit of 46 months, and a mode of 36 months. Find the probability that the project can be completed in 40 months or less.

2-14. Suppose it is known that the duration of a project is uniformly distributed between 24 months and 46 months. Find the probability that the project can be completed in 40 months or less.

2-15. Given the following project data:

Activity	Predecessor	Estimated CPM Duration, t (days)
A	-	6
B	-	5
C	-	2
D	A, B	4
E	B	5
F	C	6
G	B, F	1
H	D, E	7

If the PERT time estimates for each activity are defined as

$$a = t - 0.3t$$

$$m = t$$

$$b = t + \sqrt{t}$$

Find a deadline, T_d, such that there is 0.85 probability of finishing the project on or before the deadline. *Note*: Carry all computations to four decimal places.

2-16. Suppose we are given the data for the project below:

Activity	Predecessor	Expected PERT Duration	Variance of Duration
A	-	4	0.5000
B	A	5	1.0000
C	A	7	0.2500
D	A	2	0.3000
E	C, D	8	0.3750
F	B, E	9	0.4375

There is no penalty if the project is completed on or before the normal PERT duration. However, a penalty of $3,000 is charged for each day that the project lasts beyond the normal PERT duration. Using standard probability approach, find the *expected dollar penalty* for this project.

Note: Carry all intermediate computations to four decimal places.

2-17. Presented below is the data for a precedence diagram problem. The SS, SF, and FF relationships between pairs of activities are given.

Activity	Predecessor	Duration
A	-	5
B	A	10
C	A	4
D	B, C	15

SS(Between A & B) = 1
FF(Between A & B) = 8
SS(Between A & C) = 2
SF(Between A & C) = 8
SS(Between B & D) = 5
SS(Between C & D) = 7
FF(Between C & D) = 10

a) Perform the forward and backward computations *without* considering the precedence constraints. What is the project duration?

b) Perform the forward and backward computations considering the precedence constraints. What is the project duration?

2-18. a) What potential effect(s) does the crashing of a noncritical activity
         have on the following?
         i)   The critical path
         ii) The project duration

      b) Use a hypothetical example of a CPM project network consisting of
          seven activities to support your answer above. First show the network
          computations without crashing. Identify the critical path. Then show
          the computations with the crashing of one noncritical activity.

2-19. Assume that you are the manager responsible for the project whose data is
       presented below.

Activity	Description	Duration (Hours)	Preceding Activities
A	Develop required material list	8	-
B	Procure pipe	200	A
C	Erect scaffold	12	-
D	Remove scaffold	4	I, M
E	Deactivate line	8	-
F	Prefabricate sections	40	B
G	Install new pipes	32	F, L
H	(Deleted from work plan)	-	-
I	Fit-up pipes and valves	8	G, K
J	Procure valves	225	A
K	Install valves	8	J, L
L	Remove old pipes and valves	35	C, E
M	Insulate	24	G, K
N	Pressure test	6	I
O	Clean-up and start-up	4	D, N

      a) Draw the CPM diagram for this project.

      b) Perform the forward and backward pass calculations on the network
          and indicate the project duration.

      c) List all the different paths in the network in *decreasing* order of
          criticality index in the tabulated form shown below. Define the
          criticality index as follows:

Let S_k = sum of the total slacks on path number k
(i.e., sum of TS values for all activities on path k)
S_{max} = maximum value of S (i.e., Max$\{S_k\}$)
$C_k = [(S_{max} - S_k)/S_{max}]*100\%$
Define the most critical path as the one with $C_k = 100\%$.
Define the least critical path as the one with $C_k = 0\%$.

k	Activities in Path	Sum of TS on Path (S_k)	Path Criticality Index (C_k)
1.			100%
2.			
...	....	....	....
n			0%

2-20. Assume that we have the precedence diagramming network data below:

Activity	Predecessor	Duration
A	-	8
B	A	12
C	B	4
D	B	7
E	C, D	8
F	D	12
G	E, F	3

The following PDM restrictions are applicable to the network:
$SS_{AB} = 3$
$FF_{AB} = 12$
$FS_{BC} = 1$
$SS_{BD} = 6$
$SF_{DE} = 13$
$FS_{FG} = 3$

If the project start time is $t=5$ and the project due date is $t=52$, perform conventional CPM analysis of the network without considering the lead-lag PDM restrictions. Show both forward and backward passes. Identify the critical path. Tabulate the total slack (TS) and free slack (FS) for the activities in the network.

2-21.   Repeat Question 2-20 and consider the lead-lag PDM restrictions. Draw the Gantt chart schedule that satisfies all the lead-lag constraints.

2-22.   Draw an expanded CPM network for the Gantt chart in Question 2-21 considering the need to split activities.

2-23.   Would you classify the CPM procedure as a management by objective (MBO) approach or a management by exception (MBE) approach? Discuss.

2-24.   In activity scheduling, which of the following carries the higher priority?
        i) Activity Precedence Constraint
        ii) Resource Constraint

2-25.   For the project data in Question 2-20, assume that the given activity durations represent the most likely PERT estimates (m). Define the other PERT estimates a and b as follow:
        $a = m - 1$
        $b = m + 1$
        Disregarding the PDM lead-lag constraints, find the probability of finishing the project within 51 time units.

2-26   The *median rule* of project control refers to the due date that has a 0.50 probability of being achieved. Suppose the duration, T, of a project follows a triangular distribution with end points a and b. If the mode of the distribution is closer to b than it is to a, find a general expression for the median (denoted by m_d) such that:

$$P(T \leq m_d) = 0.50.$$

CHAPTER 3

RESOURCE-CONSTRAINED NETWORKS

This chapter addresses the problem of resource-constrained project network analysis. The differences between unconstrained PERT/CPM networks and resource-constrained networks are discussed. The resource loading and resource leveling strategies are presented. Resource idleness graph is introduced as a measure of the level of resource idleness in resource-constrained project schedules. Various resource allocation heuristics are described with illustrative examples. Techniques for assessing the complexity of project networks for scheduling purposes are also discussed. A procedure for calculating resource work rates to assess project productivity is outlined. An example of a resource-constrained PDM network is presented. The chapter introduces new graphical tools, referred to as the critical resource diagram (CRD) and the resource schedule Gantt chart. The CRD is used to represent the interrelationships among resource units as they perform their respective tasks. It is also used to identify bottleneck resources in a project network. The resource schedule Gantt chart indicates time intervals of allocation for specific resource types. The chapter concludes with examples of probabilistic evaluation of resource utilization levels.

RESOURCE ALLOCATION IN PROJECT NETWORKS

Basic CPM and PERT approaches assume unlimited resource availability in project network analysis. In this chapter, both the time and resource requirements of activities are considered in developing network schedules. As mentioned in Chapter One, projects are subject to three major constraints of time limitations, resource constraints, and performance requirements. Since these constraints are difficult to satisfy simultaneously, trade-offs must be made. The smaller the resource base, the longer the project schedule and the lower the quality of work.

Resource allocation facilitates the transition of a project from one state to another state. Figure 3-1 presents a graphical representation of the possible transition paths of a project based on resource allocation strategies.

Figure 3-1. Resource-Based Transition of Project Progress

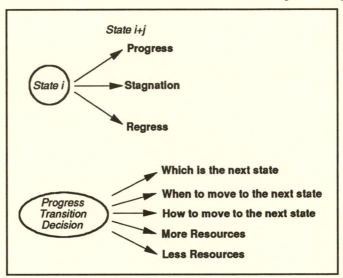

Given that the progress of a project is in an initial *state i*, three possible changes can occur. Further progress may be achieved in moving to *state i+j*, the progress may be stagnant between *state i* and *state i+j*, or the progress may regress from *state i* to *state i+j*. Planning, scheduling, and control strategies must be developed to determine what the next desired state of the project is, when the next state is expected to be reached, and how to move toward that next state. Resource availability as well as other internal and external factors will determine the nature of the progress of a project from one state to another. Network diagrams, Gantt charts, progress charts, and resource loading graphs provide visual cues that can guide resource allocation strategies.

Resource Loading Graph

Resource loading refers to the allocation of resources to work elements in a project network. A resource loading graph is a graphical representation of resource allocation over time. Figure 3-2 shows an example of a resource loading graph. Resource loading graph may be drawn for the different resources types involved in a project.

Figure 3-2. Example of Resource Loading Graph

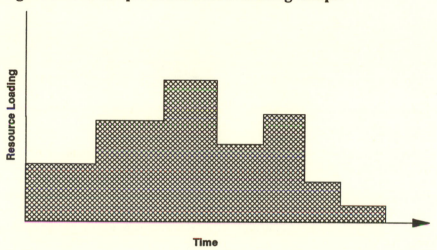

The graph provides information useful for resource planning and budgeting purposes. A resource loading graph gives an indication of the demand a project will place on an organization's resources. In addition to resource units committed to activities, the graph may also be drawn for other tangible and intangible resources of an organization. For example, a variation of the graph may be used to present information about the depletion rate of the budget available for a project. If drawn for multiple resources, it can help identify potential areas of resource conflicts. For situations where a single resource unit is assigned to multiple tasks, a variation of the resource loading graph can be developed to show the level of load (responsibilities) assigned to the resource over time. Table 3-1 shows a model of a resource availability data base. The data base is essential when planning resource loading strategies for resource-constrained projects.

Table 3-1. Format for Resource Availability Database

Resource ID	Brief Description	Special Skills	When Available	Duration of Availability	How Many
Type 1	Technician	Carpentry	8/5/93	Two Months	15
Type 2	Programmer	FORTRAN	12/25/93	Indefinite	2
Type 3	Engineer	Design	Now	Five Years	27
•	•	•	•	•	•
•	•	•	•	•	•
•	•	•	•	•	•
Type n-1	Operators	Machining	Always	Indefinite	10
Type n	Accountant	Contract Laws	9/2/93	Six Months	1

Resource Leveling

Resource leveling refers to the process of reducing the period-to-period fluctuation in a resource loading graph. If resource fluctuations are beyond acceptable limits, actions are taken to move activities or resources around in order to level out the resource loading graph. For example, it is bad for employee morale and public relations when a company has to hire and lay people off indiscriminately. Proper resource planning will facilitate a reasonably stable level of the work force. Other advantages of resource leveling include simplified resource tracking and control, lower cost of resource management, and improved opportunity for learning. Acceptable resource leveling is typically achieved at the expense of longer project duration or higher project cost. Figure 3-3 shows a somewhat leveled resource loading.

Figure 3-3. Resource Leveling Graph

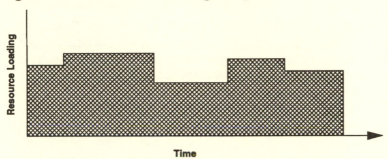

When attempting to level resources, note that:

1. Not all of the resource fluctuations can be eliminated.

2. Resource leveling often leads to an increase in project duration.

Resource leveling attempts to minimize fluctuations in resource loading by shifting activities within their available slacks. For small networks, resource leveling can be attempted manually through trial and error procedures. For large networks, resource leveling is best handled by computer software techniques. Most of the available commercial project management software packages have internal resource leveling routines. One heuristic procedure for leveling resources, known as *Burgess's Method* (Woodworth and Willie, 1975), is based on the technique of minimizing the sum of the squares for the resource requirements in each period.

Resource Idleness Graph

A resource idleness graph is similar to a resource loading graph except that it is drawn for the number of unallocated resource units over time. The area covered by the resource idleness graph may be used as a measure of the effectiveness of the scheduling strategy employed for a project. Suppose two scheduling strategies yield the same project duration, and suppose a measure of the resource utilization under each strategy is desired as a means to compare the strategies. Figure 3-4 shows two hypothetical resource idleness graphs for the alternate strategies. The areas are computed as follows:

Area A = 6(5) + 10(5) + 7(8) + 15(6) + 5(16) = 306 resource-units-time.

Area B = 5(6) + 10(9) + 3(5) + 6(5) + 3(3) + 12(12) = 318 resource-units-time.

Since Area A is less than Area B, it is concluded that Strategy A is more effective for resource utilization than Strategy B. Similar measures can be developed for multiple resources. However, for multiple resources, the different resource units must all be scaled to dimensionless quantities before computing the areas bounded by the resource idleness graphs.

Figure 3-4. Resource Idleness Graphs for Resource Allocation

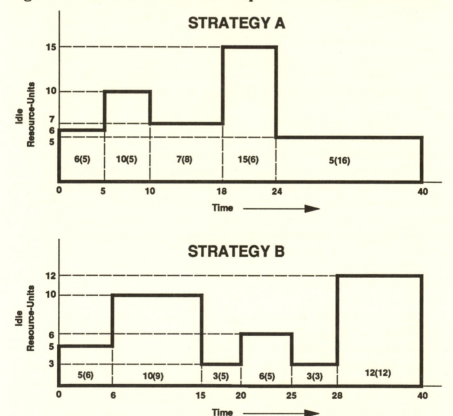

RESOURCE-CONSTRAINED SCHEDULING

A resource-constrained scheduling problem arises when the available resources are not enough to satisfy the requirements of activities that can be performed concurrently. To satisfy this constraint, sequencing rules (also called priority rules, activity urgency factor, scheduling rules, or scheduling heuristics) are used to determine which of the competing activities will have priority for resource allocation. Several optimum-yielding techniques are available for generating resource-constrained schedules. Unfortunately, the optimal techniques are not generally used in practice because of the complexity involved in implementing them for large projects. Even using a computer to generate an optimal schedule is sometimes cumbersome because of the modeling requirements, the drudgery of lengthy data entry, and the combinatorial nature of interactions among activities.

Most of the available mathematical techniques are based on integer programming that formulates the problem using 0 and 1 indicator variables. The variables indicate whether or not an activity is scheduled in specific time periods. Three of the common objectives in project network analysis are:

1. To minimize project duration
2. To minimize total project cost
3. To maximize resource utilization

One or more of the above objectives are attempted subject to one or more of the following constraints:

1. Limitation on resource availability
2. Precedence restrictions
3. Activity-splitting restrictions
4. Nonpreemption of activities
5. Project deadlines
6. Resource substitutions
7. Partial resource assignments
8. Mutually exclusive activities
9. Variable resource availability
10. Variable activity durations

Instead of using mathematical formulations, a scheduling heuristic uses logical rules to prioritize and assign resources to competing activities. Many scheduling rules have been developed in recent years. Some of the most frequently used ones are discussed later in this chapter.

RESOURCE ALLOCATION EXAMPLE

Table 3-2 presents an example of PERT project data with resource requirements. The project data was used in the preceding chapter without resource limitations. There is one resource type (operators) in the project data and there are only ten units of it available. The PERT estimates for the activity durations are expressed in terms of days. It is assumed that the resource units are reusable. Each resource unit is reallocated to a new activity at the completion of its previous assignment. Resource units can be idle if there are no eligible activities for scheduling or if enough units are not available to start a new activity. For simplification, it is assumed that the total units of resource required by an activity must be available before the activity can be scheduled. If partial resource allocation is allowed, then the work rate of the partial resources must be determined. A methodology for determining resource work rates is presented in a later section of this chapter.

Table 3-2. PERT Project Data with Resource Requirements

Activity	Predecessor	PERT Estimates a	m	b	Number of Operators Required
A	-	1	2	4	3
B	-	5	6	7	5
C	-	2	4	5	4
D	A	1	3	4	2
E	C	4	5	7	4
F	A	3	4	5	2
G	B, D, E	1	2	3	6
					$Z_1 = 10$

The unconstrained PERT duration was found earlier to be 11 days. The resource limitations are considered when creating the Gantt chart for the resource-constrained schedule. For this example, we will use the "longest-duration-first" heuristic to prioritize activities for resource allocation. Other possible heuristics are *shortest-duration-first*, *critical-activities-first*, *maximum-predecessors-first*, and so on. For very small project networks, many of the heuristics will yield identical schedules.

Longest-Duration-First Heuristic

The initial step is to rank the activities in decreasing order of their PERT durations, t_e. This yields the following priority order:

$$B, E, F, C, D, A, G$$

At each scheduling instant, only the eligible activities are considered for resource allocation. Eligible activities are those whose preceding activities have been completed. Thus, even though activity B has the highest priority for resource allocation, it can compete for resources only if it has no pending predecessors. Referring to the PERT network shown in Chapter 2, note that activities A, B, and C can start at time zero since they all have no predecessors. These three activities require a total of 12 operators (3+5+4) altogether. But we have only 10 operators available. So, a resource allocation decision must be made. We check our priority order and find that B and C have priority over A. So, we schedule B with 5 operators and C with 4 operators. The remaining one operator is not enough to meet the need of any of the remaining activities. The two scheduled activities are drawn on the Gantt chart as shown in Figure 3-5.

We have one operator idle from time zero until time 3.83, when activity C finishes and releases 4 operators. At time 3.83, we have 5 operators available. Since activity E can start after activity C, it has to compete with activity A for resources. According to the established priority, E has priority over A. So, 4 operators are assigned to E. The remaining one operator is not enough to perform activity A, so it has to wait while one operator remains idle. If E had required more operators than were available, activity A would have been able to get resources at time 3.83. No additional scheduling is done until time 6, when activity B finishes and releases 5 operators. So, we now have 6 operators available and there are no activities to compete with A for resources. Thus, activity A is finally scheduled at time 6 and we are left with 3 idle operators. Even though the 3 operators are enough to start either activity D or activity F, neither of these can start until activity A finishes, because of the precedence requirement.

Figure 3-5. Resource-Constrained PERT Schedule

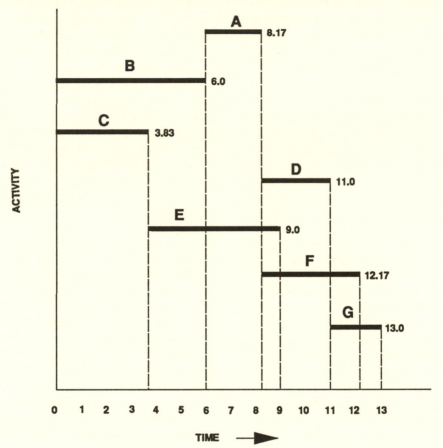

When activity A finishes at time 8.17, D and F are scheduled. Activity G is scheduled at time 11 and finishes at time 13 to complete the project. Figure 3-5 shows the complete project schedule. Note that our assumption is that activity splitting and partial resource assignments are not allowed. An activity cannot start until all the units of resources required are available. In real project situations, this assumption may be relaxed so that partial resource assignment are permissible. If splitting and partial assignments are allowed, the scheduling process will still be the same except that more record keeping will be required to keep track of pending jobs.

Resource allocation may be affected by several factors including duration of availability, skill level required, cost, productivity level, and priority strategy. Ranking of activities for resource allocation may be done under *parallel priority* or *serial priority*. In serial priority, the relative ranking of all activities is done at the beginning prior to starting the scheduling process. The activities maintain their relative priority ranking throughout the scheduling process. In the parallel priority approach, relative ranking is done at each scheduling instant and it is done only for the activities that are eligible for scheduling at that instant. Thus, under the parallel priority approach, the relative ranking of an activity may change at any time, depending on which activities it is competing with for resources at that time. The illustrative example above uses the serial priority approach. If desired, any other resource allocation heuristic could be used for the scheduling example. Some of the available resource allocation rules are presented in the following section.

RESOURCE ALLOCATION HEURISTICS

Resource allocation heuristics facilitate ease of scheduling large projects subject to resource limitations. Some heuristics are very simple and intuitive, while others require computer implementations. Several scheduling heuristics have been developed in recent years (Wiest, 1967; Elsayed, 1982; Slowinski, 1980; Kurtulus and Davis, 1982; Patterson, 1984; Davis and Patterson, 1975; Thesen, 1976; Fisher, 1980; Robert A. Russell, 1986; Cooper, 1976; Holloway et al., 1979; Badiru, 1988c). Many of these are widely applied to real projects. Many project management software packages use proprietary resource allocation rules that are not transparent to the user. A good scheduling heuristic should be simple, unambiguous, easily understood, and easily executable by those who must use it. The heuristic must be flexible and capable of resolving schedule conflicts. When users trust and use a scheduling heuristic, then project scheduling becomes an effective communication tool in project management. Some of the most used scheduling rules are presented below.

ACTIM (Activity-Time)
ACTIM (Whitehouse and Brown, 1979) is one of the earlier activity sequencing rules. The rule was developed by George H. Brooks and used in his algorithm, Brooks' Algorithm (Brooks and White, 1965; Bedworth, 1973). The original algorithm considered only the single project, single resource case, but it lends itself to extensions for the multi-resource cases. The ACTIM scheduling heuristic represents the maximum time that an activity controls in the project network on any one path. It is computed for each project activity by subtracting the activity's latest start time from the critical path time as shown below:

ACTIM = (Critical Path Time) - (Activity Latest Start Time).

ACTRES (Activity-Resource)

ACTRES is a scheduling heuristic proposed by Bedworth (1973). This is a combination of the activity time and resource requirements. It is computed as:

ACTRES = (Activity Time)*(Resource Requirement).

For multiple resources, the computation of ACTRES can be modified to account for various resource types. For this purpose, the resource requirement can be replaced by a scaled sum of resource requirements over different resource types.

TIMRES (Time-Resources)

TIMRES is another priority rule proposed by Bedworth (1973). It is composed of equally weighted portions of ACTIM and ACTRES. It is expressed as:

TIMRES = 0.5(ACTIM) + 0.5(ACTRES).

GENRES

GENRES is a search technique proposed by Whitehouse and Brown (1979) as an extension of Brooks' Algorithm (Brooks and White, 1965). It is a modification of TIMRES with various weighted combinations of ACTIM and ACTRES. GENRES is implemented as a computer search technique whereby iterative weights (w) between 0 and 1 are used in the expression below:

GENRES = (w)(ACTIM) + (1 - w)(ACTRES).

ROT (Resource Over Time)

ROT is a scheduling criterion proposed by Elsayed (1982). It is calculated as the resource requirement divided by the activity time as given below:

$$\text{ROT} = \frac{\text{Resource Requirement}}{\text{Activity Time}}.$$

The resource requirement can be replaced by the scaled sum of resource requirements in the case of multiple resource types with different units.

CAF (Composite Allocation Factor)

CAF is a comprehensive rule developed by Badiru (1988c). For each activity i, CAF is computed as a weighted and scaled sum of two components RAF (Resource Allocation Factor) and SAF (Stochastic Activity Duration Factor) as follows:

$$CAF_i = (w)RAF_i + (1-w)SAF_i,$$

where w is a weight between 0 and 1. RAF is defined for each activity i as:

$$RAF_i \;=\; \frac{1}{t_i} \sum_{j=1}^{R} \frac{x_{ij}}{y_j},$$

where:

x_{ij} = number of resource type j units required by activity i

y_j = $\underset{j}{Max}\{x_{ij}\}$, maximum units of resource type j required

t_i = the expected duration of activity i

R = the number of resource types.

RAF is a measure of the expected resource consumption per unit time. In the case of multiple resource types, the different resource units are scaled by the y_j component in the formula for RAF. This yields dimensionless quantities that can be summed in the formula for RAF. The RAF formula yields real numbers that are expressed per unit time. To eliminate the time-based unit, the following scaling method is used:

$$scaled \; RAF_i \;=\; \frac{RAF_i}{Max\{RAF_i\}}(100).$$

The above scaling approach yields unit-less values of RAF between 0 and 100 for the activities in the project. Resource-intensive activities have larger magnitudes of RAF and, therefore, require a higher priority in the scheduling process. To incorporate the stochastic nature of activity times in a project schedule, SAF is defined for each activity i as:

$$SAF_i \;=\; t_i \;+\; \frac{s_i}{t_i},$$

where:

t_i = expected duration for activity i

s_i = standard deviation of duration for activity i

s_i/t_i = coefficient of variation of the duration of activity i.

It should be noted that the formula for SAF has one component (t_i) with units of time and one component s_i/t_i with no units. To facilitate the required arithmetic operation, each component is scaled as shown below:

$$scaled \;\; t_i \;=\; \frac{t_i}{Max\{t_i\}}(50)$$

$$\text{scaled} \quad (s_i/t_i) \quad = \quad \frac{(s_i/t_i)}{\text{Max}\{s_i/t_i\}}(50)$$

When the above scaled components are plugged into the formula for SAF, we automatically obtain unit-less scaled SAF values that are on a scale of 0 to 100. However, the 100 weight will be observed only if the same activity has the highest scaled t_i value and the highest scaled s_i/t_i value at the same time. Similarly, the 0 weight will be observed only if the same activity has the lowest scaled t_i value and the lowest scaled s_i/t_i value at the same time. The scaled values of SAF and RAF are now inserted in the formula for CAF as shown below:

$$\text{CAF}_i \quad = \quad (w)\{\text{scaled RAF}_i\} \quad + \quad (1-w)\{\text{scaled SAF}_i\}.$$

To ensure that the resulting CAF values range from 0 to 100, the following final scaling approach is applied:

$$\text{scaled CAF}_i \quad = \quad \frac{\text{CAF}_i}{\text{Max}\{\text{CAF}_i\}}(100).$$

It is on the basis of the magnitudes of CAF that an activity is assigned a priority for resource allocation in the project schedule. Activities with larger values of CAF have higher priorities for resource allocation. An activity that lasts longer, consumes more resources, and varies more in duration will have a larger magnitude of CAF.

RSM (Resource Scheduling Method)

RSM was developed by Brand, Meyer, and Shaffer (1964). The rule gives priority to the activity with the minimum value of d_{ij} calculated as indicated below:

d_{ij} = increase in project duration when activity j follows activity i

= Max $\{0, (EC_i - LS_j)\}$,

where EC_i is the earliest completion time of activity i and LS_j is the latest start time of activity j. Competing activities are compared two at a time in the resource allocation process.

GRD (Greatest Resource Demand)

This rule gives priority to the activity with the largest total resource-unit requirements. The GRD measure is calculated as:

$$g_j = d_j \sum_{i=1}^{n} r_{ij},$$

where

g_j = priority measure for activity j
d_j = duration of activity j
r_{ij} = units of resource type i required by activity j per period
n = number of resource types (Resource units are expressed in common units).

GRU (Greatest Resource Utilization)

The GRU rule assigns priority to activities that, if scheduled, will result in maximum utilization of resources or minimum idle time. For large problems, computer procedures are often required to evaluate the various possible combinations of activities and the associated utilization levels.

Most Possible Jobs

This approach assigns priority in such a way that the greatest number of activities are scheduled in any period.

Other Scheduling Rules

- Most Total Successors
- Most Critical Activity
- Most Immediate Successors
- Any activity that will finish first
- Minimum Activity Latest Start (Min LS)
- Maximum Activity Latest Start (Max LS)
- Minimum Activity Earliest Start (Min ES)
- Maximum Activity Latest Completion (Max LC)
- Minimum Activity Earliest Completion (Min EC)
- Maximum Activity Earliest Completion (Max EC)
- Minimum Activity Latest Completion (Min LC)
- Maximum Activity Earliest Start (Max ES)
- Minimum Activity Total Slack (Min TS)
- Maximum Activity Total Slack (Max TS)

- Any activity that can start first
- Minimum Activity Duration
- Maximum Activity Duration

The project analyst must carefully analyze the prevailing project situation and decide which of the several rules will be most suitable for the resource allocation requirements. Since there are numerous rules, it is often difficult to know which rule to apply. Experience and intuition are often the best guide for selecting and implementing scheduling heuristics. Some of the shortcomings of heuristics include subjectivity of the technique, arbitrariness of the procedures, lack of responsiveness to dynamic changes in the project scenario, and over simplified assumptions.

There are advantages and disadvantages to using specific heuristics. For example, the shortest duration heuristic is useful for quickly reducing the number of pending activities. This may be important for control purposes. The smaller the number of activities to be tracked, the lower the burden of project control. The longest duration heuristic, by contrast, has the advantage of scheduling the biggest tasks in a project first. This permits the lumping of the smaller activities into convenient work packages later on in the project. Decomposition of large projects into subprojects can enhance the application of heuristics that are only effective for small project networks.

Example of ACTIM

Brooks' Algorithm uses ACTIM to determine which activities should receive limited resources first. The algorithm considers the single project, single resource case. Whitehouse and Brown (1979) used the following example to illustrate the use of the ACTIM scheduling heuristic. Figure 3-6 presents a project network based on the activity-on-arrow (AOA) convention. The arrows represent activities, while the nodes represent activity end points. Each activity is defined by its end points as *i-j*. The two numbers within parentheses represent activity duration and resource requirement (*t, r*) respectively. The network consists of seven actual activities and one dummy activity. The dummy activity (3-4) is required to show that activities (1-3) and (2-3) are predecessors for activity (4-5). Table 3-3 presents the tabular implementation of the steps in the algorithm for three units of resource.

Figure 3-6. Network One for ACTIM Example

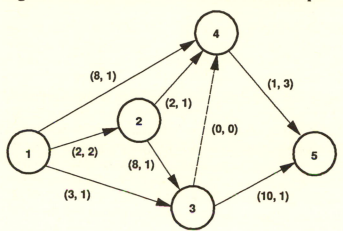

STEP 1: Develop the project network as in CPM. Identify activities, their estimated durations, and resource requirements.

STEP 2: Determine for each activity the maximum time it controls through the network on any one path. This is equivalent to the critical path time minus the latest start time of the starting node of the activity. These times are then scaled from 0 to 100. This scaled network control time is designated as ACTIM.

STEP 3: Rank the activities in decreasing order of ACTIM as shown in Table 3-3. The duration and resources required for each activity are those determined in the first step. The rows TEARL, TSCHED, TFIN, TNOW are explained below:

TEARL is the earliest time of an activity determined by traditional CPM calculations. TSCHED is the actual scheduled starting time of an activity as determined by Brooks' Algorithm. TFIN is the completion time of each activity. TNOW is the time at which the resource allocation decision is being made.

STEP 4: Set TNOW to 0. The allowable activities (ACT. ALLOW) to be considered for scheduling at TNOW of zero are those activities with TEARL of 0. These are 1-2, 1-3, 1-4. These are placed in the ACT. ALLOW. row in decreasing order of ACTIM. Ties are broken by scheduling the activity with longest duration first. The number of resources initially available (i.e., 3) is placed in the resources available column.

STEP 5: Determine if the first activity in ACT. ALLOW. (i.e., 1-2) can be scheduled. Activity 1-2 requires two resource units and three are available. So, 1-2 is scheduled. A line is drawn through 1-2 to indicate that it has been scheduled and the number of resources available is decreased by two. TSCHED and TFIN are then set for activity 1-2. This process is repeated for the remaining activities in ACT. ALLOW. until the resources available are depleted.

STEP 6: TNOW is raised to the next TFIN time of 2, which occurs at the completion of activity 1-2. The resources available are now 2. ACT. ALLOW. includes those activities not assigned at the previous TNOW (i.e., 1-4) and those new activities whose predecessors have been completed (i.e., 2-3 and 2-4).

STEP 7: Repeat this assignment process until all activities have been scheduled. The latest TFIN gives the duration of the project. For this example, the duration is 21 days. Figure 3-7 presents the Gantt chart for the final schedule.

Table 3-3. Example of ACTIM Heuristic in Brooks' Algorithm

$Z_1 = 3$							
Activity	1-2	2-3	1-3	3-5	1-4	2-4	4-5
Duration	2	8	3	10	8	2	1
ACTIM	20	18	13	10	9	3	1
Scaled ACTIM	100	90	65	50	45	15	5
Resources Reqd.	2	1	1	1	1	1	3
TEARL	0	2	0	10	0	2	10
TSCHED	0	2	0	10	2	3	20
TFIN	2	10	3	20	10	5	21
TNOW	0	2	3	5	10	20	
Resources Available	3,1,0	2,1,0	1,0	1	3,2	3,0	
ACT. ALLOW.	1-2 1-3 1-4	2-3 1-4 2-4	2-4	--	3-5 4-5	4-5	
Iteration No.	1	2	3	4	5	6	

Figure 3-7. Gantt Chart ACTIM Schedule

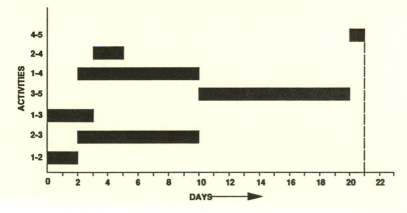

Comparison of ACTIM, ACTRES, and TIMRES

Brooks' Algorithm can be implemented with any other heuristic apart from ACTIM. Whitehouse and Brown (1979) used the example network in Figure 3-8 to compare the schedules generated by ACTIM, ACTRES, and TIMRES. Tables 3-4, 3-5, and 3-6 present the tabular of the implementation of Brooks' Algorithm with scaled values of ACTIM, ACTRES, and TIMRES. Note that each heuristic yields a different project schedule. Even though the project durations obtained from ACTRES and TIMRES are the same (13 days), the specific scheduled times are different for the activities in each schedule. The larger the project network, the more the schedules generated by different heuristics can be expected to differ.

Figure 3-8. Network for ACTIM, ACTRES, and TIMRES Comparison

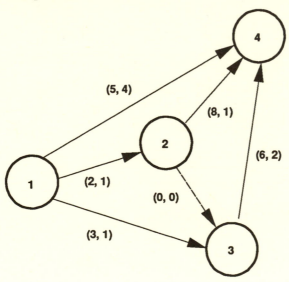

Table 3-4. ACTIM Schedule for Comparative Network

$Z_1 = 5$

Activity	1-2	1-3	2-4	3-4	1-4
Duration	2	3	8	6	5
ACTIM	10	9	8	6	5
Scaled ACTIM	100	90	80	60	50
Resources Reqd.	1	1	1	2	4
TEARL	0	0	2	3	0
TSCHED	0	0	2	3	9
TFIN	2	3	10	9	14
TNOW	0	2	3	9	
Resources Available	5, 4, 3	4, 3	4, 2	4	
ACT. ALLOW.	1-2 1-3 1-4	2-4 1-4	3-4 1-4	1-4	
Iteration No.	1	2	3	4	

Table 3-5. ACTRES Schedule for Comparative Network

$Z_1 = 5$					
Activity	1-4	1-3	1-2	3-4	2-4
Duration	5	3	2	6	8
ACTRES	20	15	14	12	8
Scaled ACTRES	100	75	70	60	40
Resources Reqd.	4	1	1	2	1
TEARL	0	0	0	5	5
TSCHED	0	0	3	5	5
TFIN	5	3	5	11	13
TNOW	0	3	5		
Resources Available	5, 1, 0	1, 0	5, 3, 2		
ACT. ALLOW.	1-4 1-3 1-2	1-2	3-4 2-4		
Iteration No.	1	2	3		

Table 3-6. TIMRES Schedule for Comparative Network

$Z_1 = 5$					
Activity	1-2	1-3	1-4	2-4	3-4
Duration	2	3	5	8	6
TIMRES	85	82.5	75	60	60
Scaled TIMRES	100	97	88	71	59
Resources Reqd.	1	1	4	1	2
TEARL	0	0	0	2	3
TSCHED	0	0	2	3	7
TFIN	2	3	7	11	13
TNOW	0	2	3	7	
Resources Available	5, 4, 3	4, 0	1, 0	4, 2	
ACT. ALLOW.	1-2 1-3 1-4	1-4 2-4	2-4 3-4	3-4	
Iteration No.	1	2	3	4	

COMPLEXITY OF PROJECT NETWORKS

The performance of a scheduling heuristic will be greatly influenced by the complexity of the project network. The more activities there are in the network and the more resource types are involved, the more complex the scheduling effort. Numerous analytical experiments (Badiru 1988c) have revealed the lack of consistency in heuristic performances. Some heuristics perform well for both small and large projects. Some perform well only for small projects. Still, some heuristics that perform well for certain types of small projects may not perform well for other projects of comparable size. The implicit network structure based on precedence relationships and path interconnections influences network complexity and, hence, the performance of scheduling heuristics. The complexity of a project network may indicate the degree of effort that has been devoted to planning the project.

The better the planning for a project, the lower the complexity of the project network can be expected to be. This is because many of the redundant interrelationships among activities can be identified and eliminated through better planning.

There have been some attempts to quantify the complexity of project networks. Since the structures of projects vary from very simple to very complex, it is desirable to have a measure of how difficult it will be to schedule a project. Kaimann (1974) presented the following coefficients of network complexity (C):

For PERT networks:

$$C = \text{(Number of Activities)}^2/\text{(Number of Events)},$$

where an event is defined as an end point (or node) of an activity.

For precedence networks:

$$C = \text{(Preceding Work Items)}^2/\text{(Work Items)}.$$

The above expressions represent simple measures of the degree of interrelationship of the project network. Davies (1974) presented the following measure for network complexity:

$$C = 2(A - N + 1)/(N - 1)(N - 2),$$

where A is the number of activities and N is the number of nodes in the project network. T. J. R. Johnson (1967) presented a measure defined as the Total Activity Density, D, to convey the complexity of a project network. The network density is defined as:

$$D = \sum_{i=1}^{N} \text{Max}\{0, (p_i - s_i)\},$$

where N is the number of activities, p_i is the number of predecessor activities for activity i, and s_i is the number of successor activities for activity i. Davis (1975) presented an alternate measure of network complexity (C), a measure of network density (D), a measure of total work content for resource type j (w_j), an obstruction factor (O), which is a measure of the ratio of excess resource requirements to total work content, adjusted obstruction per period based on earliest start time schedule (O_{est}), adjusted obstruction per period based on latest start time schedule (O_{lst}), and a resource utilization factor (U). These measures are presented below:

$$C = \frac{\text{number of activities}}{\text{number of nodes}}$$

$$D = \frac{\text{sum of job durations}}{\text{sum of job durations} + \text{total free slack}}$$

$$w_j = \sum_{i=1}^{N} d_i r_{ij}$$

$$= \sum_{t=1}^{CP} r_{jt} \,,$$

where

d_i = duration of job i
r_{ij} = per-period requirement of resource type j by job i
t = time period
N = number of jobs
CP = original critical path duration
r_{jt} = total resource requirements of resource type j in time period t.

$$O = \sum_{j=1}^{M} O_j$$

$$= \frac{\sum_{t=1}^{CP} \text{Max}\{0, \quad r_{jt} - A_j)}{w_j} \,,$$

where:

O_j = the obstruction factor for resource type j
CP = original critical path duration
A_j = units of resource type j available per period
M = number of different resource types
w_j = total work content for resource type j
r_{jt} = total resource requirements of resource type j in time period t

$$O_{est} = \sum_{j=1}^{m} \left[\frac{\sum_{t=1}^{CP} \text{Max}\{0, \quad r_{jt(est)} - A_j\}}{(M)(CP)} \right] ,$$

where $r_{jt(est)}$ is the total resource requirements of resource type j in time period t based on earliest start times.

$$O_{est} = \sum_{j=1}^{m} \left[\frac{\sum_{t=1}^{CP} \text{Max}\{0, \quad r_{jt(\text{lst})} - A_j\}}{(M)(CP)} \right],$$

where $r_{jt(\text{lst})}$ is the total resource requirements of resource type j in time period t based on latest start times. The measures O_{est} and O_{lst} incorporate the calculation of excess resource requirements adjusted by the number of periods and the number of different resource types.

$$U = \text{Max}_{j}\{f_j\}$$

$$= \text{Max}_{j} \left\{ \frac{w_j}{(CP)(A_j)} \right\},$$

where f_j is the resource utilization factor for resource type j. This measures the ratio of the total work content to the total work initially available. Badiru (1988a) defined another measure of the complexity of a project network as:

$$\lambda = \frac{p}{d} \left[\left(1 - \frac{1}{L} \right) \sum_{i=1}^{L} t_i + \sum_{j=1}^{R} \left(\frac{\sum_{i=1}^{L} t_i x_{ij}}{Z_j} \right) \right],$$

where:

λ = project network complexity
L = number of activities in the network
t_i = expected duration for activity i
R = number of resource types
x_{ij} = units of resource type j required by activity i
Z_j = maximum units of resource type j available
p = maximum number of immediate predecessors in the network
d = PERT duration of the project with no resource constraint.

The terms in the expression for the complexity are explained as follows: The maximum number of immediate predecessors, p, is a multiplicative factor that increases the complexity and potential for bottlenecks in a project network. The $(1-1/L)$ term is a fractional measure (between 0.0 and 1.0) that indicates the time intensity or work content of the project. As L increases, the quantity $(1-1/L)$ increases, and a larger fraction of the total time requirement (sum of t_i) is charged to the network complexity. Conversely, as L decreases, the network complexity decreases proportionately with the total time requirement. The sum of $(t_i x_{ij})$ indicates the time-based consumption of a given resource type j relative to the maximum availability. The term is summed over all the different resource types. Having PERT duration in the denominator helps to express the complexity as a dimensionless quantity by cancelling out the time units in the numerator. In addition, it gives the network complexity per unit of total project duration.

In addition to the approaches presented above, other project network complexity measures have been proposed in the literature (Patterson, 1976; Elmaghraby and Herroelen, 1980). There is always a debate as to whether or not the complexity of a project can be accurately quantified. There are several quantitative and qualitative factors with unknown interactions that are present in any project network. As a result, any measure of project complexity should be used as a relative measure of comparison rather than as an absolute indication of the difficulty involved in scheduling a given project. Since the performance of a scheduling approach can deteriorate sometimes with the increase in project size, a further comparison of the rules may be done on the basis of a collection of large projects. A major deficiency in the existing measures of project network complexity is that there is a lack of well-designed experiments to compare and verify the effectiveness of the measures. Also, there is usually no guideline as to whether a complexity measure should be used as an ordinal or a cardinal measure, as is illustrated in the following example.

Network Complexity Example

Table 3-7 presents a sample project for illustrating the network complexity measure presented by Badiru (1988a).

Table 3-7. Data for Project Complexity Example

Activity Number	PERT Estimates (a, m, b)	Preceding Activities	Required Resources (x_{i1}, x_{i2})
1	1, 3, 5	-	1, 0
2	0.5, 1, 3	-	1, 1
3	1, 1, 2	-	1, 1
4	2, 3, 6	Activity 1	2, 0
5	1, 3, 4	Activity 2	1, 0
6	1.5, 2, 2	Activity 3	4, 2

$$Z_1 = 5, \; Z_2 = 2$$

Using the formulation for network complexity presented by Badiru (1988a), we obtain:

$$p = 1 \qquad L = 6 \qquad d = 6.33$$

$$\sum_{i=1}^{6} t_i = 13.5, \qquad \sum_{i=1}^{6} t_i x_{i1} = 22.5, \qquad \sum_{i=1}^{6} t_i x_{i2} = 6.3$$

$$\lambda = \frac{1}{6.33}\left[\left(\frac{6-1}{6}\right)(13.5) + \left(\frac{22.5}{5} + \frac{6.3}{2}\right)\right]$$

$$= 2.99.$$

If the above complexity measure is to be used as an ordinal measure, then it must be used to compare and rank alternate project networks. For example, when planning a project, one may use the complexity measure to indicate the degree of simplification that has been achieved in each iteration of the project plan. Similarly, when evaluating project options, one may use the ordinal complexity measure to determine which network option will be easiest to manage. If the complexity measure is to be used as a cardinal measure, then a benchmark value must be developed. In order words, control limits will be needed to indicate when a project network can be classified as simple, medium, or complex. For Badiru's complexity measure, the following classification ranges are suggested:

Simple network: $0 \leq \lambda \leq 5.0$

Medium network: $5.0 < \lambda \le 12.0$

Complex network: $\lambda > 12.0$.

The above ranges are based on the result of an experimental investigation involving 30 alternate projects of various degrees of network complexity. Of course, the ranges cannot be argued to be universally applicable, because consistency of measurement cannot be assured from one project network to another. Users can always determine what ranges will best suit their needs. The complexity measure can then be used accordingly. Perhaps the greatest utility of a complexity measure is obtained when evaluating computer implementation of network analysis. This is addressed further by the discussion that follows.

Solution Time Analysis

Using solution time as a performance measure, another comparison of the scheduling heuristics may be conducted. Computer processing time should be recorded for each scheduling rule under each test problem. The following procedure may then be used to perform the solution time analysis. We let τ_{mn} denote computer processing time for scheduling heuristic m for test problem n. The sum of the processing times over the set of test problems is expressed as:

$$\psi_n = \sum_m \tau_{mn}, \quad n = 1, 2, \ldots, N; \quad m = 1, 2, \ldots, M,$$

where m, n, M, and N are as previously defined. Then,

$$\mu_n = \frac{\psi_n}{M}$$

denotes the average time for scheduling project n, where M is the number of rules considered. The normalized solution time for heuristic m under test problem n can then be denoted as:

$$\Omega_{mn} = \frac{\tau_{mn}}{\mu_n}.$$

Each heuristic m is ranked on the basis of the sum of normalized solution times over all test problems. That is,

$$\theta_m = \sum_n \Omega_{mn}, \quad m = 1, 2, \ldots, M; \quad n = 1, 2, \ldots, N.$$

It is obvious that the solution time of each scheduling heuristic depends on its computational complexity. The computations for ACTRES, ROT, and HNIS (Highest Number of Immediate Successors), for example, do not require a prior analysis of the PERT network. Since CAF, on the other hand, considers several factors in the activity sequencing process, its computations are more complex than many other scheduling heuristics. The solution time analysis results should, thus, be coupled with schedule effectiveness in order to judge the overall acceptability of any given heuristic. Prior analysis and selection of the most effective scheduling heuristic for a given project can help minimize schedule changes and delays often encountered in impromptu scheduling practices.

Rule Performance Measures

In addition to comparing scheduling heuristics on the basis of project durations, the following aggregate measures may also be used. The first one is an evaluation of the ratio of the minimum project duration observed to the project duration obtained under each heuristic. For each heuristic m, the ratio under each test problem n is computed as:

$$\rho_{mn} = \frac{q_n}{PL_{mn}}, \quad m = 1, 2, \ldots, M; \quad n = 1, 2, \ldots, N,$$

where:

ρ_{mn} = the efficiency ratio for heuristic m under test problem n

q_n = $\underset{m}{\text{Min}}\{PL_{mn}\}$ (i.e., minimum duration observed for test problem n)

PL_{mn} = the project duration for test problem n under heuristic m
M = the number of scheduling heuristics considered
N = the number of test problems.

From the above definitions, the maximum value for the ratio is 1.0. Thus, it is alternately referred to as the Rule Efficiency Ratio. The value q_n is, of course, not necessarily the global minimum project duration for test problem n. Rather, it represents the local minimum based on the particular scheduling heuristics considered. If the global minimum duration for a project is known (probably from an optimization model), then it should be used in the expression for ρ_{mn}. Rules can be compared on the basis of the absolute values for ρ_{mn} or on the basis of the sums of ρ_{mn}. The sums of ρ_{mn} over the index n are defined as:

$$\Phi_m = \sum_{n=1}^{N} \rho_{ij}, \quad m = 1, 2, \ldots, M.$$

The use of the sums of ρ_{mn} is a practical approach to comparing scheduling heuristics. It is possible to have a scheduling rule that will consistently yield near minimum project durations for all test problems. On the other hand, there may be another rule that performs very well for some test problems while performing poorly for other problems. A weighted sum helps to average out the overall performance over several test problems. The other comparison measure involves the calculation of the percentage deviations from the observed minimum project duration. The deviations are computed as:

$$S_{mn} = \left(\frac{PL_{mn} - q_n}{q_n} \right)(100), \quad m = 1, 2, \ldots, M; \quad n = 1, 2, \ldots, N,$$

which denotes the percentage deviation from the minimum project duration for rule m under test problem n. A project analyst will need to consider the several factors discussed above when selecting and implementing scheduling heuristics. The potential variability in the work rates of resources is another complicating factor in the project scheduling problem. A methodology for analyzing resource work rates is presented in the next section.

RESOURCE WORK RATE

Work rate and work time are essential components of estimating the cost of specific tasks in project management. Given a certain amount of work that must be done at a given work rate, the required time can be computed. Once the required time is known, the cost of the task can be computed on the basis of a specified cost per unit time. Work rate analysis is important for resource substitution decisions. The analysis can help identify where and when the same amount of work can be done with the same level of quality and within a reasonable time span by a less expensive resource. The results of learning curve analysis can yield valuable information about expected work rate. The general relationship between work, work rate, and time is given by:

Work done = (Work Rate)x(Time).

This is expressed mathematically as:

$$w = rt,$$

where:

$w =$ the amount of actual work done expressed in appropriate units. Example of work units are miles of road completed, lines of computer code typed, gallons of oil spill cleaned, units of widgets produced, and surface area painted.

$r =$ the rate at which the work is accomplished

$t =$ the total time required to perform the work excluding any embedded idle times

It should be noted that work is defined as a physical measure of accomplishment with uniform density. That means, for example, that one line of computer code is as complex and desirable as any other line of computer code. Similarly, cleaning one gallon of oil spill is as good as cleaning any other gallon of oil spill within the same work environment. The production of one unit of a product is identical to the production of any other unit of the product. If uniform work density cannot be assumed for the particular work being analyzed, then the relationship presented above may lead to erroneous conclusions. Uniformity can be enhanced if the scope of the analysis is limited to a manageable size. The larger the scope of the analysis, the more the variability from one work unit to another, and the less uniform the overall work measurement will be. For example, in a project involving the construction of 50 miles of surface road, the work analysis may be done in increments of 10 miles rather than the total 50 miles at a time. If the total amount of work to be analyzed is defined as one whole unit, then the relationship below can be developed for the case of a single resource performing the work:

Resource	Work Rate	Time	Work Done
Machine A	$1/x$	t	1.0

where $1/x$ is the amount of work accomplished per unit time. For a single resource to perform the whole unit of work, we must have the following:

$$\left(\frac{1}{x}\right)t \;=\; 1.0 \,.$$

That means the magnitude of x must equal the magnitude of t. For example, if Machine A is to complete one work unit in 30 minutes, it must work at the rate of $1/30$ of work per unit time. If the magnitude of x is greater than the magnitude of t, then only a fraction of the required work will be performed. The information about the proportion of work completed may be useful for productivity measurement purposes. In the case of multiple resources performing the work simultaneously, the work relationship is as presented below:

Resource, i	Work Rate, r_i	Time, t_i	Work Done, w
Machine A	r_1	t_1	$(r_1)(t_1)$
Machine B	r_2	t_2	$(r_2)(t_2)$
....	....	....	....
Machine n	r_n	t_n	$(r_n)(t_n)$
		Total	1.0

Even though the multiple resources may work at different rates, the sum of the work they all performed must equal the required whole unit. In general, for multiple resources, we have the following relationship:

$$\sum_{i=1}^{n} r_i t_i = 1.0,$$

n = number of different resource types
r_i = work rate of resource type i
t_i = work time of resource type i

For partial completion of work, the relationship is:

$$\sum_{i=1}^{n} r_i t_i = p,$$

where p is the proportion of the required work actually completed.

EXAMPLE: Machine A, working alone, can complete a given job in 50 minutes. After Machine A has been working on the job for 10 minutes, Machine B was brought in to work with Machine A in completing the job. Both machines working together finished the remaining work in 15 minutes. What is the work rate for Machine B?

Solution
The amount of work to be done is 1.0 whole unit.
The work rate of Machine A is 1/50.
The amount of work completed by Machine A in the 10 minutes it worked alone is $(1/50)(10) = 1/5$ of the required total work.
Therefore, the remaining amount of work to be done is 4/5 of the required total work.
The two machines working together for 15 minutes yield the following results:

Resource, i	Work Rate, r_i	Time, t_i	Work Done, w
Machine A	1/50	15	15/50
Machine B	r_2	15	$15(r_2)$
		Total	4/5

$$\frac{15}{50} \ + \ 15(r_2) \ = \ \frac{4}{5} \ ,$$

which yields $r_2 = 1/30$. Thus, the work rate for Machine B is 1/30. That means Machine B, working alone, could perform the same job in 30 minutes. In this example, it is assumed that both machines produce identical quality of work. If quality levels are not identical, then the project analyst must consider the potentials for quality/time trade-offs in performing the required work. The relative costs of the different resource types needed to perform the required work may be incorporated into the analysis as shown below:

Resource i	Work Rate r_i	Time t_i	Work Done w	Pay rate p_i	Pay P_i
Machine A	r_1	t_1	$(r_1)(t_1)$	p_1	P_1
Machine B	r_2	t_2	$(r_2)(t_2)$	p_2	P_2
....	....	....	....	....	....
Machine n	r_n	t_n	$(r_n)(t_n)$	p_n	P_n
		Total	1.0		Budget

Using the above relationship for work rate and cost, the work crew can be analyzed to determine the best strategy for accomplishing the required work, within the required time, and within a specified budget.

RESOURCE-CONSTRAINED PDM NETWORK

The conventional precedence diagramming network with no resource limitations was presented in Chapter 2. In this section, we extend the example presented in Figure 2-33 (Chapter 2) to a resource-constrained problem with probabilistic activity durations. Table 3-8 presents the modified project data after the activities are partitioned into segments (or subactivities) based on the lead-lag PDM restrictions. There are three main activities. These are partitioned into seven subactivities. Two resource types are involved in this example. There are 8 units of resource type 1 available and 10 units of resource type 2 available. The resource requirements for the individual segments of each activity are shown in the last two columns of the table. The seven activity segments are ranked by the CAF heuristic in the following priority order for resource allocation purposes:

Activity 6 (C1): CAF = 100
Activity 2 (A2): CAF = 71.7
Activity 5 (B3): CAF = 65.2
Activity 3 (B1): CAF = 49.6
Activity 7 (C2): CAF = 45.2
Activity 4 (B2): CAF = 29.6
Activity 1 (A1): CAF = 28.7

Figure 3-9 presents the resulting Gantt chart for the resource-constrained schedule. Note that the expected project duration is 24.08 time units. This may be compared to the duration of 18 time units obtained in Chapter 2 (Figure 2-32) without resource limitations.

Table 3-8. Resource-Constrained PDM Network Data

Act. No.	Name	Predecessors	Duration	Duration Variance	Resource 1 Required	Resource 2 Required
1	A1	-	1.79	0.11	3	0
2	A2	A1	8.17	0.10	5	4
3	B1	A1	0.63	0.11	4	1
4	B2	B1	3.01	0.12	2	0
5	B3	A2, B2	0.75	0.11	4	3
6	C1	B1	11.20	0.13	2	7
7	C2	B3, C1	2.29	0.09	6	2
					$Z_1 = 8$	$Z_2 = 10$

Figure 3-9. Resource-Constrained PDM Schedule

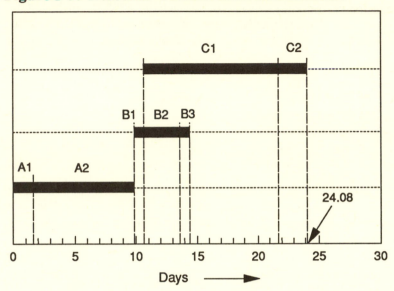

CRITICAL RESOURCE DIAGRAM

Resource management is a major function in any organization. In a project management environment, project goals are achieved through the strategic allocation of resources to tasks. Several analytical and graphical tools are available for activity planning, scheduling, and control. Examples are the critical path method (CPM), the program evaluation and review technique (PERT), and the precedence diagramming method (PDM). Unfortunately, similar tools are not available for resource management. There is a need for simple tools for resource allocation planning, scheduling, tracking, and control. In this section, a simple extension of the CPM diagram is developed for resource management purposes. The extension, called the critical resource diagram (CRD), is a graphical tool that brings the well-known advantages of the CPM diagram to resource scheduling. The advantages of CRD include simplified resource tracking and control, better job distribution, better information to avoid resource conflicts, and better tools for resource leveling.

Resource Management Constraints

Resource management is a complex task that is subject to several limiting factors including the following:

- Resource interdependencies
- Conflicting resource priorities
- Mutual exclusivity of resources
- Limitations on resource availability
- Limitations on resource substitutions
- Variable levels of resource availability
- Limitations on partial resource allocation

The above factors invariably affect the criticality of certain resource types. It is logical to expect different resource types to exhibit different levels of criticality in a resource allocation problem. For example, some resources are very expensive. Some resources possess special skills. Some are in very limited supply. The relative importance of different resource types should be considered when carrying out resource allocation in activity scheduling. The critical resource diagram helps in representing resource criticality.

CRD Network Development

Figure 3-10 shows an example of a CRD for a small project requiring six different resource types. Each node identification, RES *j*, refers to a task responsibility for resource type *j*. In a CRD, a node is used to represent each resource unit. The interrelationships between resource units are indicated by arrows. The arrows are referred to as resource-relationship (R-R) arrows. For example, if the job of resource *1* must precede the job of resource *2*, then an arrow is drawn from the node for resource 1 to the node for resource 2. Task durations are included in a CRD to provide further details about resource relationships. Unlike activity diagrams, a resource unit may appear at more than one location in a CRD provided there are no time or task conflicts. Such multiple locations indicate the number of different jobs for which the resource is responsible. This information may be useful for task distribution and resource leveling purposes. In Figure 3-10, resource 1 (RES 1) and resource 4 (RES 4) appear at two different nodes, indicating that each is responsible for two different jobs within the same work scenario.

Figure 3-10. Critical Resource Diagram

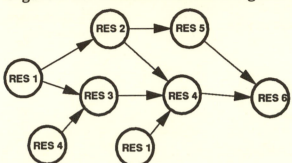

CRD Computations

The same forward and backward computations used in CPM are applicable to a CRD diagram. However, the interpretation of the critical path may be different, since a single resource may appear at multiple nodes. Figure 3-11 presents an illustrative computational analysis of the CRD network in Figure 3-10. Task durations (days) are given below the resource identifications. Earliest and latest times are computed and appended to each resource node in the same manner as in CPM analysis. RES 1, RES 2, RES 5, and RES 6 form the critical resource path. These resources have no slack times with respect to the completion of the given project. Note that only one of the two tasks of RES 1 is on the critical resource path. Thus, RES 1 has a slack time for performing one job, while it has no slack time for performing the other. Neither of the two tasks of RES 4 is on the critical resource path. For RES 3, the task duration is specified as zero. Despite this favorable task duration, RES 3 may turn out to be a bottleneck resource. RES 3 may be a senior manager whose task is signing a work order. But if he or she is not available to sign at the appropriate time, then the tasks of several other resources may be adversely affected. A major benefit of a CRD is that both senior level and lower level resources can be included in the resource planning network.

Figure 3-11. CRD Network Analysis

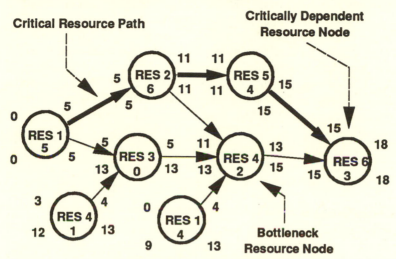

CRD Node Classifications

A *bottleneck* resource node is defined as a node at which two or more arrows merge. In Figure 3-11, RES 3, RES 4, and RES 6 have bottleneck resource nodes. The tasks to which bottleneck resources are assigned should be expedited in order to avoid delaying dependent resources. A *dependent* resource node is a node whose job depends on the job of immediately preceding nodes. A *critically dependent* resource node is defined as a node on the critical resource path at which several arrows merge. In Figure 3-11, RES 6 is both a critically dependent resource node and a bottleneck resource node. As a scheduling heuristic, it is recommended that activities that require bottleneck resources be scheduled as early as possible. A *burst* resource node is defined as a resource node from which two or more arrows emanate. Like bottleneck resource nodes, burst resource nodes should be expedited, since their delay will affect several following resource nodes.

Resource Schedule Chart

The critical resource diagram has the advantage that it can be used to model partial assignment of resource units across multiple tasks in single or multiple projects. A companion chart for this purpose is the resource schedule (RS) Chart. Figure 3-12 shows an example of an RS chart based on the earliest times computed in Figure 3-11. A horizontal bar is drawn for each resource unit or resource type. The starting point and the length of each resource bar indicate the interval of work for the resource. Note that the two jobs of RES 1 overlap over a four-day time period. By comparison, the two jobs of RES 4 are separated by a period of six days. If RES 4 is not to be idle over those six days, "fill-in" tasks must be assigned to it. For resource jobs that overlap, care must be taken to ensure that the resources do not need the same tools (e.g., equipment, computers, lathe, etc.) at the same time. If a resource unit is found to have several jobs overlapping over an extensive period of time, then a task reassignment may be necessary to offer some relief for the resource. The RS chart is useful for a graphical representation of the utilization of resources. Although similar information can be obtained from a conventional resource loading graph, the RS chart gives a clearer picture of where and when resource commitments overlap. It also shows areas where multiple resources are working concurrently.

Figure 3-12. Resource Schedule Chart

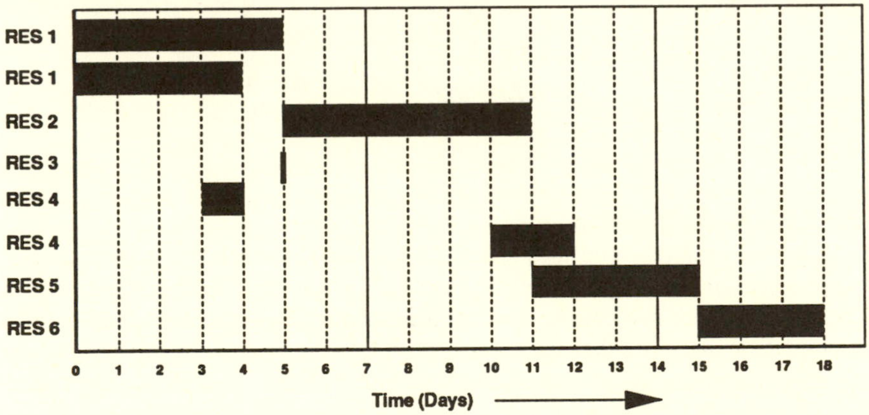

CRD and Work Rate Analysis

When resources work concurrently at different work rates, the amount of work accomplished by each may be computed by the procedure for work rate analysis presented earlier in this chapter. The critical resource diagram and the resource schedule chart provide information to identify when, where, and which resources work concurrently.

EXAMPLE: Suppose the work rate of RES 1 is such that it can perform a certain task in 30 days. It is desired to add RES 2 to the task so that the completion time of the task can be reduced. The work rate of RES 2 is such that it can perform the same task alone in 22 days. If RES 1 has already worked 12 days on the task before RES 2 comes in, find the completion time of the task. Assume that RES 1 starts the task at time 0.

Solution

The amount of work to be done is 1.0 whole unit (i.e., the full task).

The work rate of RES 1 is 1/30 of the task per unit time.

The work rate of RES 2 is 1/22 of the task per unit time.

The amount of work completed by RES 1 in the 12 days it worked alone is (1/30)(12) = 2/5 (or 40%) of the required work.

Therefore, the remaining work to be done is 3/5 (or 60%) of the full task.

Let T be the time for which both resources work together.

The two resources working together to complete the task yield the following table:

Resource Type i	Work Rate, r_i	Time, t_i	Work Done, w_i
RES 1	1/30	T	$T/30$
RES 2	1/22	T	$T/22$
		Total	3/5

Thus, we have:

$$T/30 + T/22 = 3/5,$$

which yields $T = 7.62$ days. Thus, the completion time of the task is $(12+T) = 19.62$ days from time zero. The results of this example are summarized graphically in Figure 3-13. It is assumed that both resources produce identical quality of work and that the respective work rates remain consistent. The respective costs of the different resource types may be incorporated into the work rate analysis. The CRD and RS charts are simple extensions of very familiar tools. They are simple to use and they convey resource information quickly. They can be used to complement existing resource management tools. Users can find innovative ways to modify or implement them for specific resource planning, scheduling, and control purposes. For example, resource-dependent task durations and resource cost can be incorporated into the CRD and RS procedures to enhance their utility for resource management decisions.

Figure 3-13. Resource Schedule Charts for RES 1 and RES 2

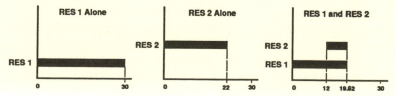

NON-DETERMINISTIC RESOURCE MANAGEMENT

In a non-deterministic project environment, probability information can be used to analyze resource utilization characteristics. Suppose the level of availability of a resource is probabilistic in nature. For simplicity, we will assume that the level of availability, X, is a continuous variable whose probability density function is defined by $f(x)$. This is true for many resource types such as funds, natural resources, and raw materials. If we are interested in the probability that resource availability will be within a certain range of x_1 and x_2, then the required probability can be computed as:

$$P(x_1 \leq X \leq x_2) = \int_{x_1}^{x_2} f(x)dx .$$

Similarly, a probability density function can be defined for the utilization level of a particular resource. If we denote the utilization level by U and its probability density function by $f(u)$, then we can calculate the probability that the utilization will exceed a certain level, u_0, by the following expression:

$$P(U \geq u_0) = \int_{u_0}^{\infty} f(u)du .$$

Example

Suppose a critical resource is leased for a large project. There is a graduated cost associated with using the resource at a certain percentage level, U. The cost is specified as \$10,000 per 10% increment in utilization level above 40%. A flat cost of \$5,000 is charged for utilization levels below 40%. The utilization intervals and the associated costs are presented below:

$U < 40\%$, \$5,000
$40\% <= U < 50\%$, \$10,000
$50\% <= U < 60\%$, \$20,000
$60\% <= U < 70\%$, \$30,000
$70\% <= U < 80\%$, \$40,000
$80\% <= U < 90\%$, \$50,000
$90\% <= U < 100\%$, \$60,000.

Thus, a utilization level of 50% will cost \$20,000, while a level of 49.5% will cost \$10,000.

Suppose the utilization level is a normally distributed random variable with a mean of 60% and a variance of 16% squared (i.e., standard deviation of 4%). Find the expected cost of using this resource.

Solution

The solution procedure involves finding the probability that the utilization level will fall within each of the specified ranges. The expected value formula will then be used to compute the expected cost as shown below:

$$E[C] \;=\; \sum_{k} x_k P(x_k),$$

where x_k represents the kth interval of utilization. The standard deviation of utilization is 4%.

$$P(U \;<\; 40) \;=\; P\!\left(z \;\le\; \frac{40-60}{4}\right) \;=\; P(z \;\le\; -5) \;=\; 0.0$$

$$
\begin{aligned}
P(40 \;\le\; U \;<\; 50) &= P\!\left(z \;<\; \frac{50-60}{4}\right) \;-\; P\!\left(z \;\le\; \frac{40-60}{4}\right)\\
&= P(z \;\le\; -2.5) \;-\; P(z \;\le\; -5)\\
&= 0.0062 \;-\; 0.0\\
&= 0.0062
\end{aligned}
$$

$$
\begin{aligned}
P(50 \;\le\; U \;<\; 60) &= P\!\left(z \;<\; \frac{60-60}{4}\right) \;-\; P\!\left(z \;\le\; \frac{50-60}{4}\right)\\
&= P(z \;\le\; 0) \;-\; P(z \;\le\; -2.5)\\
&= 0.5000 \;-\; 0.0062\\
&= 0.4938
\end{aligned}
$$

$$
\begin{aligned}
P(60 \;\le\; U \;<\; 70) &= P\!\left(z \;<\; \frac{70-60}{4}\right) \;-\; P\!\left(z \;\le\; \frac{60-60}{4}\right)\\
&= P(z \;\le\; 2.5) \;-\; P(z \;\le\; 0)\\
&= 0.9938 \;-\; 0.5000\\
&= 0.4938
\end{aligned}
$$

$$P(70 \leq U < 80) = P\left(z < \frac{80-60}{4}\right) - P\left(z \leq \frac{70-60}{4}\right)$$

$$= P(z \leq 5) - P(z \leq 2.5)$$

$$= 1.0 - 0.9938$$

$$= 0.0062$$

$$P(80 \leq U < 90) = P\left(z < \frac{90-60}{4}\right) - P\left(z \leq \frac{80-60}{4}\right)$$

$$= P(z \leq 7.5) - P(z \leq 5)$$

$$= 1.0 - 1.0$$

$$= 0.0$$

$$E(C) = \$5,000(0.0) + \$10,000(0.0062) + \$20,000(0.4938)$$

$$+ \$30,000(0.4938) + \$40,000(0.0062) + \$50,000(0.0)$$

$$= \$25,000.$$

Thus, it can be expected that leasing this critical resource will cost $25,000 in the long run. A decision can be made whether to lease or buy the resource. Resource substitution may also be considered on the basis of the expected cost of leasing.

This chapter has presented various approaches to the resource-constrained project scheduling problem. The specific methods of implementing these approaches will depend on the prevailing project scenario at the time of scheduling. The project analyst should consider the various options available and then select what is most relevant to his or her project. The next chapter presents schedule optimization techniques.

QUESTIONS AND EXERCISES

3-1. For the project data in Table 3-3, redefine the activity durations in terms of PERT estimates as presented below:

Activity	a, m, b
1-2	1, 2, 3
2-3	7, 8, 9
1-3	2, 3, 4
3-5	9, 10, 11
1-4	7, 8, 9
2-4	1, 2, 3
4-5	0, 1, 2

If the other activity data are the same as presented in Table 3-3, compute the scaled CAF for each activity in the project and use the CAF criterion to schedule the project. Compare the CAF schedule to the ACTIM schedule obtained in the example of Table 3-3.

3-2. Presented below is the activity data for a project that is subject to variable resource availability. It is assumed that the scaled CAF weights for the activities are already known as given in the last column of the tabulated data. There are two resource types. Resource availability varies from day to day on the basis of the resource schedule tabulated after the project data.

Activity	Predecessor	Duration (Day)	Resource Reqmt. (Type 1, Type 2)	Scaled CAF
A	-	6	2, 5	50.1
B	-	5	1, 3	57.1
C	-	2	3, 1	56.8
D	A, B	4	2, 0	100
E	B	5	1, 4	53.2
F	C	6	3, 1	51.8
G	B, F	1	4, 3	44.9
H	D, E	7	2, 3	54.9

Variable Resource Availability for Project in Question 2

Time Period (Days)	Units Available (Type 1, Type 2)
0 to 5	3, 5
5$^+$ to 10	2, 3
10$^+$ to 14	3, 4
14$^+$ to 20	4, 4
20$^+$ to 22	5, 3
22$^+$ to 30	4, 5
30$^+$ to 99	6, 6

Use the CAF weights to develop the Gantt chart for the project considering the daily resource availability. A task that is already in progress will be temporarily suspended whenever there are not enough units of resources to continue it. The task will resume (without increasing its duration) whenever enough resources become available.

3-3. Use the Minimum Total Slack (Min TS) heuristic to schedule the resource-constrained project below. If a tie occurs, use minimum activity duration to break the tie.

Units of Resource Type 1 available = 10
Units of Resource Type 2 available = 15

Activity	Predecessor	a	m	b	Resource Units Type 1	Type 2
A	-	1	2	4	3	0
B	-	5	6	7	5	4
C	-	2	4	5	4	1
D	A	1	3	4	2	0
E	C	4	5	7	4	3
F	A	3	4	5	2	7
G	B, D, E	1	2	3	6	2

3-4. For Question 3-3, draw the resource loading diagram for each resource type on the same graph. Which resource type exhibits more fluctuations in resource loading?

3-5. Using the computational approach presented in this chapter, compute the scaled CAF weight for each activity in Question 3-3.

3-6. Schedule the project in Question 3-3 using each of the following heuristics: CAF, LS, ES, LC, EC, TS, GRD, ACTIM. What is the shortest project duration obtained? Which heuristics yield that shortest project duration?

3-7. Draw the resource loading graph for each schedule in Question 3-6.

3-8. Draw the resource idleness graph for each schedule in Question 3-6.

3-9. Use the computational measure presented in this chapter to compute the resource utilization level (area) for each schedule in Question 3-6.

3-10. Use Badiru's approach to compute the project network complexity for the data in Question 3-3.

3-11. For the project data below, use Badiru's approach to compute the network complexity for the following alternate levels of resource availability: 2, 3, 4,5,6,7,8,9,10,11,12. Plot the complexity measures against the respective resource availability levels. Discuss your findings.

Activity Number	PERT Estimates (a, m, b)	Preceding Activities	Required Resources
1	1, 3, 5	-	1
2	0.5, 1, 3	-	2
3	1, 1, 2	-	1
4	2, 3, 6	Activity 1	2
5	1, 3, 4	Activity 2	1
6	1.5, 2, 2	Activity 3	2

3-12. For the project data below, use Badiru's approach to compute the network complexity for all possible combinations of resource availability (Z_1, Z_2), where the possible values of Z_1 are 4, 6, 7, 8, and 9 and the possible values of Z_2 are 2, 3, 4, 5, and 6. Note that this will generate 25 network complexity values. Fit an appropriate multiple regression function to the data you generated, where network complexity is the dependent variable and Z_1 and Z_2 are the independent variables.

Activity Number	PERT Estimates (a, m, b)	Preceding Activities	Required Resources (x_{i1}, x_{i2})
1	1, 3, 5	-	1, 0
2	0.5, 1, 3	-	1, 1
3	1, 1, 2	-	1, 1
4	2, 3, 6	Activity 1	2, 0
5	1, 3, 4	Activity 2	1, 0
6	1.5, 2, 2	Activity 3	4, 2

3-13. Three project crews are awarded a contract to construct an automated plant. The crews can work simultaneously on the project if necessary. Crew One, working alone, can complete the project in 82 days. Crew Two, working alone, can complete the project in 50 days. Crew Three, working alone, can complete the project in 64 days. Crew Two started the project. Ten days after the project started, Crew One joined the project. Fifteen days after Crew One joined the project, Crew Three also joined the project. Crew Two left the project 5 days before it was completed. Crew One is paid $500,000 per day on the project. Crew Two is paid $750,000 per day. Crew Three is paid $425,975 per day.

a) Find how many days it took to complete the project (assume that fractions of a day are permissible).

b) Based on the project participation described above, find the minimum budget needed to complete the project.

3-14. A project involves laying 100 miles of oil distribution pipe in the Alaskan wilderness. It is desired to determine the lowest-cost crew size and composition that can get the job done within 90 days. Three different types of crew are available. Each crew can work independently or work simultaneously with other crews. Crew One can lay pipes at the rate of 1 mile per day. If Crew Two is to do the whole job alone, it can finish it in 120 days. Crew Three can lay pipes at the rate of 1.7 miles per day. But this crew already has other imminent project commitments that will limit its participation in the piping project to only 35 contiguous days. All the three crews are ready, willing, and available to accept their contracts at the beginning of the project. Crew Three charges $50,000 per mile of pipes laid. Crew Two charges $35,000 per mile and Crew One charges $40,000 per mile. Contracts can be awarded only in increments of 10 miles. That is, a crew can get a contract only for 0 mile, 10 miles, 20 miles, 30 miles, and so on.

Required: Determine the best composition of the project crews and the minimum budget needed to finish the project in the shortest possible time.

3-15. Suppose the utilization level of a critical resource is defined by a normal distribution with a mean of 70 percent and a variance of 24 percent squared. Compute the probability that the utilization of the resource will exceed 85 percent.

3-16. Suppose rainfall is a critical resource for a farming project. The availability of rainfall in terms of inches during the project is known to be a random variable defined by a triangular distribution with a lower end point of 5.25 inches, a mode of 6 inches, and an upper end point of 7.5 inches. Compute the probability that there will be between 5.5 and 7 inches of rainfall during the project.

3-17. A scarce resource is to be leased for an engineering project. There is a graduated cost associated with using the resource at a certain percentage level, U. A step function has been defined for the cost rates for different levels of utilization. The step cost function is presented below:

If $U < 50\%$, Cost = \$0
If $50\% <= U < 60\%$, \$5,000
If $60\% <= U < 67\%$, \$20,000
If $67\% <= U < 85\%$, \$45,000
If $U >= 85\%$, \$55,000.

Suppose the utilization level is a random variable following a triangular distribution with a lower limit of 40%, a mode of 70%, and an upper limit of 95%.

a) Plot the step function for the cost of leasing the resource.

b) Plot the triangular probability density function for the utilization level.

c) Find the expected cost of using this resource.

3-18. Suppose three resource types (RES 1, RES 2, and RES 3) are to be assigned to a certain task. RES 1 working alone can complete the task in 35 days, RES 2 working alone can complete the task in 40 days, and RES 3 working alone can complete the task in 60 days. Suppose one unit of RES 1 and one unit of RES 2 start working on the task together at time zero. Two units of RES 3 joined the task after 45% of the task has been completed. RES 2 quits the task when there is 15% of the task remaining. Determine the completion time of the task and the total number of days that each resource type worked on the task. Assume that work rates are constant and units of the same resource type have equal work rates.

3-19. Three resource types (RES 1, RES 2, and RES 3) are to be assigned to a certain task. RES 1 working alone can complete the task in 35 days, RES 2 working alone can complete the task in 40 days, and RES 3 working alone can complete the task in 60 days. Suppose one unit of RES 1 and one unit of RES 2 start working on the task together at time zero. Two units of RES 3 are brought in to join the task some time after time zero. RES 2 quits the task when there is 20% of the task remaining.   If the full task is desired to be completed 13 days from time zero, determine how many days from time zero the two units of RES 3 should be brought in to join the task. Assume that work rates are constant and units of the same resource type have equal work rates.

3-20. Develop a quantitative methodology for incorporating different levels of quality of work by different resource types into the procedure for work rate analysis presented in this chapter.

CHAPTER 4

PROJECT OPTIMIZATION

This chapter presents some mathematical formulations useful for project optimization. Project optimization may focus on any of several performance measures of a project. Some of these performance measures are project duration, schedule composition, cost, resource allocation, and throughput. Schedule optimization is often the major focus in project management. While heuristic scheduling is very simple to implement, it does have some limitations. The limitations of heuristic scheduling include subjectivity, arbitrariness, and simplistic assumptions. In addition, heuristic scheduling does not handle uncertainty very well. One the other hand, mathematical scheduling is difficult to apply to practical problems. However, the increasing access to low-cost high-speed computers has facilitated increased use of mathematical scheduling approaches that yield optimal project schedules. The advantages of mathematical scheduling include:

- It provides optimal solutions.
- It can be formulated to include realistic factors influencing a project.
- Its formulation can be validated.
- It has proven solution methodologies.

With the increasing availability of personal computers and software tools, there is very little need to solve optimization problems by hand nowadays. Computerized algorithms are now available to solve almost any kind of optimization problem. What is more important for the project analyst is to be aware of the optimization models available, the solution techniques available, and how to develop models for specific project optimization problems. It is crucial to know which model is appropriate for which problem and to know how to implement optimized solutions in practical settings. The presentations in this chapter concentrate on the processes for developing models for project optimization rather than the manual techniques for solving the models. Excellent books are available on optimization solution techniques. Examples are Wu and Coppins (1981), Cooper and Steinberg (1974), Stark and Mayer (1983), Johnson and Montgomery (1974), Miller and Schmidt (1984), Ravindran et al. (1987), Taha (1982), Whitehouse and Wechler (1976), and Jelen and Black (1983).

GENERAL PROJECT SCHEDULING FORMULATION

Several mathematical models can be developed for project scheduling problems, depending on the specific objective of interest and the prevailing constraints. One general formulation is presented below:

Minimize $\{ \underset{\forall \ i}{\text{Max}} \ \{ s_i \ + \ d_i \} \}$

Subject to: $s_i \ \geq \ \underset{j \in P_i}{\text{Max}} \{ s_j \ + \ d_j \} \quad \forall i$

$$R_k \ \geq \ \sum_{i \in A_t} r_{ik} \quad \forall t; \ \forall k \ ,$$

where:
s_i = start time of activity i
d_i = duration of activity i
P_i = set of activities which must precede activity i
R_i = availability level of resource type k
A_t = set of activities ongoing at time t
r_{ik} = number of units of resource type k required by activity i.

The objective of the above model is to minimize the completion time of the last activity in the project. Since the completion time of the last activity determines the project duration, the project duration is indirectly minimized. The first constraint set ensures that all predecessors of activity i are completed before activity i may start. The second constraint set ensures that resource allocation does not exceed resource availability. The general model may be modified or extended to consider other project parameters. Examples of other factors that may be incorporated into the scheduling formulation include cost, project deadline, activity contingency, mutual exclusivity of activities, activity crashing requirements, and activity subdivision. The objective functions may involve any of the following:

- *Minimize project duration.*

- *Minimize project cost.*

- *Minimize number of late jobs.*

- *Minimize idle resource time.*
- *Maximize project revenue.*
- *Maximize net present worth.*

LINEAR PROGRAMMING FORMULATION

Linear programming is one of the most widely used quantitative techniques. It is a mathematical technique for finding the optimum solution to a linear objective function of two or more quantitative decision variables subject to a set of linear constraints. The technique is applicable to a wide range of decision-making problems. Its wide applicability is due to the fact that its formulation is not tied to any particular class of problems, as the CPM and PERT techniques are. Numerous research and application studies of linear programming are available in the literature.

The objective of a linear programming model is to optimize an objective function by finding values for a set of decision variables subject to a set of constraints. We can define the optimization problem mathematically as:

Optimize: $\quad z = c_1 x_1 + c_2 x_2 + \ldots + c_n x_n$

Subject to: $\quad a_{11} x_1 + a_{12} x_2 + \ldots + a_{1n} x_n \ \{\leq, \ =, \ \geq\} \ b_1$

$\qquad\qquad a_{21} x_1 + a_{22} x_2 + \ldots + a_{2n} x_n \ \{\leq, \ =, \ \geq\} \ b_2$

$$\cdot \quad \cdot \quad \cdot$$

$$\cdot \quad \cdot \quad \cdot$$

$\qquad\qquad a_{m1} x_1 + a_{m2} x_2 + \ldots + a_{mn} x_n \ \{\leq, \ =, \ \geq\} \ b_m$

$\qquad\qquad x_1, \ x_2, \ \ldots \ x_n \ \geq \ 0 \ ,$

where:
Optimize is replaced by *maximize* or *minimize* depending on the objective,
z is the value of the objective function for specified values of the decision variables,
$x_1, x_2, \ldots, x_n$ are the *n decision variables*,
$c_1, c_2, \ldots, c_n$ are the *objective function coefficients*,
$b_1, b_2, \ldots, b_n$ are the limiting values of the constraints (*right-hand-side*), and
$a_{11}, a_{12}, \ldots, a_{mn}$ are the *constraint coefficients* (per-unit usage rates).

The word *programming* in LP does not refer to computer programming, as some people think. Rather, it refers to choosing a *program of action*. The word *linear* refers to the *linear relationships* between the variables in the model. The characteristics of an LP formulation are explained below:

Quantitative Decision Variables: A decision variable is a factor that can be manipulated by the decision maker. Examples are number of resource units assigned to a task, number of product types in a product mix, and number of units of a product to produce. Each decision variable must be defined numerically in some unit of measurement.

Linear Objective Function: The objective function relates to the measure of performance to be minimized or maximized. There is a linear relationship between the variables that make up the objective function. The coefficient of each variable in the objective function indicates its per-unit contribution (positive or negative) toward the value of the objective function.

Linear Constraints: Every decision problem is subject to some specific limitations or constraints. The constraints specify the restrictions on how the decision maker may manipulate the decision variables. Examples of decision constraints are capacity limitations, maximum number of resource units available, demand and supply requirements, and number of work hours per day. The relationships between the variables in a constraint must be expressed as linear functions represented as equations or inequalities.

Non-negativity Constraint: The non-negativity constraint is common to all linear programming problems. This requires that all decision variables are restricted to non-negative values.

The general procedure for using a linear programming model to solve a decision problem involves an LP formulation of the problem and a selection of a solution approach. The procedure is summarized as follows:

1. Determine the decision variables in the problem.

2. Determine the objective of the problem.

3. Formulate the objective function as an algebraic expression.

4. Determine the real-world restrictions on the problem scenario.

5. Write each of the restrictions as an algebraic constraint.

6. Select a solution approach. The *graphical method* and the *simplex technique* are the two most popular approaches. The graphical method is easy to apply when the LP model contains just two decision variables. Several computer software packages are available for solving LP problems. Examples are LINDO, Linear Optimizer, LP88, MathPro, What-if Solver, and Turbo-Simplex. A comprehensive survey by Sharda (1992) lists several of the available LP packages.

An important aspect of using LP models is the interpretation of the results to make decisions. An LP solution that is optimal analytically may not be practical in a real-world decision scenario. The decision maker must incorporate his or her own subjective judgment when implementing LP solutions. Final decisions are often based on a combination of quantitative and qualitative factors. The examples presented in this chapter illustrate the application of optimization models to project planning and scheduling problems.

ACTIVITY PLANNING EXAMPLE

Activity planning is a major function in project management. Linear programming can be used to determine the optimal allocation of time and resources to the activities in a project. The example presented here is an adaptation of an example presented by Wu and Coppins (1981). Suppose a program planner is faced with the problem of planning a five-day development program for a group of managers in a manufacturing organization. The program includes some combination of four activities: seminar, laboratory work, case studies, and management games. It is estimated that each day spent on an activity will result in productivity improvement for the organization. The productivity improvement will generate annual cost savings as shown in Table 4-1. The program will last five days and there is no time lost between activities. In order to balance the program, the planner must make sure that not more than three days are spent on active or passive elements of the program. The active and passive percentages of each activity are also shown in the table. The company wishes to spend at least half a day on each of the four activities. A total budget of $1,500 is available. The cost of each activity is shown in the tabulated data.

Table 4-1. Data for Activity Planning Problem

Activity	Cost Savings ($/year)	% Active	% Passive	Cost ($/day)
Seminar	3,200,000	10	90	400
Laboratory Work	2,000,000	40	60	200
Case Studies	400,000	100	0	75
Management Games	2,000,000	60	40	100

The program planner must determine how many days to spend on each of the four activities. The following variables are defined for the problem:

x_1 = number of days spent on seminar

x_2 = number of days of laboratory work

x_3 = number of days for case studies

x_4 = number of days with management games.

The objective is to maximize the estimated annual cost savings. That is,

Maximize: $f = 3200x_1 + 2000x_2 + 400x_3 + 2000x_4$

Subject to the following constraints:

1. The program lasts exactly 5 days:
$$x_1 + x_2 + x_3 + x_4 = 5$$

2. Not more than 3 days can be spent on active elements:
$$0.10x_1 + 0.40x_2 + x_3 + 0.60x_4 \leq 3$$

3. Not more than 3 days can be spent on passive elements:
$$0.90x_1 + 0.60x_2 + 0.40x_4 \leq 3$$

4. At least 0.5 day must be spent on each of the four activities:
$$x_1 \geq 0.50 \qquad\qquad x_3 \geq 0.50$$
$$x_2 \geq 0.50 \qquad\qquad x_4 \geq 0.50$$

5. The budget is limited to $1,500:
$$400x_1 + 200x_2 + 75x_3 + 100x_4 \leq 1500.$$

The complete linear programming model for the example is presented below:

Maximize: $f = 3200x_1 + 2000x_2 + 400x_3 + 2000x_4$

Subject to:
$$
\begin{aligned}
x_1 + x_2 + x_3 + x_4 &= 5 \\
0.1x_1 + 0.4x_2 + x_3 + 0.6x_4 &\leq 3 \\
0.9x_1 + 0.6x_2 + 0x_3 + 0.4x_4 &\leq 3 \\
x_1 &\geq 0.5 \\
x_2 &\geq 0.5 \\
x_3 &\geq 0.5 \\
x_4 &\geq 0.5 \\
400x_1 + 200x_2 + 75x_3 + 100x_4 &\leq 1500 \\
x_1, x_2, x_3, x_4 &\geq 0.
\end{aligned}
$$

The optimal solution to the problem is shown in Table 4-2. Most of the conference time must be allocated to the seminar (2.20 days). The expected annual cost savings due to this activity is $7,040,000. That is, 2.20 days x $3,200,000/year/day. Management games is the second most important activity. A total of 1.8 days for management games will yield annual cost savings of $3,600,000. Fifty percent of the remaining time (0.5 day) should be devoted to laboratory work, which will result in annual cost savings of $1,000,000. Case studies also require half a day with a resulting annual savings of $200,000. The total annual savings, if the LP solution is implemented, is $11,840,000. Thus, an investment of $1,500 in management training for the personnel can generate annual savings of $11,840,000: a huge rate of return on investment!

Table 4-2. LP Solution to the Activity Planning Example

Activity	Cost Savings ($/year)	Number of Days	Annual Cost Savings
Seminar	3,200,000	2.20	7,040,000
Laboratory Work	2,000,000	0.50	1,000,000
Case Studies	400,000	0.50	200,000
Management Games	2,000,000	1.80	3,600,000
Total		5	11,840,000

RESOURCE COMBINATION EXAMPLE

This example illustrates the use of LP for energy resource allocation (Badiru, 1991a). Suppose an industrial establishment uses energy for heating, cooling, and lighting. The required amount of energy is presently being obtained from conventional electric power and natural gas. In recent years, there have been frequent shortages of gas, and there is a pressing need to reduce the consumption of conventional electric power. The director of the energy management department is considering a solar energy system as an alternate source of energy. The objective is to find an optimal mix of three different sources of energy to meet the plant's energy requirements. The three energy sources are:

- Natural gas
- Conventional electric power
- Solar power

It is required that the energy mix yield the lowest possible total annual cost of energy for the plant. Suppose a forecasting analysis indicates that the minimum KWH (kw-hr) needed per year for heating, cooling, and lighting, are 1,800,000 KWH, 1,200,000 KWH, and 900,000 KWH respectively. The solar energy system is expected to supply at least 1,075,000 KWH annually. The annual use of conventional electric power must be at least 1,900,000 KWH, due to a prevailing contractual agreement for energy supply. The annual consumption of the contracted supply of gas must be at least 950,000 KWH. The cubic foot unit for natural gas has been converted to KWH (1 cu. ft. of gas = 0.3024 KWH).

The respective rates of \$6/KWH, \$3/KWH, and \$2/KWH are applicable to the three sources of energy. The minimum individual annual savings desired are \$600,000 from solar power, \$800,000 from conventional electric power, and \$375,000 from natural gas. The savings are associated with the operating and maintenance costs. The energy cost per KWH is \$0.30 for conventional electric power, \$0.20 for natural gas, and \$0.40 for solar power. The initial cost of the solar energy system has been spread over its useful life of ten years with appropriate cost adjustments to obtain the rate per KWH. The problem data is summarized in Table 4-3. If we let x_{ij} be the KWH used from source i for purpose j, then would have the data organized as shown in Table 4-4.

Table 4-3. Energy Resource Combination Data

Energy Source	Supply (1000's KWH)	Savings (1000's $)	Unit Savings ($/KWH)	Unit Cost ($/KWH)
Solar power	1,075	600	6	0.40
Electric power	1,900	800	3	0.30
Natural gas	950	375	2	0.20

Table 4-4. Tabulation of Data for LP Model

Energy Source	Type of Use			Constraint
	Heating	Cooling	Lighting	
Solar power	x_{11}	x_{12}	x_{13}	$\geq 1075K$
Electric power	x_{21}	x_{22}	x_{23}	$\geq 1900K$
Natural gas	x_{31}	x_{32}	x_{33}	$\geq 950K$
Constraint	$\geq 1800K$	$\geq 1200K$	$\geq 900K$	

The optimization problem involves the minimization of the total cost function, Z. The mathematical formulation of the problem is presented below.

Minimize:
$$Z = 0.4 \sum_{j=1}^{3} x_{1j} + 0.3 \sum_{j=1}^{3} x_{2j} + 0.2 \sum_{j=1}^{3} x_{3j}$$

Subject to:
$$x_{11} + x_{21} + x_{31} \geq 1800$$
$$x_{12} + x_{22} + x_{32} \geq 1200$$
$$x_{13} + x_{23} + x_{33} \geq 900$$
$$6(x_{11} + x_{12} + x_{13}) \geq 600$$
$$3(x_{21} + x_{22} + x_{23}) \geq 800$$
$$2(x_{31} + x_{32} + x_{33}) \geq 375$$
$$x_{11} + x_{12} + x_{13} \geq 1075$$
$$x_{21} + x_{22} + x_{23} \geq 1900$$
$$x_{31} + x_{32} + x_{33} \geq 950$$
$$x_{ij} \geq 0, \quad i,j = 1, 2, 3.$$

Using the LINDO LP computer package, the solution presented in Table 4-5 was obtained. The table shows that solar power should not be used for cooling and lighting if the lowest cost is to be realized. The use of conventional electric power should be spread over the three categories of uses. The solution indicates that natural gas should be used only for cooling purposes. In pragmatic terms, this LP solution may have to be modified before being implemented on the basis of the prevailing operating scenarios and the technical aspects of the units involved.

Table 4-5. LP Solution to the Resource Combination Example

	Type of Use		
Energy Source	Heating	Cooling	Lighting
Solar power	1,075	0	0
Electric power	750	250	900
Natural gas	0	950	0

RESOURCE REQUIREMENTS ANALYSIS

Suppose a manufacturing project requires that a certain number of workers be assigned to a work station. The workers produce identical units of the same product. The objective is to determine the number of workers to assign to the work station in order to minimize the total production cost per shift. Each shift is eight hours long. Each worker can be assigned a variable number of hours and/or variable production rates to work during a shift. Four different production rates are possible: *slow rate, normal rate, fast rate,* and *high pressure rate.* Each worker is capable of working at any of the production rates during a shift. The total number of work hours available per shift is determined by multiplying the number of workers assigned by the eight hours available in a shift.

There is a variable cost and a level of percent defective associated with each production rate. The variable cost and the percent defective increase as the production rate increases. At least 450 units of the product must be produced during each shift. It is assumed that the workers' performance levels are identical. The production rates and the respective costs and percent defective are presented below:

Operating Rate 1 (Slow):
  $r_1 = 10$ units per hour
  $c_1 = \$5$ per hour
  $d_1 = 5\%$

Operating Rate 2 (Normal):
    $r_2 = 18$ units per hour
    $c_2 = \$10$ per hour
    $d_2 = 8\%$

Operating Rate 3 (Fast):
    $r_3 = 30$ units per hour
    $c_3 = \$15$ per hour
    $d_3 = 12\%$

Operating Rate 4 (High pressure):
    $r_4 = 40$ units per hour
    $c_4 = \$25$ per hour
    $d_4 = 15\%$

LP Formulation
Let x_i represent the number of hours worked at production rate i.
Let n represent the number of workers assigned.
Let u_i represent the number of good units produced at operation rate i.
    $u_1 = 10$ units/hour $(1 - 0.05) = 9.50$ units/hour
    $u_2 = 18$ units/hour $(1 - 0.08) = 16.56$ units/hour
    $u_3 = 30$ units/hour $(1 - 0.12) = 25.40$ units/hour
    $u_4 = 40$ units/hour $(1 - 0.15) = 34.00$ units/hour

Minimize: $z = 5x_1 + 10x_2 + 15x_3 + 25x_4$
Subject to: $x_1 + x_2 + x_3 + x_4 \leq 8n$
        $9.50x_1 + 16.56x_2 + 25.40x_3 + 34.00x_4 \geq 450$
        $x_1, x_2, x_3, x_4 \geq 0.$

The solution will be obtained by solving the LP model for different values of n. A plot of the minimum costs versus values of n can then be used to determine the optimum assignment policy. The complete solution is left as an exercise at the end of this chapter.

THE KNAPSACK PROBLEM

The *Knapsack Problem* is a famous operations research problem dealing with resource allocation. The general nature of the problem is as follows:
Suppose that n items are being considered for inclusion in a travel supply bag (knapsack). Each item has a certain per-unit value to the traveller. Each item also has a per-unit weight that contributes to the overall weight of the knapsack. There is a limitation on the total weight that the traveller can carry. Figure 4-1 shows a representation of the problem. The objective is to maximize the total value of the knapsack subject to the total weight limitation.

Figure 4-1. The Knapsack Problem

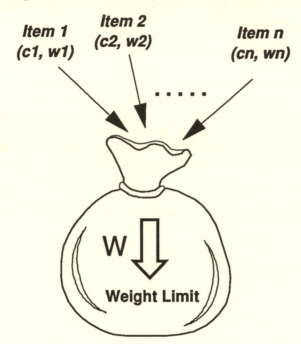

Mathematical formulation: For $j = 1, \ldots, n$, let $c_j > 0$ be the value per unit for item j. Let $w_j > 0$ be the weight per unit of item j. If the total weight limitation is W, then the problem of maximizing the total value of the knapsack is:

Maximize $z = \displaystyle\sum_{j=1}^{n} c_j x_j$

Subject to: $\displaystyle\sum_{j=1}^{n} w_j x_j \leq W$

$x_j \geq 0$ integer, $j = 1, \ldots, n,$

where x_j is the number of units of item j included in the knapsack. All data in the knapsack formulation are assumed to be integers. The Knapsack Problem can be solved by any of the available general Integer Linear Programming (ILP) algorithms. However, because it has only one constraint, more efficient solution algorithms are possible. For very simple models, the problem can be solved by inspection. For some special problems, such as project scheduling, it may be necessary to solve a large number of Knapsack problems sequentially. Even though each Knapsack formulation and solution may be simple, the overall problem structure may still be very complex.

KNAPSACK FORMULATION

The Knapsack Problem formulation can be applied to a project scheduling problem that is subject to resource constraints. In this case, each activity to be scheduled at a specific instant is modeled as an "item" to be included in the Knapsack. The composition of the activities in a scheduling window is viewed as the "Knapsack." Figure 4-2 presents a representation of a scheduling window with its composition of scheduled activities at a given instant.

Figure 4-2. The Knapsack Formulation of Project Scheduling

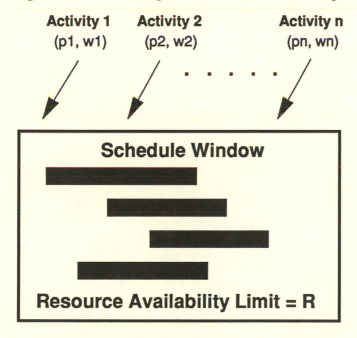

One important aspect of the Knapsack formulation for activity scheduling is that only one unit of each activity (item) can be included in the schedule at any given scheduling time. This is because the same activity cannot be scheduled more than once at the same time. However, in certain applications, such as concurrent engineering, it may be desired to have multiple executions of the same activity concurrently. For such cases, each execution of the activity may be modeled as a separate entity with one additional constraint to force concurrent execution. The formulation of the Knapsack Problem for activity scheduling is done at each and every scheduling time t. The objective is to schedule as many activities of high priority as possible while satisfying activity precedence relationships, without exceeding the resource availability limitations. The activity precedence requirements are used to determine the activities that are eligible for scheduling at a given scheduling time.

For $j = 1, \ldots, N$ activities, let $p_j > 0$ be the priority value for activity j. The priority value is used to prioritize activities for resource allocation when activities compete for limited resources. It is assumed that the priority values for the activities do not change during the scheduling process. This is referred to as *fixed prioritization* of activities. If the activity priority values can change depending on the state and time of the scheduling problem, then the activity prioritization is referred to as *variable prioritization* of activities. Let $r_{ij} \geq 0$ be the number of units of resource type i (weight) required by activity j. It is also assumed that the resource requirements do not change during the scheduling process. Let R_{it} be limit on the units of resource type i available at time t. The formulation of the scheduling problem is as follows:

Maximize $\quad z_t \quad = \quad \sum_{j=1, j \in S_t}^{N} p_j x_{jt}$

Subject to: $\quad \sum_{j=1, j \in S_t}^{N} r_{ij} x_{jt} \quad \leq \quad R_{it}, \quad i \quad = \quad 1, \ldots, k$

$\quad\quad\quad \zeta(S_t) \quad = \quad n_t,$

$\quad\quad\quad x_{jt} \quad = \quad 0 \quad \text{or} \quad 1, \quad j \quad = \quad 1, \ldots, N,$

where:
z_t = overall performance measure of the schedule generated at time t,
p_j = the priority measure (value) for activity j,
t = current time of scheduling,
x_{jt} = indicator variable specifying whether or not activity j is scheduled at time t,
N = total number of activities,
n_t = number of activities eligible for scheduling at time t ($n_t \leq N$),
S_t = set of activities eligible for scheduling at time t,
$\zeta(S_t)$ = cardinality of set S at time t,
k = number of different resource types,
r_{ij} = units of resource type i required by activity j,

R_{it} = units of resource type i available at time t.
The next scheduling time, t, is determined as the minimum of the finishing times of the currently scheduled activities.

KNAPSACK SCHEDULING EXAMPLE

Suppose we have a project consisting of seven activities: Activities A, B, C, D, E, F, and G, which are labeled 1 through 7.

The activity durations are specified as d_j:
$d_1 = 2.17, d_2 = 6, d_3 = 3.83, d_4 = 2.83, d_5 = 5.17, d_6 = 4, d_7 = 2$

The scaled priority values of the activities are specified as p_j:
$p_1 = 55.4, p_2 = 100, p_3 = 72.6, p_4 = 54, p_5 = 88, p_6 = 66.6, p_7 = 75.3$

There are two resource types with the following availability levels at time t, R_{ji}:
$R_{1,0} = 10, R_{2,0} = 15$

Units of *resource type* 1 required by the activities are specified as r_{1j}:
$r_{11} = 3, r_{12} = 5, r_{13} = 4, r_{14} = 2, r_{15} = 4, r_{16} = 2, r_{17} = 6$

Units of *resource type* 2 required by the activities are specified as r_{2j}:
$r_{21} = 0, r_{22} = 4, r_{23} = 1, r_{24} = 0, r_{25} = 3, r_{26} = 7, r_{27} = 2$

The precedence relationships between the activities are represented as $P(.) = \{$set of predecessors$\}$:
$P(A) = \phi, P(B) = \phi, P(C) = \phi, P(D) = \{A\}, P(E) = \{C\}, P(F) = \{A\}, P(G) = \{B, D, E\}$

The successive Knapsack formulations and solutions for the problem are presented below:

$\underline{t = 0:}$
$S_0 = \{A, B, C\}$
Maximize: $z_0 = 55.4x_A + 100x_B + 72.6x_C$
Subject to: $3x_A + 5x_B + 4x_C \leq 10$
$0x_A + 4x_B + 1x_C \leq 15$
$x_A, x_B, x_C = 0$ or 1,

whose solution yields $x_A = 0, x_B = 1, x_C = 1$. Thus, activity B is scheduled at $t=0$ and it will finish at $t = 6$; C is scheduled at $t = 0$ and it will finish at $t = 3.83$. The next scheduling time is $t = $ Min $\{3.38, 6\} = 3.83$.

$t = 3.83$:
$S_{3.83} = \{A, E\}$
Maximize: $z_{3.83} = 55.4x_A + 88.0x_E$
Subject to: $3x_A + 4x_E \leq 5$
 $0x_A + 3x_E \leq 11$
 $x_A, x_E = 0 \text{ or } 1,$

whose solution yields $x_A = 0, x_E = 1$. Thus, activity E is scheduled at $t = 3.83$ and it will finish at $t = 9$. The next scheduling time is $t = \text{Min } \{6, 9\} = 6$.

$t = 6$:
$S_6 = \{A\}$
Maximize: $z_6 = 55.4x_A$
Subject to: $3x_A \leq 6$
 $x_A = 0 \text{ or } 1,$

whose solution yields $x_A = 1$. Thus, activity A is scheduled at $t = 6$ and it will finish at $t = 8.17$. The next scheduling time is $t = \text{Min } \{8.17, 9\} = 8.17$.

$t = 8.17$:
$S_{8.17} = \{D, F\}$
Maximize: $z_{8.17} = 54x_D + 66.6x_F$
Subject to: $2x_D + 2x_F \leq 6$
 $0x_D + 7x_F \leq 12$
 $x_D, x_F = 0 \text{ or } 1,$

whose solution yields $x_D = 1, x_F = 1$. Thus, activities D and F are scheduled at $t = 8.17$. D will finish at $t = 11$. F will finish at $t = 12.17$. The next scheduling time is $t = \text{Min } \{9, 11, 12.17\} = 9$.

$t = 9$:
$S_9 = \phi$
No activity is eligible for scheduling at $t = 9$, since G cannot be scheduled until E finishes. The next scheduling time is $t = \text{Min } \{11, 12.17\} = 11$.

$t = 11$:
$S_{11} = \{G\}$
Maximize: $z_9 = 75.3x_G$
Subject to: $6x_G \leq 8$
 $2x_G \leq 8$
 $x_G = 0 \text{ or } 1,$

whose solution yields $x_G = 1$. Thus, activity G is scheduled at $t = 11$ and it will finish at $t = 13$. All activities have been scheduled. The project completion time is $t = \text{Max} \{12.17, 13\} = 13$. Figure 4-3 shows the Gantt chart of the completed schedule.

Figure 4-3. Gantt Chart of Knapsack Schedule

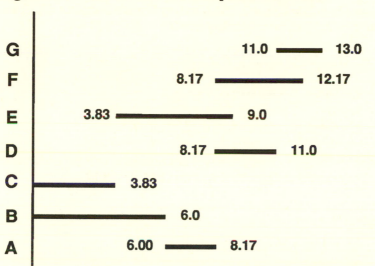

TRANSPORTATION PROBLEM

The *transportation problem* is a special class of optimization problem dealing with the distribution of items from sources of supply to locations of demand. This type of problem can occur in large or multiple project scheduling environments where supplies must be delivered to various project sites in a coordinated fashion to meet scheduling requirements. A specific algorithm, known as the *transportation method*, is available for solving transportation problems that satisfy the following assumptions:

1. The problem must concern a single product type to be transported.

2. There must be several *sources* from which the product is to be transported.

3. The amount of *supply* available at each source must be known.

4. There must be several *destinations* to which the product is to be transported.

5. The *demand* at each destination must be known.

6. The per-unit cost of transporting the product from any source to any destination must be known.

    The general format of the transportation problem, referred to as the *transportation tableau*, is presented in Figure 4-4.

Figure 4-4. General Layout of the Transportation Problem

Destinations

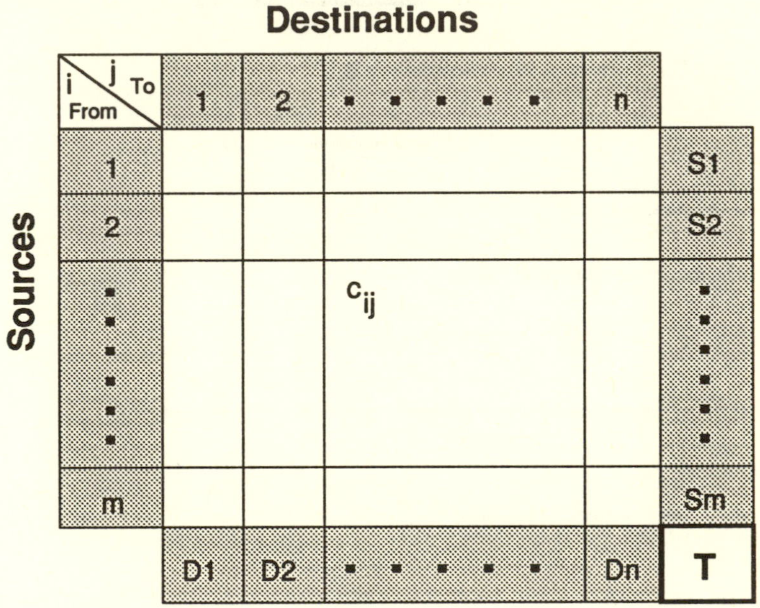

The objective of the transportation method is to determine the minimum cost plan to transport units from origins to destinations while satisfying all supply limitations and demands. The following notation is used:

$Src\,i$ = Source i, $i = 1, 2, \ldots, m$
$Des\,j$ = Destination j, $j = 1, 2, \ldots, n$
S_i = Available Supply from Source i, $i = 1, 2, \ldots, m$
D_j = Total Demand for Destination j, $j = 1, 2, \ldots, n$
c_{ij} = Cost of transporting one unit of the product from source i to destination j

x_{ij} = Number of units of the product transported from source i to destination j.
A linear programming formulation of the transportation problem is presented below:

$$\text{Minimize} \quad z = \sum_{i=1}^{m} \sum_{j=1}^{n} c_{ij} x_{ij}$$

$$\text{Subject to:} \quad \sum_{j=1}^{n} x_{ij} \leq S_i, \quad i = 1, 2, ..., m$$

$$\sum_{i=1}^{m} x_{ij} \geq D_j, \quad j = 1, 2, ..., n$$

$$x_{ij} \geq 0.$$

The first set of constraints indicates that the sum of the shipments from a source cannot exceed its supply. The second set of constraints indicates that the sum of shipments to a destination must satisfy its demand. The above LP model implies that the total supply must at least equal the total demand. Although it is possible to model and solve a transportation problem as a linear programming problem, the special structure of the problem makes it possible to use the *transportation method* as a more efficient solution method. Like the LP simplex method, the transportation method is an iterative solution procedure, moving from one trial solution to another less costly trial solution. The iterative solution continues until the optimal solution is reached. Unlike the simplex method, however, the transportation method is limited to only certain types of problems.

Balanced Versus Unbalanced Transportation Problems

A transportation problem is said to be *balanced* if the total available supply is equal to the total demand. For a balanced problem, the inequality constraints in the model will be modified to equality constraints. That is:

$$\sum_{j=1}^{n} x_{ij} = S_i, \quad i = 1, 2, ..., m$$

$$\sum_{i=1}^{m} x_{ij} = D_j, \quad j = 1, 2, ..., n.$$

A transportation problem is *unbalanced* when total supply is not equal to total demand. Unbalanced transportation problems are more realistic in practical situations. A modification of the initial transportation tableau is required for unbalanced transportation problems. If total supply is greater than total demand, we will add one extra *dummy destination* to the initial tableau. The dummy destination is assigned a demand, D_{n+1}, that is equal to total available supply minus the total demand: That is:

$$D_{n+1} = \sum_{i=1}^{m} S_i - \sum_{j=1}^{n} D_j.$$

The dummy destination serves to balance the problem. Allocations to cells associated with the dummy destination are simply not shipped from the sources. These unshipped units represent excess supply. The magnitude of the excess supply can be used for making capacity adjustment decisions at the sources if no "real" destinations can be found to absorb the excess units.

If total supply is less than total demand, then some of the demands cannot be fulfilled. In such a case, a *dummy source* is included in the formulation. Other options are to reduce demand levels or increase supply capacities. The supply from the dummy source may be viewed as subcontracted supply. If supply and demand levels are fixed, then the supply to be subcontracted out, S_{m+1}, will be:

$$S_{m+1} = \sum_{j=1}^{n} D_j - \sum_{i=1}^{m} S_i.$$

Initial Solution to the Transportation Problem

To use the transportation method, we must first identify an *initial feasible solution*. The *northwest-corner technique* is one way to obtain an initial solution to a transportation problem. The technique makes the first allocation to the northwest corner cell in the transportation tableau. As much allocation as possible is made to that northwest corner cell. This technique is a simple method to determine a *feasible solution* to the transportation problem. The feasible solution satisfies all supply and demand restrictions. The initial solution may not be optimal, but it serves as a starting point for procedures that are designed to find the optimal solution. A summary of the northwest-corner technique is presented below:

NORTHWEST-CORNER TECHNIQUE

Step 1: Set up tableau and enter the S_i, D_j, and c_{ij} values.
    a.   Allocate $u_{11} = $ Min $\{S_1, D_1\}$.
    b.   Update supply and demand: $S_1 = S_1 - u_{11}$ and $D_1 = D_1 - u_{11}$.

Step 2: Move to a new cell.
    a.   If current $S_1 = 0$, move down one cell.
    b.   If current $D_1 = 0$, move one cell to the right.

Step 3: Make allocation to the new cell ij
   a.   Allocate x_{ij} = Min $\{S_i, D_j\}$
   b.   Update supply and demand: $S_i = S_i - x_{ij}$ and $D_j = D_j - x_{ij}$.

Step 4: Repeat Steps 2 and 3 until all available supply and all demand have been allocated to cells within the initial tableau. That is, until $S_i = 0$ and $D_j = 0$ $(i = 1, 2, \ldots, m; j = 1, 2, \ldots, n)$.

The northwest-corner method, although very simple and fast, usually does not yield a good initial solution because it totally ignores costs. Better initial approximation methods are available. These other methods include the *least-Cost method*, *Vogel's approximation method (VAM)*, and *Russell's approximation method* (Taha, 1982; Hillier and Lieberman, 1974).

LEAST-COST METHOD

The least-cost method uses the cell costs as the basis for making allocations to the cells in the transportation tableau.

Step 1: Assign as much as possible to the variable with the smallest unit cost in the tableau. Break ties arbitrarily. Cross out the satisfied row or column.

Step 2: If both a row and a column are satisfied simultaneously, only one may be crossed out. Adjust the supply and demand for all uncrossed rows and columns.

Step 3: Repeat the process by assigning as much as possible to the cell with the smallest uncrossed unit cost.

Step 4: The procedure is complete when only one row or column remains uncrossed.

VOGEL'S APPROXIMATION

Vogel's approximation (Reinfeld and Vogel, 1958) is better than the northwest-corner method. In fact, the method usually yields an optimal or close to optimal starting solution to the transportation problem. The steps of the method are presented below:

Step 1: Set up the transportation tableau and evaluate the row or column penalty.

   a. For each row, subtract the smallest cost element from the next smallest cost element in the same row.

   b. For each column subtract the smallest cost element from the next smallest cost element in the same column.

Step 2: Identify the row or column with the largest penalty (break ties arbitrarily).

    a. Allocate as much as possible to the cell with the least cost in the selected row or column. That is, assign the smaller of row supply and column demand.

    b. If there is only one cell remaining in a row or column, choose the cell and allocate as many units as possible to it.

    c. Adjust the supply and demand and cross out the satisfied row or column.

Step 3: Determine satisfied rows or columns.

    a. If a row supply becomes zero, cross out the row and calculate the new column penalties. The other row penalties are not affected.

    b. If a column demand becomes zero, cross out the column and calculate new row penalties.

    c. If both a row supply and a column demand become zero at the same time, cross out only one of them. The one remaining will have a supply or demand or zero, which means an assignment of zero units in a subsequent step.

Step 4: Repeat Steps 2 and 3 until an initial basic feasible solution has been obtained.

RUSSELL'S APPROXIMATION METHOD

Russell's approximation method (E. Russell, 1969) is another approach to obtaining an initial solution for the transportation problem. The steps of the method are presented below:

Step 1: For each source row i remaining under consideration, determine u_i as:
u_i = Max $\{c_{ij}\}$ still remaining in that row.
For each destination column j remaining under consideration, determine v_j as:
v_j = Max $\{c_{ij}\}$ still remaining in that column.

Step 2: For each cell not previously selected in the rows and columns, calculate $(c_{ij} - u_i - v_j)$.

Step 3: Select the cell having the largest negative value of $(c_{ij} - u_i - v_j)$. Break ties arbitrarily. Assign as many units as possible to the cell.

Step 4: Repeat Steps 1-3 until an initial solution is obtained.

The Transportation Algorithm

The transportation algorithm generates an optimal solution to the transportation problem. The algorithm gets to the optimal solution by improving on an initial feasible solution. The steps of the algorithm are summarized below:

Step 1: Find an initial basic feasible solution.

Step 2: Define a row index, u_i, and a column index, v_j.
This is called the MODI (modified distribution) or the uv method.
There are m of the u_i ($i = 1, 2, \ldots, m$) and n of the v_j ($i = 1, 2, \ldots, m$).
The indices are composed so that for each *basic cell* $c_{ij} = u_i + v_j$.
A basic cell has $x_{ij} > 0$. There must be $m+n-1$ basic cells. Thus, there are $m+n-1$ equations in $m+n$ unknowns. This means that we can arbitrarily assign any value to one of the row or column indices (e.g., $u_1 = 0$).

Step 3: After setting $u_1 = 0$, solve for the remaining indices by using the relationship $u_i + v_j = c_{ij}$ iteratively for each basic cell. Each time one index is computed, there will be another one that is immediately defined. Place the value of each index in the appropriate cell in the tableau.

Step 4: Calculate the reduced cost of each non-basic cell as follows:
$$c_{ij} - z_{ij} = c_{ij} - (u_i + v_j) = c_{ij} - u_i - v_j.$$
Circle the $c_{ij} - (u_i + v_j)$ values in for the non-basic cells. Because this is a cost minimization problem, the current basis is optimal if:
$$c_{ij} - z_{ij} = c_{ij} - u_i - v_j \geq 0$$
for all non-basic variables. Stop if optimal.

Step 5: Select the non-basic variable with the most negative reduced cost to enter the basis. That is, select x_{ij} to enter the basis so that:
$$c_{ij} - z_{ij} = \text{Min}_{pq} \{c_{pq} - z_{pq}\}.$$

Step 6: Use the *stepping-stone method* to determine the loop formed by the non-basic cell (*ij*) and the basic cells. The stepping-stone method "steps" through cells in a closed loop path in the tableau based on the following rules:

a. Only one non-basic variable (i.e., the entering variable) is included in the stepping-stone path.

b. The path is unique.

c. Start by placing a plus sign in the cell of the entering variable. The plus sign indicates that this variable will increase.

d. Place a minus sign in the cell of a basic variable so that the column or row of the incoming variable is balanced with one plus sign and one minus sign. The minus sign indicates that the cell will increase by one unit for every unit increase in the entering variable.

e. Continue the assignment of plus and minus signs in the basic cells in such a way that each row and each column of the tableau contains either no signs or exactly one plus sign and one minus sign.

d. The stepping-stone path ends when both the row and the column of the entering variable are balanced. Basic variables that are not in the path contain no sign and will not change as the entering variable increases.

Step 7: Determine the exiting variable. This is the basic variable containing a minus sign and having the smallest x_{ij} value.
Set $K = \text{Min}_{ij} \{x_{ij} \mid \text{sign is minus}\}$.

Step 8: Update the transportation tableau as follows:
Add K units to each cell that has a plus sign in the closed path.
Subtract K units from each that has a minus sign in the closed path.

Step 9: Return to Step 2.

Example of Transportation Problem

Suppose four project sites are to be supplied with units of a certain product from three different sources. It is desired to minimize the total cost of supplying the sites with the required units. The supply and demand data and the shipment costs are summarized as follows:
$S_1 = 30, S_2 = 50, S_3 = 40$
$D_1 = 30, D_2 = 20, D_3 = 40, D_4 = 30$
$c_{11} = \$5, c_{12} = \$8, c_{13} = \$3, c_{14} = \$6$
$c_{21} = \$4, c_{22} = \$5, c_{23} = \$7, c_{24} = \$4$
$c_{31} = \$6, c_{32} = \$2, c_{33} = \$4, c_{34} = \$5.$

Figure 4-5 shows the layout of the problem. This is a balanced transportation problem. The initial feasible solution obtained through the northwest-corner method is shown in Figure 4-6.

Figure 4-5. Cost Matrix for Transportation Problem Example

Destinations

	1	2	3	4	
1	5	8	3	6	30
2	4	5	7	4	50
3	6	2	4	5	40
	30	20	40	30	120

(Sources)

Figure 4-6. Tableau 1 for Transportation Example

Destinations

	1	2	3	4	
1	5 30	8	3	6	30
2	4	5 20	7 30	4	50
3	6	2	4 10	5 30	40
	30	20	40	30	120

(Sources)

There are only $5 \neq m+n-1 = 6$ positive x_{ij}. Therefore, choose an independent cell for a zero allocation. Let $u_2 = 0$. Determine the remaining u_i and v_j values for the basic cells using the relationship $c_{ij} = (u_i + v_j)$. Using the u_i and v_j already available, compute $c_{ij} - (u_i + v_j)$ for each of the non-basic cells. The resulting tableau is shown in Figure 4-7.

Figure 4-7. Tableau 2 for Transportation Example

		1	2	3	4	
		v1 = 4	**v2 = 5**	**v3 = 7**	**v4 = 8**	
u1 = 1	1	5 ⌐ 30	8 ⌐ 2	3 ⌐ -5	6 ⌐ -3	30
u2 = 0	2	4 ⌐ 0	5 ⌐ 20	7 ⌐ 30	4 ⌐ -4	50
u3 = -3	3	6 ⌐ 5	2 ⌐ 0	4 ⌐ 10	5 ⌐ 30	40
		30	20	40	30	120

If all the $c_{ij} - (u_i + v_j)$ values for the non-basic cells were positive, the solution would be optimal. Cell (1,3) has the most negative value. So, it enters the solution. This is shown in Figure 4-8a. Note that cell (2, 1) is treated as a basic cell since an "allocation" of zero has been made to it. Allocate as much as possible to the entering cell, cell (1, 3), without violating the supply and demand constraints. The new solution is shown in Figure 4-8b.

Figure 4-8a. Part (a) of Tableau 3 for Transportation Example

	1	2	3	4	
1	5 ⌐ -K 30	8 ⌐ 2	3 ⌐ -5 +K	6 ⌐ -3	30
2	4 ⌐ +K 0	5 ⌐ 20	7 ⌐ -K 30	4 ⌐ -4	50
3	6 ⌐ 5	2 ⌐ 0	4 ⌐ 10	5 ⌐ 30	40
	30	20	40	30	120

Figure 4-8b. Part (b) of Tableau 3 for Transportation Example

	1	2	3	4	
1	5 ⌐ 0	8 ⌐	3 ⌐ -5 30	6 ⌐	30
2	4 ⌐ 30	5 ⌐ 20	7 ⌐	4 ⌐	50
3	6 ⌐	2 ⌐	4 ⌐ 10	5 ⌐ 30	40
	30	20	40	30	120

The tableau generated by a return to step 2 of the algorithm is shown in Figure 4-9.

Figure 4-9. Tableau 4 for Transportation Example

		v1 = 5	v2 = 6	v3 = 3	v4 = 4	
		1	2	3	4	
u1 = 0	1	5 ⌐ 0	8 ⌐ 2	3 ⌐ 30	6 ⌐ 2	30
u2 = -1	2	4 ⌐ 30	5 ⌐ 20	7 ⌐ 5	4 ⌐ 1	50
u3 = 1	3	6 ⌐ 0	2 ⌐ -5	4 ⌐ 10	5 ⌐ 30	40
		30	20	40	30	120

The optimal solution has not been reached. Therefore, continue with the algorithm steps. Figures 4-10 through 4-14 show the subsequent tableaus of the solution. Figure 4-15 shows the final tableau and the optimal solution.

Figure 4-10. Tableau 5 for Transportation Example

	1	2	3	4	
1	5 $_0$-K	8	3 $_{30}$+K	6	30
2	4 +K 30	5 -K 20	7	4	50
3	6	2	4 10	5 30	40
	30	20	40	30	120

Figure 4-11. Tableau 6 for Transportation Example

	1	2	3	4	
1	5 0	8	3 30	6	30
2	4 30	5 20	7	4	50
3	6	2	4 10	5 30	40
	30	20	40	30	120

Figure 4-12. Tableau 7 for Transportation Example

	v1 = 1 1	v2 = 2 2	v3 = 4 3	v4 = 5 4	
u1 = 1 1	5 5	8 7	3 30	6 2	30
u2 = 3 2	4 30	5 20	7 0	4 -4	50
u3 = 0 3	6 5	2 0	4 10	5 30	40
	30	20	40	30	120

Figure 4-13. Tableau 8 for Transportation Example

	1	2	3	4	
1	5	8	3 30	6	30
2	4 30	5 -K 20	7	4 +K	50
3	6	2 +K 0	4 10	5 -K 30	40
	30	20	40	30	120

Figure 4-14. Tableau 9 for Transportation Example

	1	2	3	4	
1	5	8	3 30	6	30
2	4 30	5 20	7	4	50
3	6	2 0	4 10	5 30	40
	30	20	40	30	120

Figure 4-15. Tableau 10 for Transportation Example

	v1 = 5	v2 = 2	v3 = 4	v4 = 5	
	1	2	3	4	
u1 = 1 1	5 1	8 7	3 30	6 2	30
u2 = -1 2	4 30	5 4	7 4	4 20	50
u3 = 0 3	6 1	2 20	4 10	5 10	40
	30	20	40	30	120

The solution indicates that we should ship 30 units from source 1 to destination 3, 30 units from source 2 to destination 1, 20 units from source 2 to destination 4, 20 units from source 3 to destination 2, 10 units from source 3 to destination 3, and 10 units from source 3 to destination 4. The minimum cost is:

$$z = 3(30) + 4(30) + 4(20) + 2(20) + 4(10) + 5(10) = 420.$$

Transshipment Formulation

The transshipment problem is a general model of the transportation problem. In this model, there can be *pure sources, pure destinations,* and *transshipment points,* which can serve as both sources and destinations. It is possible for any source or destination to ship to any other source or destination. Thus, there may be many different ways of shipping from point i to point j in addition to the direct route. In the transportation problem, the way in which units are distributed from source i to destination j must be known in advance so that the corresponding cost per unit, c_{ij}, can be determined ahead of time. In the transshipment problem, units may go through intermediate points that offer lower total shipment cost. For example, instead of shipping units directly from source 2 to destination 3, it may be cheaper to include the units going to destination 3 with the units going to destination 4 and then ship those units from destination 4, which now serves as a source, to destination 3. A mathematical formulation of the transshipment problem is as follows: Let

x_{ij} = amount shipped from point i to point j, $i,j = 1, 2, \ldots, n$; $i \neq j$
c_{ij} = cost of shipping from point i to point j, $c_{ij} \geq 0$
r_i = net requirement at point i.

Each point must satisfy a balance equation stating that the amount shipped minus the amount received equals the net requirement at the point. It is also required that total demand equal total supply. Thus, we have:

$$\text{Minimize} \quad z = \sum_{i=1}^{n} \sum_{j=1}^{n} c_{ij} x_{ij}, \quad i \neq j$$

$$\text{Subject to:} \quad \sum_{j=1, j \neq i}^{n} x_{ij} - \sum_{j=1, j \neq i}^{n} x_{ji} = r_i, \quad i = 1, 2, \ldots, n$$

$$\sum_{i=1}^{n} r_i = 0$$

$$x_{ij} \geq 0, \quad j = 1, 2, \ldots, n; \quad i \neq j.$$

ASSIGNMENT PROBLEM

Suppose there are n tasks which must be performed by n workers. The cost of worker i performing task j is c_{ij}. If is desired to assign workers to the tasks in a fashion that minimizes the cost of completing the tasks. This problem scenario is referred to as the *assignment problem.* The technique for finding the optimal solution to the problem is called the *assignment method*. Like the transportation method, the assignment method is an iterative procedure that arrives at the optimal solution by improving on a trial solution at each stage of the procedure.

CPM and PERT can be used in controlling projects to ensure that the project will be completed on time. As was mentioned in Chapters 2 and 3, these two techniques do not consider the assignment of resources to the tasks that make up a project. The *assignment method* can be used to achieve an optimal assignment of resources to specific tasks in a project. Although the assignment method is cost-based, task duration can be incorporated into the modeling in terms of time-cost relationships. Of course, task precedence requirements and other scheduling restrictions will have to be accounted for in the final scheduling of the tasks. The objective is to minimize the total cost. Thus, the formulation of the assignment problem is as follows: Let

$x_{ij} = 1$ if worker i is assign to task j, $i, j = 1, 2, . . .,n$
$x_{ij} = 0$ if worker i is not assigned to task j
$c_{ij} = $ cost of worker i performing task j.

Minimize $z = \sum_{i=1}^{n} \sum_{j=1}^{n} c_{ij} x_{ij}$

Subject to: $\sum_{j=1}^{n} x_{ij} = 1, \quad i = 1, 2, ..., n$

$\sum_{i=1}^{n} x_{ij} = 1, \quad j = 1, 2, ..., n$

$x_{ij} \geq 0, \quad i, j = 1, 2, ..., n.$

It can be seen that the above formulation is a transportation problem with $m = n$ and all supplies and demands are equal to 1. Note that we have used the non-negativity constraint, $x_{ij} \geq 0$, instead of the integer constraint, $x_{ij} = 0$ or 1. However, the solution of the model will still be integer-valued (Cooper and Steinberg, 1974). Hence, the assignment problem is a special case of the transportation problem with $m = n$, $a_i = 1$, and $a_i = 1$. Conversely (Dantzig, 1963), the transportation problem can also be viewed as a special case of the assignment problem. A transportation problem can be modeled as an assignment problem and vice versa. The basic requirements of an assignment problem are:

1.   There must be two or more tasks to be completed.

2.   There must be two or more resources that can be assigned to the tasks.

3. The cost of using any of the resources to perform any of the tasks must be known.

4. Each resource is to be assigned to one and only one task.

If the number of tasks to be performed is greater than the number of workers available, we will need to add *dummy workers* to balance the problem. Similarly, if the number of workers is greater than the number of tasks, we will need to add *dummy tasks* to balance the problem. If there is no problem of overlapping, a worker's time may be split into segments so that the worker can be assigned more than one task. In this case, each segment of the worker's time will be modeled as a separate resource in the assignment problem. Thus, the assignment problem can be extended to consider partial allocation of resource units to multiple tasks.

Although the assignment problem can be formulated for and solved by the simplex method or the transportation method, a more efficient algorithm has been developed specifically for the assignment problem. The method, known as the *Hungarian method* (Kuhn, 1956), is a simple iterative technique. The method is based on the assignment theory developed by Egervary, a Hungarian mathematician. It is based on properties of matrices and relationships between primal and dual problems. Kuhn (1956) discusses several modifications of the Hungarian method. Further details on the method can also be found in Bazaraa and Jarvis (1977). The steps of the assignment method are summarized below:

Step 1: Develop the $n \times n$ cost matrix, in which rows represent workers and columns represent tasks.

Step 2: For each row of the cost matrix, subtract the smallest number in the row from each and every number in the row. For each column of the resulting matrix, subtract the smallest number from each and every number in the column. The resulting matrix is called the *matrix of reduced costs*.

Step 3: Find the minimum number of lines through the rows and columns of the reduced-cost matrix such that all zeros have a line through them. If the number of lines is *n*, the optimal solution has been reached; stop. Otherwise, go to Step 4.

Step 4: Define a new reduced-cost matrix as follows: Determine the smallest number in the matrix which does not have a line through it. Subtract this number from all the "un-lined" numbers and add it to all the numbers which have two lines through them (i.e, numbers located at the intersection of two lines in the matrix). Go to Step 3.

Example of Assignment Problem

To adapt an example presented by Wu and Coppins (1981), suppose five workers are to be assigned to five tasks on the basis of the cost matrix presented in Figure 4-16. Let us use the algorithm steps presented above to solve this assignment problem.

Figure 4-16. Cost Matrix for Assignment Problem

Tasks

		1	2	3	4	5
	1	$200	$400	$500	$100	$400
	2	$400	$700	$800	$1,100	$700
Worker	3	$300	$900	$800	$1,000	$500
	4	$100	$300	$500	$100	$400
	5	$700	$100	$200	$100	$200

For convenience, we can divide each cost element by 100. When the smallest number in each row of the resulting simplified matrix is subtracted from all the elements in the row, we obtain Figure 4-17. When the smallest number in each column of Figure 4-17 is subtracted from all the elements in the column, we obtain Figure 4-18.

Figure 4-17. Tableau 1 for Assignment Problem

Tasks

Worker		1	2	3	4	5
	1	1	3	4	0	3
	2	0	3	4	7	3
	3	0	6	5	7	2
	4	0	2	4	0	3
	5	6	0	1	0	1

Figure 4-18. Tableau 2 for Assignment Problem

Tasks

Worker		1	2	3	4	5
	1	1	3	3	0	2
	2	0	3	3	7	2
	3	0	6	4	7	1
	4	0	2	3	0	2
	5	6	0	0	0	0

The minimum number of lines required to cover all the zeros is three. This is shown in Figure 4-19. The smallest uncovered number in Figure 4-19 is 1. When this "1" is subtracted from the other uncovered numbers and added to the numbers that are covered by two lines, we obtain the new reduced-cost matrix shown in Figure 4-20.

Figure 4-19. Tableau 3 for Assignment Problem

Tasks

	1	2	3	4	5
1	1	3	3	0	2
2	0	3	3	7	2
3	0	6	4	7	1
4	0	2	3	0	2
5	0	0	0	0	0

Worker

Figure 4-20. Tableau 4 for Assignment Problem

Tasks

	1	2	3	4	5
1	1	2	2	0	1
2	0	2	2	7	1
3	0	5	3	7	0
4	0	1	2	0	1
5	7	0	0	1	0

Worker

The minimum number of lines needed to cover all the zeros in Figure 4-20 is 4. The smallest uncovered number is 1. After repeating the appropriate steps of the algorithm, we obtain Figure 4-21. Since $n = 5$ lines are needed to cover all the zeros, the optimal solution has been found.

Figure 4-21. Final Tableau for Assignment Problem

Tasks

	1	2	3	4	5
1	1	1	1	0	1
2	0	1	1	1	1
3	0	4	2	1	0
4	0	0	1	0	1
5	0	0	0	2	1

Worker

To determine the optimal assignment, first make assignments to the rows and columns with only one zero. In Figure 4-21, if we start with the rows, we will make assignments in cell (1, 4) and cell (2, 1). Then, considering the columns, we will make assignments in cell (5, 3) and cell (3, 5). The only remaining assignment is for cell (4, 2). These optimal assignments are shown crossed in the figure. The minimum cost is $1,900.

TRAVELLING RESOURCE FORMULATION

The travelling salesman problem is a special case of the assignment problem. The problem is stated as follows: Given a set of n cities, numbered 1 through n, a salesman must determine a *minimum-distance* route, called a *tour*, which begins in city 1, goes through each of the other $(n-1)$ cities exactly once, and then returns to city 1. There are $(n-1)!$ possible tours. Thus, complete enumeration of the tours to find the minimum distance is impractical for most application scenarios.

The travelling salesman problem may be viewed as a *travelling resource problem* in project scheduling whereby a single resource unit is expected to perform tasks at several project sites. The formulation of the travelling salesman problem is as follows: Let

$x_{ij} = 1$ if route includes going from city i to city j, $i, j = 1, 2, \ldots, n$; $i \neq j$
$x_{ij} = 0$ otherwise
$c_{ij} = $ distance between city i and city j.

Minimize $z = \sum_{i=1}^{n} \sum_{j=1}^{n} c_{ij} x_{ij}, \quad i \neq j$

Subject to: $\sum_{j=1}^{n} x_{ij} = 1, \quad i = 1, 2, ..., n$

$\sum_{i=1}^{n} x_{ij} = 1, \quad j = 1, 2, ..., n$

$x_{ij} = 0, 1, \quad i, j = 1, 2, ..., n; \quad i \neq j.$

The first constraint represents the salesman's departures, while the second constraint represents his arrivals. Although the above formulation can be solved as an assignment problem, a feasible assignment solution does not necessarily represent a *valid tour*. Specifically, a solution of the assignment problem may include subtours, which are disconnected tour cycles. One approach to formulating the salesman problem is to add additional constraints to the assignment problem formulation to eliminate the possibility of subtours. Several techniques are available in the literature for solving the travelling salesman problem. Interested readers should refer to Bellmore and Nemhauser (1968), Little et al. (1963), and other publications on the subject.

SHORTEST-PATH PROBLEM

The *shortest-path* problem involves finding the shortest path from a specified origin to a specified destination in an acyclic network. A *network* consists of a set of *nodes* (or vertices) and a set of *arcs* (or edges or links) which connect the nodes. Arc (i, j) represents the link from node i to node j. It is often assumed that the arcs are *directed*. That is, each arc has a specific orientation. A *path* is a collection of arcs from one node to another without regard to their directions. A *directed chain* from one node to another is a set of arcs which are all oriented in a specific direction. A directed chain beginning and ending at the same node is a *directed cycle*. A network which has no directed cycles is said to be *acyclic*. In acyclic networks, $i < j$ for all arcs (i, j).

Practical network problems involve assigning costs, profits, distances, capacity restrictions, or other performance measures to arcs. Supply and demand levels can also be associated with nodes in the network. Let us consider a directed network with a distance d_{ij} associated with each arc (i, j). It is assumed that the distances between arcs are non-negative. When no arc exists from node i to node j, the length of the *dummy arc (i, j)* is set to M, where $M >>> 0$. The shortest-path problem consists of finding the shortest directed chain from a specified origin to a specified destination.

In project planning, transportation and equipment routing between project sites are suitable problems for the application of the shortest-path algorithm. Possible extensions of the basic shortest-path problem may include the following:

Smartest path between two project sites: In some applications, the shortest path may not be the best path in terms of ease of transportation, resource requirement, and other performance considerations. The objective here is to quantify "smartness" and incorporate the measure into the shortest-path procedure.

Safest path between two project sites: In this case, the objective is to find the path that offers the highest measure of safety. We will need to quantify "safety" so that the measure can be incorporated into the shortest-path procedure.

Cheapest path between project sites: For some problems, the shortest path may turn out to be the most expensive. Commuters using toll roads are familiar with this dilemma. The objective in the cheapest-path problem is to find the least-cost path between two points. Distance-cost relationships can be used as the basis for obtaining quantitative measures to incorporate into the conventional shortest-path procedure so as to minimize cost rather than distance.

Dreyfus (1969) discusses various shortest-path problem scenarios and solution algorithms. Some examples of path-to-path problems of interest are:
Shortest path between the originating node and the terminal node.
Shortest path between the origin and all nodes in the network.
Shortest paths between all nodes in the network.
The n shortest paths from the origin to the terminal node.
The steps of one algorithm for solving the shortest-path problem are presented below:

Step 1: Assign to the origin (node 1), the *permanent* label $y_1 = 0$, and assign to every other node the *temporary* label $y_j = M$. Set $i = 1$.

Step 2: From node i, recompute the temporary labels $y_i = \text{Min}\ \{y_j,\ y_i + d_{ij}\}$, where node j is temporarily labeled and $d_{ij} < M$.

Step 3: Find the smallest of the temporary labels, say y_i. Label node i permanently with value y_i.

Step 4: If all nodes are permanently labeled, stop. Otherwise, go to Step 2.

GOAL PROGRAMMING

One major shortcoming of linear programming is that only one objective can be considered at a time. In many real-world situations, the decision maker is faced with problems involving more than one objective. Goal programming is one model that permits a consideration of multiple goals at the same time. What is required is the assignment of relative priorities to the goals being considered. The multiple goals do not have to be on the same measurement scale. For example, cost minimization, revenue maximization, and minimization of project duration may all coexist as goals in a goal programming problem. Goal programming solution techniques choose the values of the decision variables in such a way that deviations from the goals are minimized. If all the goals cannot be satisfied, goal programming will attempt to satisfy them in order of priority. Goal programming has been applied to various problems ranging from activity planning to resource allocation (Tingley and Liebman, 1984; Goodman, 1974; Hannan, 1978; Ignizio, 1976; Kornbluth, 1973; Lee, 1972; Lee, 1979). Moore et al. (1978) presented a goal programming project crashing model for the installation of a paper processing system at a bank. Many similar practical applications of goal programming can be found in the literature.

The formulation of goal programming problems is similar to that of linear programming problems except for the following requirements:
1. Explicit consideration of multiple goals
2. A measure of deviation from desired goals
3. Relative prioritization of the multiple goals

The objective of goal programming is to minimize the deviations from the desired goals. The priorities assigned to the goals are considered to be *preemptive*. Lower-priority goals are satisfied only after higher-priority goals have been satisfied. The general formulation of the goal programming model with preemptive weights is presented below: Let

n = number of goals to be considered.

x_i = value of the ith decision variable in the problem.

d_i^+ = amount by which goal i is exceeded.

d_i^- = amount by which goal i is underachieved.

P_i = priority factor for the goal having the ith priority (The goal with the highest priority has a priority factor of P_1.)

$P_i >>> P_{i+1}$ so that there is no number $k > 0$ such that $nP_{i+1} \geq P_i$.

That is, P_i is infinitely larger than P_{i+1}.

The priority factors are included in the objective function with the appropriate deviational variables.

z is the objective function,

$x_1, x_2, \ldots, x_n$ are the n *decision variables*,

$c_1, c_2, \ldots, c_n$ are coefficients of decision variables in the *objective function*,

$a_{i1}, a_{i2}, \ldots, a_{in}$ are *coefficients* of decision variables in the ith constraint.

b_i are the right-hand-side constants of the ith constraint $(i = 1, 2, \ldots, m)$.

$$\text{Minimize} \quad z \;=\; \sum_i P_k w_{i,k}^+ d_i^+ \;+\; \sum_i P_s w_{i,s}^- d_i^-$$

$$\text{Subject to:} \quad \sum_{j=1}^{n} m_{ij} x_j \;-\; d_i^+ \;+\; d_i^- \;=\; g_i, \quad i = 1, 2, \ldots, p$$

$$\sum_{j=1}^{n} a_{ij} x_j \;\leq\; b_i, \quad i \;=\; p+1, \ldots, p+m$$

$$x_j, \;\; d_i^+, \;\; d_i^- \;\geq\; 0, \quad j \;=\; 1, \ldots, n; \;\; i \;=\; 1, \ldots, p,$$

where:

p = number of goals,

m = number of non-goal constraints,

n = number of decision variables,

$d_i^+, \;\; d_i^-$ = deviations from ith goal,

P_k, P_s = priority factors,

$w_{i,k}^+$ = relative weight of d_i^+ in the kth ranking,

$w_{i,k}^-$ = relative weight of d_i^- in the sth ranking.

The formulation of a goal programming model requires a very careful analysis. The formulation can be better seen by illustrative examples. Readers should refer to Wu and Coppins (1981), Goodman (1974), Hannan (1978), Ignizio (1976), Kornbluth (1973), and Lee (1972) for such examples.

QUESTIONS AND EXERCISES

4-1. Repeat the activity scheduling example presented in this chapter with the assumption that a 15-minute break is required between the completion of one activity and the start of the next activity.

4-2. A delivery man makes deliveries to two project sites: Site A and Site B. He receives $1,000 per delivery to Site A and $200 per delivery to Site B. He is required to make at least 5 deliveries per week to Site B. Each delivery to either Site A or Site B takes him 3 hours to complete. There is an upper limit of 35 hours of delivery time per week. The objective of the delivery man is to increase is delivery income as much as possible. Formulate his problem as an LP model.

4-3.   Solve the LP model of the example presented in this chapter on the number of workers to assign to a project work station. Discuss how you would go about implementing the LP solution in a practical setting.

4-4.   Develop and solve the *Knapsack* formulation to schedule the project presented below. Draw the Gantt chart for the schedule.

Use the following notation in your formulation:

C_t = the set of activities eligible for scheduling at time t

CAF_i = relative priority weight for activity i

R_{jt} = units of resource type j available at time t

$\overline{R}_{jt}$ = units of resource type j in use at time t

r_{ji} = units of resource type j required by activity i

x_{it} = indicator variable for scheduling activity i at time t
            $x_{it} = 1$ if activity i is scheduled at time t
            $x_{it} = 0$ if activity i is not scheduled at time t.

Activity	Predecessor	Duration (Days)	Resource Requirement (Type 1, Type 2)	Priority Weight
A	-	6	2, 5	50.1
B	-	5	1, 3	57.1
C	-	2	3, 1	56.8
D	A, B	4	2, 0	100
E	B	5	1, 4	53.2
F	C	6	3, 1	51.8
G	B, F	1	4, 3	44.9
H	D, E	7	2, 3	54.9

There are two resource types. Resource availability varies from day to day based on the schedule below:

Time Period	Units Available (Type 1, Type 2)
0 to 5	3, 5
5^+ to 10	2, 3
10^+ to 14	3, 4
14^+ to 20	4, 4
20^+ to 22	5, 3
22^+ to 30	4, 5
30^+ and up	6, 6

4-5. Solve the resource assignment problem with the following cost matrix:

$$\begin{bmatrix} 3 & 7 & 2 & 4 \\ 3 & 6 & 5 & 7 \\ 6 & 4 & 5 & 6 \\ 4 & 3 & 4 & 5 \end{bmatrix}$$

4-6. Starting with Vogel's approximation as the starting solution, solve the transportation problem example presented in this chapter. The example was previously solved with the northwest-corner starting solution.

4-7. Boomer-Sooner, Inc., produces three styles of portable stadium seats: High-Rider Style, Low-Rider Style, and Line-Hugger Style. The seats are made of high-impact composite material and are produced in two steps: Assembly and Painting. The schedule for labor and material inputs for each seat style are as follows:

Assembly labor:
  1 hour per high-rider seat
  3 hours per low-rider seat
  1.5 hours per line-hugger seat
Painting labor:
  1.5 hour per high-rider seat
  1.5 hours per low-rider seat
  4 hours per line-hugger seat
Material requirement:
  4 pounds per high-rider seat
  3 pounds per low-rider seat
  6 pounds per line-hugger seat

2,000 hours of assembly labor hours are available per month.
1,000 hours of painting labor hours are available per month.
The contributions to profit for the styles are $35, $40, and $65 respectively. The company has two equally desirable goals: minimization of idle time in painting, and making a monthly profit of $20,000. Set up this problem as a goal programming problem and show the initial tableau.

4-8.   A project manager has four crews which can be hired on a temporary basis during peak construction periods. The manager currently has three projects more than can be handled with his regular crews. It is desired to determine the crew assignments that will minimize the total project cost. The costs of using certain crews for certain projects are presented below:

Crew 1:   Project A; $4,000
          Project B; $3,000
          Project C; $9,000

Crew 2:   Project A; $7,000
          Project B; $1,000
          Project C; $8,000

Crew 3:   Project A; $2,000
          Project B; $6,000
          Project C; $4,000

Crew 4:   Project A; $9,000
          Project B; $5,000
          Project C; $5,000

4-9.   Find the shortest path between the originating node and the terminal node for the following acyclic network:

Arc	Duration
1-2	7
1-3	6
1-4	10
2-3	2
2-4	4
3-4	2
3-5	7
4-5	3

4-10.   Develop a computer program for finding the shortest path between all pairs of nodes in a directed acyclic network. Use the program to verify your solution to Question 4-9.

4-11. Develop a general LP formulation for scheduling the project below. Resource requirements and precedence relationships must be satisfied in the model.

Activity	Predecessor	Duration (Days)	Resource Requirement (Type 1, Type 2)
A	-	3	0, 3
B	A	4	2, 1
C	A	2	1, 1
D	B, C	7	5, 2

4-12. Use any software tool available to you to solve the LP model in Problem 4-11.

CHAPTER 5

PROJECT ECONOMICS

This chapter presents techniques of economic analysis for project planning and control. Topics covered include basic cash flow analysis, break even analysis, minimum revenue requirement analysis, and capital budgeting. For further details on these and related topics, readers may consult some of the numerous references available on engineering economic analysis. Selected examples are Bussey and Eschenbach (1992), White et al. (1989), Newnan (1991), Canada and Sullivan (1989), Fleischer (1984), Gonen (1990), Grant et al. (1982), DeGarmo et al. (1988), Park and Sharp-Bette (1990), Riggs and West (1986), Sprague and Whittaker (1986), Steiner (1988), and Stevens (1979).

BASIC CASH FLOW ANALYSIS

The time value of money is an important factor in project planning and control. This is particularly crucial for long-term projects that are subject to changes in several cost parameters. The basic reason for performing economic analysis is to make a choice between mutually exclusive projects that are competing for limited resources. The cost performance of each project will depend on the timing and levels of its expenditures. The techniques of computing cash flow equivalence permit us to bring competing project cash flows to a common basis for comparison. The common basis depends on the prevailing interest rate. Two cash flows that are equivalent at a given interest rate will not be equivalent at a different interest rate.

Cash Flow Conversion Factors

Cash flow conversion involves the transfer of project funds from one point in time to another. The following notation is used for the variables involved in the conversion process:

$i =$ interest rate per period
$n =$ number of interest periods
$P =$ a present sum of money
$F =$ a future sum of money
$A =$ a uniform end-of-period cash receipt or disbursement
$G =$ a uniform arithmetic gradient increase in period-by-period payments or disbursements.

In many cases, the interest rate used in performing economic analysis is set equal to the minimum attractive rate of return (MARR) of the decision maker. The MARR is also sometimes referred to as hurdle rate, required internal rate of return (IRR), return on investment (ROI), or discount rate. The value of MARR is chosen with the objective of maximizing the economic performance of a project.

COMPOUND AMOUNT FACTOR

The procedure for the single payment compound amount factor finds a future sum of money, F, that is equivalent to a present sum of money, P, at a specified interest rate, i, after n periods. This is calculated as:

$$F = P(1 + i)^n.$$

A graphic representation of the relationship between P and F is shown below:

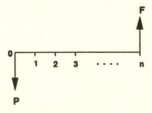

Example
A sum of $5,000 is deposited in a project account and left there to earn interest for 15 years. If the interest rate per year is 12%, the compound amount after 15 years can be calculated as shown below:

$$F = \$5,000(1 + 0.12)^{15}$$

$$= \$27,367.85.$$

PRESENT WORTH FACTOR

The present worth factor computes P when F is given. The present worth factor is obtained by solving for P in the equation for the compound amount factor. That is,

$$P = F(1 + i)^{-n}.$$

Suppose it is estimated that $15,000 would be needed to complete the implementation of a project five years from now, how much should be deposited in a special project fund now so that the fund would accrue to the required $15,000 exactly five years from now? If the special project fund pays interest at 9.2% per year, the required deposit would be:

$$P = \$15,000(1 + 0.092)^{-5}$$

$$= \$9,660.03.$$

CAPITAL RECOVERY FACTOR

The capital recovery formula is used to calculate the uniform series of equal end-of-period payments, A, that are equivalent to a given present amount, P, as shown in the diagram below.

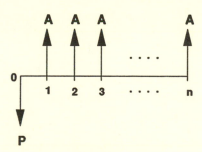

The capital recovery amount is calculated as:

$$A = P\left[\frac{i(1 + i)^n}{(1 + i)^n - 1}\right].$$

Example

Suppose a piece of equipment needed to launch a project must be purchased at a cost of $50,000. The entire cost is to be financed at 13.5% per year and repaid on a monthly installment schedule over four years. It is desired to calculate what the monthly loan payments will be. It is assumed that the first loan payment will be made exactly one month after the equipment is financed. If the interest rate of 13.5% per year is compounded monthly, then the interest rate per month will be 13.5%/12 = 1.125% per month. The number of interest periods over which the loan will be repaid is 4(12) = 48 months. Consequently, the monthly loan payments are calculated to be:

$$A = \$50,000\left[\frac{0.01125(1+0.01125)^{48}}{(1+0.01125)^{48} - 1}\right]$$

$$= \$1,353.82.$$

UNIFORM SERIES PRESENT WORTH FACTOR

The series present worth factor is used to calculate the present worth equivalent, P, of a series of equal end-of-period amounts, A. This is the converse of the capital recovery factor. The equation for the series present worth factor is obtained by solving for P from the capital recovery factor as shown below:

$$P = A\left[\frac{(1+i)^n - 1}{i(1+i)^n}\right].$$

Example

Suppose the sum of $12,000 must be withdrawn from an account to meet the annual operating expenses of a multi-year project. The project account pays interest at 7.5% per year compounded on an annual basis. If the project is expected to last ten years, how much must be deposited in the project account now so that the operating expenses of $12,000 can be withdrawn at the end of every year for ten years? The project fund is expected to be depleted to zero by the end of the last year of the project. The first withdrawal will be made one year after the project account is opened, and no additional deposits will be made in the account during the project life cycle. The required deposit is calculated to be:

$$P = \$12,000\left[\frac{(1+0.075)^{10} - 1}{0.075(1+0.075)^{10}}\right]$$

$$= \$82,368.92.$$

UNIFORM SERIES SINKING FUND FACTOR

The sinking fund factor is used to calculate the uniform series of equal end-of-period amounts, A, that are equivalent to a single future amount, F. The graphic representation of the relationship between A and F is shown below:

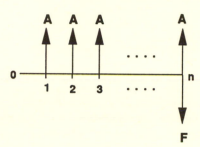

Note that the future amount occurs at the same point in time as the last amount in the uniform series of payments. The equation relating A to F is shown below:

$$A = F\left[\frac{i}{(1+i)^n - 1}\right].$$

Example
How large are the end-of-year equal amounts that must be deposited into a project account so that a balance of \$75,000 will be available for withdrawal immediately after the twelfth annual deposit is made? The initial balance in the account is zero at the beginning of the first year. The account pays 10% interest per year. Using the formula for the sinking fund factor, the required annual deposits are:

$$A = \$75,000\left[\frac{0.10}{(1+0.10)^{12} - 1}\right]$$

$$= \$3,507.25.$$

UNIFORM SERIES COMPOUND AMOUNT FACTOR

The series compound amount factor is the converse of the series sinking fund factor. It is used to calculate a single future amount that is equivalent to a uniform series of equal end-of-period payments. The factor is written as:

$$F = A\left[\frac{(1+i)^n - 1}{i}\right].$$

Example
If equal end-of-year deposits of $,5000 are made to a project fund paying 8% per year for ten years. How much can be expected to be available for withdrawal from the account for capital expenditure immediately after the last deposit is made?

$$F = \$5,000\left[\frac{(1+0.08)^{10} - 1}{0.08}\right]$$

$$= \$72,432.50.$$

CAPITALIZED COST FORMULA

Capitalized cost refers to the present value of a single amount that is equivalent to a perpetual series of equal end-of-period payments. This is an extension of the series present worth factor with an infinitely large number of periods. This is shown graphically below:

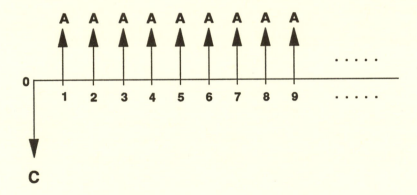

Using the limit theorem from calculus as n approaches infinity, the series present worth factor reduces to the following formula for the capitalized cost:

$$P = \frac{A}{i}.$$

Example
How much should be deposited in a general fund to service a recurring public service project to the tune of $6,500 per year forever if the fund yields an annual interest rate of 11%? Using the capitalized cost formula, the required one-time deposit to the general fund is:

$$P = \frac{\$6,500}{0.11}$$

$$= \$59,090.91.$$

The formulas presented above represent the basic cash flow conversion factors. The factors are widely tabulated, for convenience, in engineering economy books. Several variations and extensions of the factors are available. Such extensions include the arithmetic gradient series factor and the geometric series factor. Variations in the cash flow profiles include situations where payments are made at the beginning of each period rather than at the end and situations where a series of payments contains unequal amounts. Conversion formulas can be derived mathematically for those special cases by using the basic factors presented above.

Time Required for Investment to Double

The time is takes an amount to reach a certain multiple of its initial level is often of interest in many investment scenarios. The "Rule of 72" is one simple approach to calculating how long it will take an amount to double in value at a given interest rate per period. The Rule of 72 gives the following formula for estimating the doubling period:

$$n = \frac{72}{i},$$

where i is the interest rate expressed in percentage. Referring to the single payment compound amount factor, we can set the future amount equal to twice the present amount and then solve for n, the number of periods. That is, $F = 2P$. Thus,

$$2P = P(1+i)^n.$$

Solving for n in the above equation yields an expression for calculating the exact number of periods required to double P:

$$n = \frac{\ln(2)}{\ln(1+i)},$$

where i is the interest rate expressed in decimals. For example, at an interest rate of 5% per year, it will take any given amount 14.21 years to double in value. This, of course, assumes that the interest rate will remain constant throughout the planning horizon. Table 5-1 presents a tabulation of the values calculated from both approaches. Figure 5-1 shows a graphical comparison of the Rule of 72 to the exact calculation.

Table 5-1. Evaluation of the Rule of 72

$i\%$	n (Rule of 72)	n (Exact Value)
0.25	288.00	277.61
0.50	144.00	138.98
1.00	72.00	69.66
2.00	36.00	35.00
5.00	14.20	17.67
8.00	9.00	9.01
10.00	7.20	7.27
12.00	6.00	6.12
15.00	4.80	4.96
18.00	4.00	4.19
20.00	3.60	3.80
25.00	2.88	3.12
30.00	2.40	2.64

Figure 5-1. Graphical Evaluation of Rule of 72

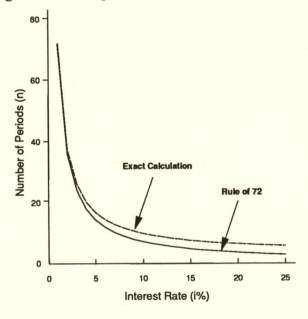

PROJECT BREAK EVEN ANALYSIS

Break even analysis refers to the determination of the balanced performance level where project income is equal to project expenditure. The total cost of an operation is expressed as the sum of the fixed and variable costs with respect to output quantity. That is,

$$TC(x) = FC + VC(x),$$

where x is the number of units produced, $TC(x)$ is the total cost of producing x units, FC is the total fixed cost, and $VC(x)$ is the total variable cost associated with producing x units. The total revenue resulting from the sale of x units is defined as:

$$TR(x) = px,$$

where p is the price per unit. The profit due to the production and sale of x units of the product is calculated as:

$$P(x) = TR(x) - TC(x).$$

The break even point of an operation is defined as the value of a given parameter that will result in neither profit nor loss. The parameter of interest may be the number of units produced, the number of hours of operation, the number of units of a resource type allocated, or any other measure of interest. At the break even point, we have the following relationship:

$$TR(x) = TC(x)$$
$$\text{or}$$
$$P(x) = 0.$$

In some cases, there may be a known mathematical relationship between cost and the parameter of interest. For example, there may be a linear cost relationship between the total cost of a project and the number of units produced. The cost expressions facilitate straightforward break even analysis. Figure 5-2 shows an example of a break even point for a single project. Figure 5-3 shows examples of multiple break even points that exist when multiple projects are compared. When two project alternatives are compared, the break even point refers to the point of indifference between the two alternatives. In Figure 5-3, x1 represents the point where projects A and B are equally desirable, x2 represents where A and C are equally desirable, and x3 represents where B and C are equally desirable. The figure shows that if we are operating below a production level of $x2$ units, then project C is the preferred project among the three. If we are operating at a level more than $x2$ units, then project A is the best choice.

Figure 5-2. Break even Point for a Single Project

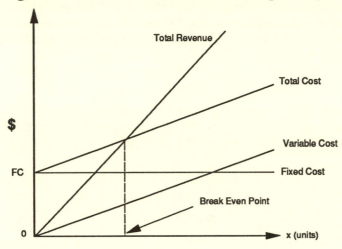

Figure 5-3. Break even Points for Multiple Projects

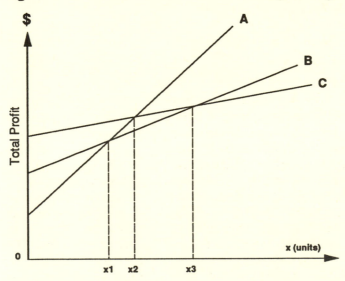

Example

Three project alternatives are being considered for producing a new product. The required analysis involves determining which alternative should be selected on the basis of how many units of the product are produced per year. Based on past records, there is a known relationship between the number of units produced per year, x, and the net annual profit, $P(x)$, from each alternative. The level of production is expected to be between 0 and 250 units per year. The net annual profits (in thousands of dollars) are given below for each alternative:

Project A: $P(x) = 3x - 200$

Project B: $P(x) = x$

Project C: $P(x) = (1/50)x^2 - 300$.

This problem can be solved mathematically by finding the intersection points of the profit functions and evaluating the respective profits over the given range of product units. It can also be solved by a graphical approach. Figure 5-4 shows a plot of the profit functions. Such a plot is called a break even chart. The plot shows that Project B should be selected if between 0 and 100 units are to be produced. Project A should be selected if between 100 and 178.1 units (178 physical units) are to be produced. Project C should be selected if more than 178 units are to be produced. It should be noted that if less than 66.7 units (66 physical units) are produced, Project A will generate net loss rather than net profit. Similarly, Project C will generate losses if less than 122.5 units (122 physical units) are produced.

Figure 5-4. Plot of Profit Functions

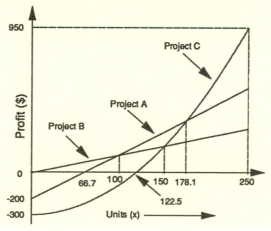

Measuring Profit Ratio

Break even charts offer opportunities for several different types of analysis. In addition to the break even points, other measures of worth or criterion measures may be derived from the charts. A measure, called *profit ratio* (Badiru, 1991a), is presented here for the purpose of obtaining a further comparative basis for competing projects. Profit ratio is defined as the ratio of the profit area to the sum of the profit and loss areas in a break even chart. That is,

$$\text{Profit Ratio} = \frac{\text{Area of Profit Region}}{\text{Area of Profit Region} + \text{Area of Loss Region}}.$$

For example, suppose the expected revenue and the expected total cost associated with a project are given, respectively, by the following expressions:

$R(x) = 100 + 10x$
$TC(x) = 2.5x + 250,$

where x is the number of units produced and sold from the project. Figure 5-5 shows the break even chart for the project. The break even point is shown to be 20 units. Net profits are realized from the project if more than 20 units are produced, and net losses are realized if less than 20 units are produced. It should be noted that the revenue function in Figure 5-5 represents an unusual case where a revenue of $100 is realized when zero units are produced.

Figure 5-5. Area of Profit versus Area of Loss

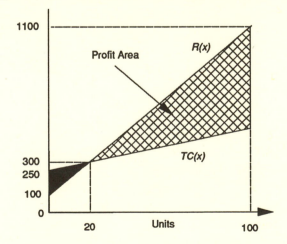

Suppose it is desired to calculate the profit ratio for this project if the number of units that can be produced is limited to between 0 and 100 units. From Figure 5-5, the surface area of the profit region and the area of the loss region can be calculated by using the standard formula for finding the area of a triangle: Area = (1/2)(Base)(Height). Using this formula, we have the following:

$$\text{Area of Profit Region} \quad = \quad \frac{1}{2}(\text{base})(\text{height})$$

$$= \quad \frac{1}{2}(1100 - 500)(100 - 20)$$

$$= \quad 24,000 \quad \text{square units.}$$

$$\text{Area of Loss Region} \quad = \quad \frac{1}{2}(\text{base})(\text{height})$$

$$= \quad \frac{1}{2}(250 - 100)(20)$$

$$= \quad 1,500 \quad \text{square units.}$$

Thus, the profit ratio is computed as:

$$\text{Profit Ratio} \quad = \quad \frac{2400}{24000 \ + \ 1500}$$

$$= \quad 0.9411$$

$$= \quad 94.11\%.$$

The profit ratio may be used as a criterion for selecting among project alternatives. If this is done, the profit ratios for all the alternatives must be calculated over the same values of the independent variable. The project with the highest profit ratio will be selected as the desired project. For example, Figure 5-6 presents the break even chart for an alternate project, say Project II. It is seen that both the revenue and cost functions for the project are nonlinear. The revenue and cost are defined as follows:

$R(x) = 160x - x^2$

$TC(x) = 500 + x^2.$

Figure 5-6. Break even Chart for Revenue and Cost Functions

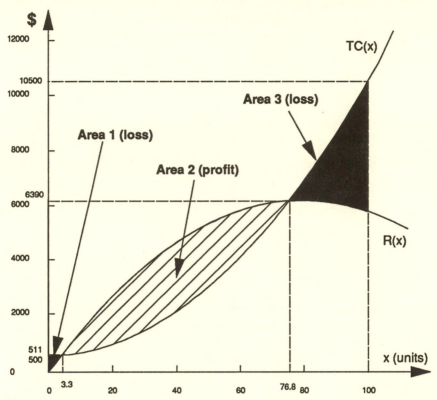

If the cost and/or revenue functions for a project are not linear, the areas bounded by the functions may not be easily determined. For those cases, it may be necessary to use techniques such as definite integrals to find the areas. Figure 5-6 indicates that the project generates a loss if less than 3.3 units (3 actual units) or more than 76.8 units (76 actual units) are produced. The respective profit and loss areas on the chart are calculated as shown below:

$$\text{Area 1 (loss)} \quad = \quad \int_0^{3.3} [(500 + x^2) \ - \ (160x - x^2)]dx$$

$$= \quad 802.8 \quad unit - dollars$$

$$\text{Area 2 (profit)} \quad = \quad \int_{3.3}^{76.8} [(160x - x^2) \; - \; (500 + x^2)]dx$$

$$= \quad 132,272.08 \quad unit - dollars$$

$$\text{Area 3 (loss)} \quad = \quad \int_{76.8}^{100} [(500 + x^2) \; - \; (160x - x^2)]dx$$

$$= \quad 48,135.98 \quad unit - dollars.$$

Consequently, the profit ratio for Project II is computed as:

$$\text{Profit Ratio} \quad = \quad \frac{\text{Total Area of Profit Region}}{\text{Total Area of Profit Region} \; + \; \text{Total Area of Loss Region}}$$

$$= \quad \frac{132,272.08}{802.76 \; + \; 132,272.08 \; + \; 48,135.98}$$

$$= \quad 0.7299$$

$$= \quad 72.99\%.$$

The profit ratio approach evaluates the performance of each alternative over a specified range of operating levels. Most of the existing evaluation methods use single-point analysis with the assumption that the operating condition is fixed at a given production level. The profit ratio measure allows an analyst to evaluate the net yield of an alternative given that the production level may shift from one level to another. An alternative, for example, may operate at a loss for most of its early life, while it may generate large incomes to offset the losses in its later stages. Conventional methods cannot easily capture this type of transition from one performance level to another. In addition to being used to compare alternate projects, the profit ratio may also be used for evaluating the economic feasibility of a single project. In such a case, a decision rule may be developed. An example of such a decision rule is:

If profit ratio is greater than 75%, accept the project.
If profit ratio is less than or equal to 75%, reject the project.

ANALYSIS OF AMORTIZATION SCHEDULE

Many capital investment projects are financed with external funds. A careful analysis must be conducted to ensure that the amortization schedule can be handled by the organization involved. A computer program such as GAMPS (Graphic Evaluation of Amortization Payments) might be used for this purpose (Badiru, 1988d). The program analyzes the installment payments, the unpaid balance, principal amounts paid per period, total installment payment, and current cumulative equity. It also calculates the "equity break even point" for the debt being analyzed. The equity break even point indicates the time when the unpaid balance on a loan is equal to the cumulative equity on the loan. With the output of this program, the basic cost of servicing the project debt can be evaluated quickly. A part of the output of the program presents the percentage of the installment payment going into equity and interest charge respectively.

Computational Procedure

The computational procedure for analyzing project debt follows the steps below:

1. Given a principal amount, P, a periodic interest rate, i (in decimals), and a discrete time span of n periods, the uniform series of equal end-of-period payments needed to amortize P is computed as:

$$A = \frac{P[i(1+i)^n]}{(1+i)^n - 1} .$$

It is assumed that the loan is to be repaid in equal monthly payments. Thus, $A(t) = A$, for each period t throughout the life of the loan.

2. The unpaid balance after making t installment payments is given by:

$$U(t) = \frac{A[1-(1+i)^{t-n}]}{i} .$$

3. The amount of equity or principal amount paid with installment payment number t is given by:

$$E(t) = A(1+i)^{t-n-1}.$$

4. The amount of interest charge contained in installment payment number t is derived to be:

$$I(t) = A[1-(1+i)^{t-n-1}],$$

where $A = E(t) + I(t)$.

5. The cumulative total payment made after t periods is denoted by:

$$C(t) = \sum_{k=1}^{t} A(k)$$

$$= \sum_{k=1}^{t} A$$

$$= A*t.$$

6. The cumulative interest payment after t periods is given by:

$$Q(t) = \sum_{x=1}^{t} I(x).$$

7. The cumulative principal payment after t periods is computed as:

$$S(t) = \sum_{k=1}^{t} E(k)$$

$$= A \sum_{k=1}^{t} (1+i)^{-(n-k+1)}$$

$$= A\left[\frac{(1+i)^{t} - 1}{i(1+i)^{n}}\right],$$

where:

$$\sum_{n=1}^{t} x^{n} = \frac{x^{t+1} - x}{x - 1}.$$

8. The percentage of interest charge contained in installment payment number t is:

$$f(t) = \frac{I(t)}{A}(100\%).$$

9. The percentage of cumulative interest charge contained in the cumulative total payment up to and including payment number t is:

$$F(t) = \frac{Q(t)}{C(t)}(100\%).$$

10. The percentage of cumulative principal payment contained in the cumulative total payment up to and including payment number t is:

$$H(t) \;=\; \frac{S(t)}{C(t)}(100\%)$$

$$=\; 1 \;-\; F(t).$$

Example

Suppose a manufacturing productivity improvement project is to be financed by borrowing $500,000 from an industrial development bank. The annual nominal interest rate for the loan is 10%. The loan is to be repaid in equal monthly installments over a period of 15 years. The first payment on the loan is to be made exactly one month after financing is approved. It is desired to perform a detailed analysis of the loan schedule. The GAMPS computer program was used to analyze this problem. Table 5-2 presents a partial output of GAMPS for the loan repayment schedule.

Table 5-2. Amortization Schedule for Financed Project

t	$U(t)$	$A(t)$	$E(t)$	$I(t)$	$C(t)$	$S(t)$	$f(t)$	$F(t)$
1	498794.98	5373.04	1206.36	4166.68	5373.04	1206.36	77.6	77.6
2	497578.56	5373.04	1216.42	4156.62	10746.08	2422.78	77.4	77.5
3	496352.01	5373.04	1226.55	4146.49	16119.12	3649.33	77.2	77.4
4	495115.24	5373.04	1236.77	4136.27	21492.16	4886.10	76.9	77.3
5	493868.16	5373.04	1247.08	4125.96	26865.20	6133.18	76.8	77.2
6	492610.69	5373.04	1257.47	4115.57	32238.24	7390.65	76.6	77.1
7	491342.74	5373.04	1267.95	4105.09	37611.28	8658.61	76.4	76.9
8	490064.22	5373.04	1278.52	4094.52	42984.32	9937.12	76.2	76.9
9	488775.05	5373.04	1289.17	4083.87	48357.36	11226.29	76.0	76.8
10	487475.13	5373.04	1299.91	4073.13	53730.40	12526.21	75.8	76.7
.	.	.	.	.	.	.	.	.
170	51347.67	5373.04	4904.27	468.77	913416.80	448656.40	8.7	50.9
171	46402.53	5373.04	4945.14	427.90	918789.84	453601.54	7.9	50.6
172	41416.18	5373.04	4986.35	386.69	924162.88	458587.89	7.2	50.4
173	36388.27	5373.04	5027.91	345.13	929535.92	463615.80	6.4	50.1
174	31318.47	5373.04	5069.80	303.24	934908.96	468685.60	5.6	49.9
175	26206.42	5373.04	5112.05	260.99	940282.00	473797.66	4.9	49.6
176	21051.76	5373.04	5154.65	218.39	945655.04	478952.31	4.1	49.4
177	15854.15	5373.04	5197.61	175.43	951028.08	484149.92	3.3	49.1
178	10613.23	5373.04	5240.92	132.12	956401.12	489390.84	2.5	48.8
179	5328.63	5373.04	5284.60	88.44	961774.16	494675.44	1.7	48.6
180	0.00	5373.04	5328.63	44.41	967147.20	500004.07	0.8	48.3

The tabulated result shows a monthly payment of $5,373.04 on the loan. Considering time $t = 10$ months, one can see the following results:

$U(10) = \$487,475.13$ (unpaid balance)
$A(10) = \$5,373.04$ (monthly payment)
$E(10) = \$1,299.91$ (equity portion of the tenth payment)
$I(10) = \$4,073.13$ (interest charge contained in the tenth payment)
$C(10) = \$53,730.40$ (total payment to date)
$S(10) = \$12,526.21$ (total equity to date)
$f(10) = 75.81\%$ (percentage of the tenth payment going into interest charge)
$F(10) = 76.69\%$ (percentage of the total payment going into interest charge)

Thus, over 76 percent of the sum of the first ten installment payments goes into interest charges. The analysis shows that by time t=180, the unpaid balance has been reduced to zero. That is, $U(180) = 0.0$. The total payment made on the loan is \$967,148.40 and the total interest charge is \$967,148.20 - \$500,000 = \$467,148.20. So, 48.30% of the total payment goes into interest charges. The information about interest charges might be very useful for tax purposes. The tabulated output shows that equity builds up slowly while unpaid balance decreases slowly. Note that very little equity is accumulated during the first three years of the loan schedule. This is shown graphically in Figure 5-7. The effects of inflation, depreciation, property appreciation, and other economic factors are not included in the analysis presented above. A project analyst should include such factors whenever they are relevant to the loan situation.

Figure 5-7. Plot of Unpaid Balance and Cumulative Equity

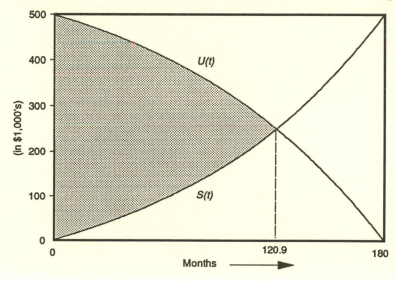

The point at which the curves intersect is referred to as the equity break even point. It indicates when the unpaid balance is exactly equal to the accumulated equity or the cumulative principal payment. For the example, the equity break even point is 120.9 months (over 10 years). The importance of the equity break even point is that any equity accumulated after that point represents the amount of ownership or equity that the debtor is entitled to after the unpaid balance on the loan is settled with project collateral. The implication of this is very important, particularly in the case of mortgage loans. The equity break even point can be calculated directly from the formula derived below:

Let the equity break even point, x, be defined as the point where $U(x) = S(x)$. That is:

$$A\left[\frac{1-(1+i)^{-(n-x)}}{i}\right] = A\left[\frac{(1+i)^x - 1}{i(1+i)^n}\right].$$

Multiplying both the numerator and denominator of the left-hand side of the above expression by $(1+i)^n$ and simplifying yields:

$$\frac{(1+i)^n - (1+i)^x}{i(1+i)^n}$$

on the left-hand side. Consequently, we have:

$$(1+i)^n - (1+i)^x = (1+i)^x - 1.$$

$$(1+i)^x = \frac{(1+i)^n + 1}{2},$$

which yields the equity break even expression:

$$x = \frac{\ln[0.5(1+i)^n + 0.5]}{\ln(1+i)},$$

where:
ln is the natural log function
n is the number of periods in the life of the loan
i is the interest rate per period.

Figure 5-8 presents a plot of the total loan payment and the cumulative equity with respect to time. The total payment starts from $0.0 at time 0 and goes up to $967,147.20 by the end of the last month of the installment payments. Since only $500,000 was borrowed, the total interest payment on the loan is $967,147.20 -

$500,000 = $467,147.20. The cumulative principal payment starts at $0.0 at time 0 and slowly builds up to $500,001.34, which is the original loan amount. The extra $1.34 is due to round-off error in the calculations.

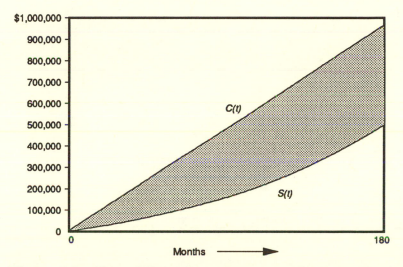

Figure 5-8. Plot of Total Loan Payment and Total Equity

Figure 5-9 presents a plot of the percentage of interest charge in the monthly payments and the percentage of interest charge in the total payment. The percentage of interest charge in the monthly payments starts at 77.55% for the first month and decreases to 0.83% for the last month. By comparison, the percentage of interest in the total payment starts also at 77.55% for the first month and slowly decreases to 48.30% by the time the last payment is made at time 180. Table 5-2 and Figure 5-9 show that an increasing proportion of the monthly payment goes into the principal payment as time goes on. If the interest charges are tax deductible, the decreasing values of $f(t)$ mean that there would be decreasing tax benefits from the interest charges in the later months of the loan.

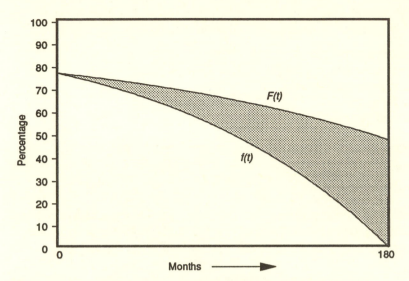

Figure 5-9. Plot of Percentage of Interest Charge

REVENUE REQUIREMENT ANALYSIS

Companies evaluating capital expenditures for proposed projects must weigh the expected benefits against the initial and expected costs over the life cycle of the project. One method that is often used is the minimum annual revenue requirements (MARR) analysis. Using the information about costs, interest payments, recurring expenditures, and other project-related financial obligations, the minimum annual revenue required by a project can be calculated. We can compute the break even point of the project. The break even point is then used to determine the level of revenue that must be produced by the project in order for it to be profitable. The analysis can be done with either the flow-through method or the normalizing method (Stevens, 1979).

The factors to be included in the analysis are initial investment cost, book salvage value, tax salvage value, annual project costs, useful life for book-keeping purposes, book depreciation method, tax depreciation method, useful life for tax purposes, rate of return on equity, rate of return on debt, capital interest rate, debt ratio, and investment tax credit. The minimum annual revenue requirement for any year *n* may be determined by means of the net cash flows expected for that year: Net Cash Flow = Income - Taxes - Principal Paid. That is,

$$X_n = (G - C - I) - I - P,$$

where
G = gross income for year n
C = expenses for year n
I = interest payment for year n
t = taxes for year n
P = principal payment for year n.

Rewriting the equation yields

$$G = X_n + C + I + t + P.$$

The above equation assumes that there are no capital requirements, salvage value considerations, or working capital changes in year n. For the minimum annual gross income, the cash flow, X_n, must satisfy the following relationship:

$$X_n = D_e + f_n,$$

where
D_e = recovered portion of the equity capital
f_n = return on the unrecovered equity capital.

It is assumed that the total equity and debt capital recovered in a year are equal to the book depreciation, D_b, and that the principal payments are a constant percentage of the book depreciation. That is,

$$P = c(D_b),$$

where c is the debt ratio. The recovery of equity capital is, therefore, given by:

$$D_e = (1 - c)D_b$$

and the annual return on equity, f_n, and interest, I, are based on the unrecovered balance as shown below:

$$f_n = (1 - c)k_e(BV_{n-1})$$

$$I = ck_d(BV_{n-1}),$$

where
c = debt ratio

k_e = required rate of return on equity
k_d = required rate of return on debt capital
BV_{n-1} = book value at the beginning of year n.

Based on the preceding equations, the minimum annual gross income, or revenue requirement, for year n can be described as:

$$R = D_b + f_n + C + I + t.$$

An expression for taxes, t, is given by:

$$t = (G - C - D_t - I)T,$$

where
D_t = depreciation for tax purposes
T = tax rate.

If the expression for R is substituted for G in the above equation, the following alternate expression for t can be obtained:

$$t = \frac{T}{1-T}(D_b + f_n - D_t).$$

The calculated minimum annual revenue requirement can be used to evaluate the economic feasibility of a project. An example of a decision criterion that may be used for that purpose is presented below:

Decision Criterion: If expected gross incomes are greater than the minimum annual revenue requirements, then the project is considered to be economically acceptable and the project investment is considered to be potentially profitable. Economic acceptance should be differentiated from technical acceptance. If, of course, other alternatives being considered have similar results, a comparison based on the margin of difference (i.e., incremental analysis) between the expected gross incomes and minimum annual revenue requirements must be made. There are two extensions to the basic analysis procedure presented above. They are the *flow-through* and *normalizing methods* (Stevens, 1979).

Flow-Through Method of MARR

This extension of the basic revenue requirement analysis allocates credits and costs in the year that they occur. That is, there are no deferred taxes and the investment tax credit is not amortized. Capitalized interest is taken as an expense in the first year. The resulting equation for calculating the minimum annual revenue requirements is:

$$R = D_b + f_e + I + gP + C + t,$$

where the required return on equity is given by:

$$f_e = k_e(1-c)K_{n-1},$$

where
k_e = implied cost of common stock
c = debt ratio
K_{n-1} = chargeable investment for the preceding year
$K_n = K_{n-1} - D_b$ (with K_0 = initial investment)
g = capitalized interest rate.

The capitalized interest rate is usually set by federal regulations. The debt interest is given by:

$$I = (c)k_d K_{n-1},$$

where
k_d = after-tax cost of capital.

The investment tax credit is calculated as:

$$C_t = i_t P,$$

where i_t is the investment tax credit. Costs, C, are estimated totals that include such items as ad valorem taxes, insurance costs, operation costs, and maintenance costs. The taxes for the flow-through method are calculated as

$$t = \frac{T}{1-T}(f_e + D_b - D_t) - \frac{C}{1-T}.$$

Normalizing Method of MARR

The normalizing method differs from the flow-through method in that deferred taxes are utilized. These deferred taxes are sometimes included as expenses in the early years of the project and then as credits in later years. This *normalized* treatment of the deferred taxes is often used by public utilities to minimize the potential risk of changes in tax rules that may occur before the end of the project, but are unforeseen at the start of the project. Also, the interest paid on the initial investment cost is capitalized. That is, it is taken as a tax deduction in the first year of the project and then amortized over the life of the project to spread out the interest costs. The resulting minimum annual revenue requirement is expressed as

$$R = D_b + d_t + C_t - A_t + I + f_e + t + C,$$

where the depreciation schedules are based on the following capitalized investment cost:

$$K = P + gP,$$

with P and g as previously defined. The deferred taxes, d_t, are the differences in taxes that result from using an accelerated depreciation model instead of a straight line rate over the life of the project. That is,

$$d_t = (D_t - D_s)T,$$

where
D_t = accelerated depreciation for tax purposes
D_s = straight line depreciation for tax purposes.

The amortized investment tax credit, A_t, is spread over the life of the project, n, and is calculated as:

$$A_t = \frac{C_t}{n} .$$

The debt interest is similar to the earlier equation for capitalized interest. However, the chargeable investment differs by taking into account the investment tax credit, deferred taxes, and the amortized investment tax credit. The resulting expressions are

$$I = k_d(c)K_{n-1}$$

$$K_n = K_{n-1} - D_b - C_t - d_t - A_t.$$

In this case, the expression for taxes, t, is given by:

$$t = \frac{T}{1-T}(f_e + D_b + d_t + C_t - A_t - D_t - gP) - \frac{C_t}{1-T}.$$

The differences between the procedures for calculating the minimum annual revenue requirements for the flow-through and the normalizing methods yield some interesting and important details (Badiru and Russell, 1987). If the MARRs are converted to uniform annual amounts (leveled), a better comparison between the effects of the calculations for each method can be made. For example, the MARR data calculated by using each method are presented in Table 5-3.

Table 5-3. Normalizing versus Flow-Through Revenue Analysis

Year	Normalizing		Flow-Through	
	R_n	R_u	R_n	R_u
1	7135	5661	5384	5622
2	6433	5661	6089	5622
3	5840	5661	5913	5622
4	5297	5661	5739	5622
5	4812	5661	5565	5622
6	4380	5661	5390	5622
7	4005	5661	5214	5622
8	3685	5661	5040	5622

The annual MARR values are denoted by R_n, and the uniform annual amounts are denoted by R_u. The uniform amounts are found by calculating the present value for each yearly amount and then converting that total amount to equal yearly amounts over the same span of time. For a given investment, the flow-through method will produce a lower levelized minimum annual revenue requirement. This is because the normalized data includes an amortized investment tax credit and also deferred taxes. The yearly data for the flow-through method should give values closer to the actual cash flows, because credits and costs are assigned in the year in which they occur and not up front as in the normalizing method.

The normalizing method, however, provides for a faster recovery of the project investment. For this reason, this method is often used by public utility companies when establishing utility rates. The normalizing method also agrees more in practice with required accounting procedures used by utility companies than does the flow-through method. Return on equity also differs between the two methods. For a given internal rate of return, the normalizing method will give a higher rate of return on equity than the flow-through method. This difference occurs because of the inclusion of deferred taxes in the normalizing method.

Example
Suppose we have the following data for a project. It is desired to perform a revenue requirement analysis using both the flow-through and the normalizing methods.

Initial Project Cost   = $100,000
Book Salvage Value   = $10,000
Tax Salvage Value   = $10,000
Book Depreciation Model   = Straight Line
Tax Depreciation Model   = Sum-of-Years Digits
Life for Book Purposes   = 10 years
Life for Tax Purposes   = 10 years
Total Costs per Year   = $4,000
Debt Ratio   = 40%
Required Return on Equity   = 20%
Required Return on Debt   = 10%
Tax Rate   = 52%
Capitalized Interest   = 0%
Investment Tax Credit   = 0%.

Tables 5-4, 5-5, 5-6, and 5-7 show the differences between the normalizing and flow-through methods for the same set of data. The different treatments of capital investment produced by the investment tax credit can be seen.

Table 5-4. Part One of MARR Analysis

	Tax Depreciation		Deferred Taxes	
Year	Normalizing	Flow-Through	Normalizing	Flow-Through
1	16363.64	16363.64	3829.09	None
2	14727.27	14727.27	2978.18	
3	13090.91	13090.91	2127.27	
4	11454.55	11454.55	1276.36	
5	9818.18	9818.18	425.45	
6	8181.82	8181.82	-425.45	
7	6545.45	6545.45	-1276.36	
8	4909.09	4909.09	-2127.27	
9	3272.73	3272.73	-2978.18	
10	1636.36	1636.36	-3829.09	

Table 5-5. Part Two of MARR Analysis

Year	Capitalized Investment		Taxes	
	Normalizing	Flow-Through	Normalizing	Flow-Through
	100000.00	100000.00	-	-
1	87170.91	91000.00	9170.91	5022.73
2	75192.73	92000.00	8354.04	5625.46
3	64065.46	73000.00	7647.78	6228.18
4	53789.90	64000.00	7052.15	6830.91
5	44363.64	55000.00	6567.13	7433.64
6	35789.09	46000.00	6192.73	8036.36
7	28065.45	37000.00	5928.94	8639.09
8	21192.72	28000.00	5775.78	9241.82
9	15170.90	19000.00	5733.24	9844.55
10	10000.00	10000.00	5801.31	10447.27

Table 5-6. Part Three of MARR Analysis

Year	Return on Debt		Return of Equity	
	Normalizing	Flow-Through	Normalizing	Flow-Through
1	4000.00	4000.00	12000.00	12000.00
2	3486.84	3640.00	10460.51	10920.00
3	3007.71	3280.00	9023.13	9840.00
4	2562.62	2920.00	7687.86	8760.00
5	2151.56	2560.00	6454.69	7680.00
6	1774.55	2200.00	5323.64	6600.00
7	1431.56	1840.00	4294.69	5520.00
8	1122.62	1480.00	3367.85	4440.00
9	847.71	1120.00	2543.13	3360.00
10	606.84	760.00	1820.51	2280.00

Table 5-7. Part Four of MARR Analysis

| Year | Mininum Annual Revenues | |
	Normalizing	Flow-Through
1	42000.00	34022.73
2	38279.56	33185.45
3	34805.89	32348.18
4	31578.98	31510.91
5	28598.84	30673.64
6	25865.45	29836.36
7	23378.84	28999.09
8	21138.98	28161.82
9	19145.89	27324.55
10	17399.56	26487.27

There is a big difference in the distribution of taxes, since most of the taxes are paid early in the investment period with the normalizing method and taxes are deferred with the flow-through method. The resulting minimum annual revenue requirements are larger for the normalizing method early in the period. However, there is a more gradual decrease with the flow-through method. Therefore, the use of the flow-through method does not put as great a demand on the project to produce high revenues early in the project life cycle as does the normalizing method. Also, the normalizing method produces a lower rate of return on equity. This fact may be of particular interest to shareholders.

COST ESTIMATION

Cost estimation and budgeting help establish a strategy for allocating resources in project planning and control. There are three major categories of cost estimation for budgeting. These are based on the desired level of accuracy. The categories are *order-of-magnitude estimates*, *preliminary cost estimates*, and *detailed cost estimates*. Order-of-magnitude cost estimates are usually gross estimates based on the experience and judgment of the estimator. They are sometimes called "ballpark" figures. These estimates are typically made without a formal evaluation of the details involved in the project. The level of accuracy associated with order-of-magnitude estimates can range from -50% to +50% of the actual cost. These estimates provide a quick way of getting cost information during the initial stages of a project.

50%(Actual Cost) ≤ Order-of-Magnitude Estimate ≤ 150%(Actual Cost).

Preliminary cost estimates are also gross estimates, but with a higher level of accuracy. In developing preliminary cost estimates, more attention is paid to some selected details of the project. An example of a preliminary cost estimate is the estimation of expected labor cost. Preliminary estimates are useful for evaluating project alternatives before final commitments are made. The level of accuracy associated with preliminary estimates can ranges from -20% to +20% of the actual cost.

80% (Actual Cost) ≤ Preliminary Estimate ≤ 120% (Actual Cost).

Detailed cost estimates are developed after careful consideration is given to all the major details of a project. Considerable time is typically needed to obtain detailed cost estimates. Because of the amount of time and effort needed to develop detailed cost estimates, the estimates are usually developed after there is firm commitment that the project will take off. Detailed cost estimates are important for evaluating actual cost performance during the project. The level of accuracy associated with detailed estimates normally range from -5% to +5% of the actual cost.

95% (Actual Cost) ≤ Detailed Cost ≤ 105% (Actual Cost).

There are two basic approaches to generating cost estimates. The first one is a variant approach, in which cost estimates are based on variations of previous cost records. The other approach is the generative cost estimation, in which cost estimates are developed from scratch without taking previous cost records into consideration.

Optimistic And Pessimistic Cost Estimates

Using an adaptation of the PERT formula, we can combine optimistic and pessimistic cost estimates. Let:
O = optimistic cost estimate
M = most likely cost estimate
P = pessimistic cost estimate.

Then, the estimated cost can be estimated as:

$$E[C] = \frac{O + 4M + P}{6}$$

and the cost variance can be estimated as:

$$V[C] = \left[\frac{P - O}{6}\right]^2 .$$

BUDGETING AND CAPITAL RATIONING

Budgeting involves sharing limited resources between several project groups or functions in a project environment. Budget analysis can serve any of the following purposes:

- A plan for resources expenditure
- A project selection criterion
- A projection of project policy
- A basis for project control
- A performance measure
- A standardization of resource allocation
- An incentive for improvement

Top-Down Budgeting

Top-down budgeting involves collecting data from upper level sources such as top and middle managers. The figures supplied by the managers may come from their personal judgment, past experience, or past data on similar project activities. The cost estimates are passed to lower level managers, who then break the estimates down into specific work components within the project. These estimates may, in turn, be given to line managers, supervisors, and lead workers to continue the process until individual activity costs are obtained. Top management provides the global budget, while the functional level worker provides specific budget requirements for project items.

Bottom-Up Budgeting

In this method, elemental activities, and their schedules, descriptions, and labor skill requirements are used to construct detailed budget requests. Line workers familiar with specific activities are requested to provide cost estimates. Estimates are made for each activity in terms of labor time, materials, and machine time. The estimates are then converted to an appropriate cost basis. The dollar estimates are combined into composite budgets at each successive level up the budgeting hierarchy. If estimate discrepancies develop, they can be resolved through the intervention of senior management, middle management, functional managers, project manager, accountants, or standard cost consultants. Figure 5-10 shows the breakup of a project into phases and parts to facilitate bottom-up budgeting and improve both schedule and cost control.

Figure 5-10. Budgeting by Project Phases

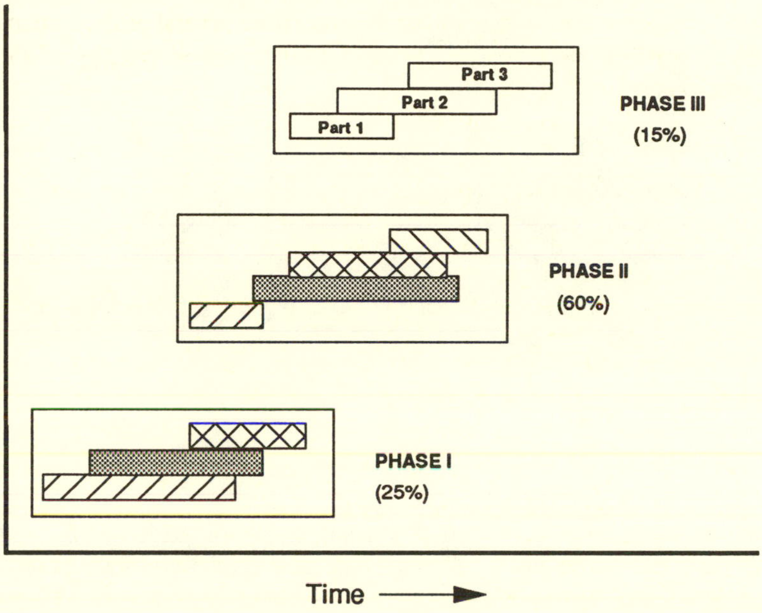

Elemental budgets may be developed on the basis of the timed progress of each part of the project. When all the individual estimates are gathered, we obtain a composite budget estimate. Figure 5-11 shows an example of the various components that may be involved in an overall budget. The bar chart appended to a segment of the pie chart indicates the individual cost components making up that particular segment. Analytical tools such as learning curve analysis, work sampling, and statistical estimation may be employed in the cost estimation and budgeting processes.

Figure 5-11. Pie and Bar Charts of Project Budget

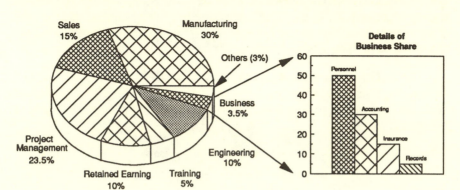

LP Formulation of Capital Rationing

Capital rationing involves selecting a combination of projects that will optimize the return on investment. A mathematical formulation of the capital budgeting problem is presented below:

$$\text{Maximize} \quad z \ = \ \sum_{i=1}^{n} v_i x_i$$

$$\text{Subject to:} \quad \sum_{i=1}^{n} c_i x_i \ \le \ B$$

$$x \ = \ 0, \ 1, \ i \ = \ 1, ..., n$$

where:
n = number of projects
v_i = measure of performance for project i (e.g., present value)
c_i = cost of project i
x_i = indicator variable for project i
B = budget availability level.

A solution of the above model will indicate which projects should be selected in combination with which projects. The example that follows illustrates a capital rationing problem.

Example of a Capital Rationing Problem

This example involves the determination of the optimal combination of project investments so as to maximize total return on investment. Suppose a project analyst is given N projects, $X_1, X_2, X_3, \ldots, X_N$, with the requirement to determine the level of investment in each project so that total investment return is maximized subject to a specified limit on available budget. The projects are not mutually exclusive.

The investment in each project starts at a base level b_i ($i = 1, 2, \ldots, N$) and increases by a variable increments k_{ij} ($j = 1, 2, 3, \ldots, K_i$), where K_i is the number of increments used for project i. Consequently, the level of investment in project X_i is defined as:

$$x_i = b_i + \sum_{j=1}^{K_i} k_{ij},$$

where:

$$x_i \geq 0 \quad \forall i.$$

For most cases, the base investment will be zero. In those cases, we will have $b_i = 0$. In the modeling procedure used for this problem,

$$X_i = \begin{cases} 1 & \text{if the investment in project } i \text{ is greater than zero} \\ 0 & \text{otherwise} \end{cases}$$

and

$$Y_{ij} = \begin{cases} 1 & \text{if } j\text{th increment of alternative } i \text{ is used} \\ 0 & \text{otherwise.} \end{cases}$$

The variable x_i is the actual level of investment in project i, while X_i is an indicator variable indicating whether or not project i is one of the projects selected for investment. Similarly, k_{ij} is the actual magnitude of the jth increment while Y_{ij} is an indicator variable that indicates whether or not the j'th increment is used for project i. The maximum possible investment in each project is defined as M_i such that:

$$b_i \leq x_i \leq M_i.$$

There is a specified limit, B, on the total budget available to invest such that:

$$\sum_i x_i \leq B.$$

There is a known relationship between the level of investment, x_i, in each project and the expected return, $R(x_i)$. This relationship will be referred to as the *utility function*, $f(.)$, for the project. The utility function may be developed through historical data, regression analysis, and forecasting models. For a given project, the utility function is used to determine the expected return, $R(x_i)$, for a specified level of investment in that project. That is,

$$R(x_i) \;=\; f(x_i)$$

$$\;=\; \sum_{j=1}^{K_i} r_{ij} Y_{ij},$$

where r_{ij} is the incremental return obtained when the investment in project i is increased by k_{ij}. If the incremental return decreases as the level of investment increases, the utility function will be *concave*. In that case, we will have the following relationship:

$$r_{ij} \;\geq\; r_{i,j+1}$$

or

$$r_{ij} \;-\; r_{i,j+1} \;\geq\; 0.$$

Thus,

$$Y_{ij} \;\geq\; Y_{i,j+1}$$

or

$$Y_{ij} \;-\; Y_{i,j+1} \;\geq\; 0,$$

so that only the first n increments ($j = 1, 2, \ldots, n$) that produce the highest returns are used for project i. Figure 5-12 shows an example of a concave investment utility function.

Figure 5-12. Utility Curve for Investment Yield

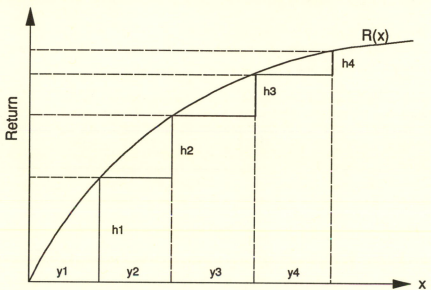

If the incremental returns do not define a concave function, $f(x_i)$, then one has to introduce the inequality constraints presented above into the optimization model. Otherwise, the inequality constraints may be left out of the model, since the first inequality, $Y_{ij} \geq Y_{i,j+1}$, is always implicitly satisfied for concave functions. Our objective is to maximize the total return. That is,

Maximize $\quad Z \;=\; \sum_i \sum_j r_{ij} Y_{ij}$

Subject to the following constraints:

$x_i \;=\; b_i \;+\; \sum_j k_{ij} Y_{ij}$

$b_i \;\leq\; x_i \;\leq\; M_i$

$Y_{ij} \;\geq\; Y_{i,j+1}$

$\sum_i x_i \leq B$

$x_i \;\geq\; 0$

$Y_{ij} \;=\; 0 \text{ or } 1.$

Now suppose we are given four projects (i.e., $N = 4$) and a budget limit of $10 million. The respective investments and returns are shown in Table 5-8, Table 5-9, Table 5-10, and Table 5-11.

Table 5-8. Investment Data for Project 1 for Capital Rationing

Stage (j)	y_{1j} Incremental Investment	x_1 Level of Investment	r_{1j} Incremental Return	$R(x_1)$ Total Return
0	-	0	-	0
1	0.80	0.80	1.40	1.40
2	0.20	1.00	0.20	1.60
3	0.20	1.20	0.30	1.90
4	0.20	1.40	0.10	2.00
5	0.20	1.60	0.10	2.10

Table 5-9. Investment Data for Project 2 for Capital Rationing

Stage (j)	y_{2j} Incremental Investment	x_2 Level of Investment	r_{2j} Incremental Return	$R(x_2)$ Total Return
0	-	0	-	0
1	3.20	3.20	6.00	6.00
2	0.20	3.40	0.30	6.30
3	0.20	3.60	0.30	6.60
4	0.20	3.80	0.20	6.80
5	0.20	4.00	0.10	6.90
6	0.20	4.20	0.05	6.95
7	0.20	4.40	0.05	7.00

Table 5-10. Investment Data for Project 3 for Capital Rationing

Stage (j)	y_{3j} Incremental Investment	x_3 Level of Investment	r_{3j} Incremental Return	$R(x_3)$ Total Return
0	0	-	-	0
1	2.00	2.00	4.90	4.90
2	0.20	2.20	0.30	5.20
3	0.20	2.40	0.40	5.60
4	0.20	2.60	0.30	5.90
5	0.20	2.80	0.20	6.10
6	0.20	3.00	0.10	6.20
7	0.20	3.20	0.10	6.30
8	0.20	3.40	0.10	6.40

Table 5-11. Investment Data for Project 4 for Capital Rationing

Stage (j)	y_{4j} Incremental Investment	x_4 Level of Investment	r_{4j} Incremental Return	$R(x_4)$ Total Return
0	-	0	-	0
1	1.95	1.95	3.00	3.00
2	0.20	2.15	0.50	3.50
3	0.20	2.35	0.20	3.70
4	0.20	2.55	0.10	3.80
5	0.20	2.75	0.05	3.85
6	0.20	2.95	0.15	4.00
7	0.20	3.15	0.00	4.00

All the values are in millions of dollars. For example, in Table 5-8, if an incremental investment of $0.20 million from stage 2 to stage 3 is made in project 1, the expected incremental return from the project will be $0.30 million. Thus, a total investment of $1.20 million in project 1 will yield a total return of $1.90 million. The question addressed by the optimization model is to determine how many investment increments should be used for each project. That is, when should we stop increasing the investments in a given project? Obviously, for a single project, we would continue to invest as long as the incremental returns are larger than the incremental investments. However, for multiple projects, investment interactions complicate the decision so that investment in one project cannot be independent of the other projects. The LP model of the capital rationing example was solved with LINDO software. The model is:

Maximize $Z = 1.4Y11 + .2Y12 + .3Y13 + .1Y14 + .1Y15 + 6Y21 + .3Y22 + .3Y23 + .2Y24 + .1Y25 + .05Y26 + .05Y27 + 4.9Y31 + .3Y32 + .4Y33 + .3Y34 + .2Y35 + .1Y36 + .1Y37 + .1Y38 + 3Y41 + .5Y42 + .2Y43 + .1Y44 + .05Y45 + .15Y46$

Subject to:

$.8Y11 + .2Y12 + .2Y13 + .2Y14 + .2Y15 - X1 = 0$
$3.2Y21 + .2Y22 + .2Y23 + .2Y24 + .2Y25 + .2Y26 + .2Y27 - X2 = 0$
$2.0Y31 + .2Y32 + .2Y33 + .2Y34 + .2Y35 + .2Y36 + .2Y37 + .2Y38 - X3 = 0$
$1.95Y41 + .2Y42 + .2Y43 + .2Y44 + .2Y45 + .2Y46 + .2Y47 - X4 = 0$
$X1 + X2 + X3 + X4 <= 10$

$Y12 - Y13 >= 0$
$Y13 - Y14 >= 0$
$Y14 - Y15 >= 0$
$Y22 - Y23 >= 0$
$Y26 - Y27 >= 0$
$Y32 - Y33 >= 0$
$Y33 - Y34 >= 0$
$Y34 - Y35 >= 0$
$Y35 - Y36 >= 0$
$Y36 - Y37 >= 0$
$Y37 - Y38 >= 0$
$Y43 - Y44 >= 0$
$Y44 - Y45 >= 0$
$Y45 - Y46 >= 0$
$X_i >= 0$ for $i = 1, 2, ..., 5$
$Y_{ij} = 0,1$ for all i and j.

The solution indicates the following values for Y_{ij}.

Project 1:
$Y11 = 1, Y12 = 1, Y13 = 1, Y14 = 0, Y15 = 0.$
Thus, the investment in project 1 is $X1 = \$1.20$ million.
The corresponding return is $1.90 million.

Project 2:
Y21 = 1, Y22 = 1, Y23 = 1, Y24 = 1, Y25 = 0, Y26 = 0, Y27 = 0.
Thus, the investment in project 2 is X2 = $3.80 million.
The corresponding return is $6.80 million.

Project 3:
Y31 = 1, Y32 = 1, Y33 = 1, Y34 = 1, Y35 = 0, Y36 = 0 , Y37 = 0.
Thus, the investment in project 3 is X3 = $2.60 million.
The corresponding return is $5.90 million.

Project 4:
Y41 = 1, Y42 = 1, Y43 = 1.
Thus, the investment in project 4 is X4 = $2.35 million.
The corresponding return is $3.70 million.

The total investment in all four projects is $9,950,000. Thus, the optimal solution indicates that not all of the $10,000,000 available should be invested. The expected return from the total investment is $18,300,000. This translates into 83.92% return on investment. Figure 5-13 presents histograms of the investments and the returns for the four projects. The individual returns on investment from the projects are shown graphically in Figure 5-14.

Figure 5-13. Histogram of Capital Rationing Example

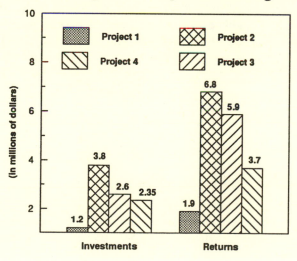

Figure 5-14. Histogram of Returns on Investments

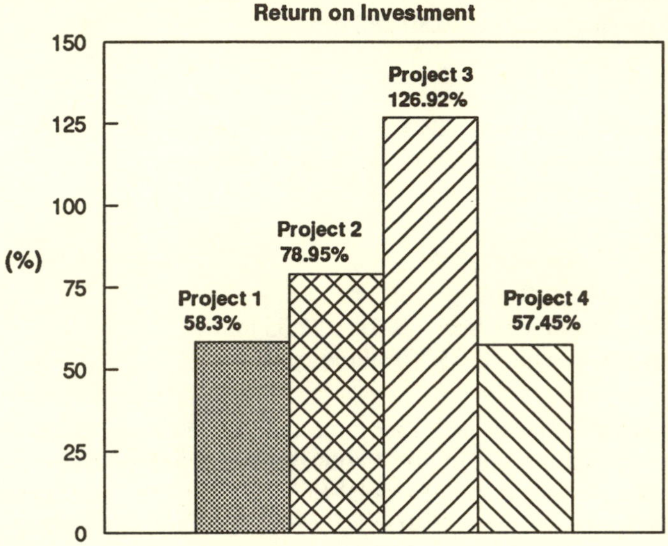

Return on Investment

The optimal solution indicates an unusually large return on total investment. In a practical setting, expectations may need to be scaled down to fit the realities of the project environment. Not all optimization results will be directly applicable to real situations. Possible extensions of the above model of capital rationing include the incorporation of risk and time value of money into the solution procedure. Risk analysis would be relevant, particularly for cases where the levels of returns for the various levels of investment are not known with certainty. The incorporation of time value of money would be useful if the investment analyis is to be performed for a given planning horizon. For example, we might need to make investment decisions to cover the next five years rather than just the current time.

COST MONITORING

As a project progresses, costs can be monitored and evaluated to identify areas of unacceptable cost performance. Figure 5-15 shows a plot of cost versus time for projected cost and actual cost. The plot permits a quick identification of when cost overruns occur in a project.

Figure 5-15. Evaluation of Actual and Projected Cost

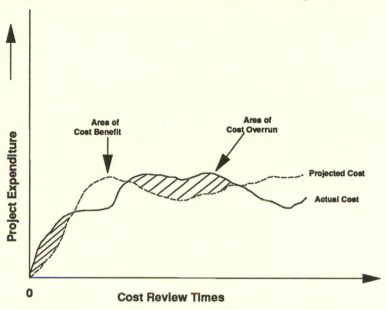

Cost plots similar to Figure 5-15 may be used to evaluate cost performance in a project. An approach similar to the profit ratio presented earlier may be used together with the plot to evaluate the overall cost performance of a project over a specified planning horizon. Presented below is a formula for *cost performance index (CPI)*:

$$CPI = \frac{\text{Area of Cost Benefit}}{\text{Area of Cost Benefit} + \text{Area of Cost Overrun}}.$$

As in the case of the profit ratio, CPI may be used to evaluate the relative performances of several project alternatives or to evaluate the feasibility and acceptability of an individual alternative.

EXERCISES

5-1.   A manufacturing company has revenue and cost functions that are defined, respectively, as follows (x is the number of units):

$$R(x) = \frac{3x}{4}$$

$$C(x) = \frac{x^3 - 8x^2 + 25x + 30}{25}$$

a) Plot the cost and revenue functions on the same graph and show the break even points.

b) At what value of x will the company's profit be maximum?

5-2. In performing a make-or-buy analysis for a piece of equipment needed for a project, the project analyst developed the following cost functions:
Alternative 1 (Make): $C(x) = 2500 + 125x - 0.025x^2$
Alternative 2 (Buy Type A): $C(x) = 5000 + 75x$
Alternative 3 (Buy Type B): $C(x) = 2000 + 100x + 0.005x^2$,

where x is the number of hours of utilization of the equipment. Determine the ranges of values of x over which each alternative is the preferred choice. Make a plot of the three cost functions on the same graph and indicate the respective preference regions.

5-3. The net present worths, in millions of dollars, for three project alternatives, A, B, and C, are given below:

NPW of A = $1.25x + 22.5$
NPW of B = $2.5x + 20$
NPW of C = 2^x,

where x represents thousands of units of a product generated by the project. Find the range of production units over which each alternative is the preferred choice. Plot the break even chart for the alternatives on the same graph and indicate the respective preference regions. What is the fixed cost of alternative C?

5-4. Find the capitalized cost of a project fund needed to provide a maintenance expense of $3,000 every two years forever if the first maintenance operation is to be conducted two years after the project fund is started. The interest rate on the fund is 9.25% per year.

5-5. Repeat Problem 3-14 with the following constraints:
There is a limit of $20,000,000 on the budget.
The project must be completed within 50 days.
Crew One and Crew Three cannot work together.

5-6. Maintenance expenditures for a 20-year project will occur at periodic outlays of $1,000 at the end of the 5th year, $2,000 at the end of the 10th year, and $3,500 at the end of the 15th year. With interest at 10% per year, find the equivalent uniform annual cost over the life of the project.

5-7. Two machines are under consideration for a manufacturing project. There is some uncertainty concerning the hours of usage of the machines. Machine A costs $3,000 and has an efficiency of 90%. Machine B costs $1,400 and has an efficiency of 80%. Each machine has a 10-year life with no salvage value. Electric service for both machines costs $1 per year per kilowatt of demand and $0.01 per kilowatt-hour of energy. The output of the motors used in the machines is expected to be 100 horsepower. The interest rate is 8% per year. At how many hours of operation per year would the machines be equally economical? If annual usage is expected to be less than this amount, which machine is preferable?

5-8. Presented below are the monthly total dollar expenditures on a community service project.

Month	Expenditure
January	$500,000
February	100,000
March	76,000
April	125,125
May	4,072
June	127,000
July	50,000
August	17,000
September	100,000
October	25,000
November	80,000
December	275,000

The total budget allocated for the project is $1,250,000. It is a one-year project, and the work content is evenly distributed over the project duration. That is, the same amount of work (in man-hours) is expected to be accomplished each month. As a cost control measure, the project manager has stipulated that the cumulative project expenditure must be directly proportional to the amount of work completed.

a) Develop a cumulative cost control chart for the project. Identify the control limits and the points where cumulative cost is out of control.

b) If the lower control limit on monthly expenditure is $20,000, identify the months where expenditures are below this control limit. Discuss the potential causes for the low expenditures and what, if any, investigation or control actions should be taken.

5-9.   Suppose you borrow $50,000 to start an engineering consulting business. The loan is to be repaid by making end-of-month payments for 48 months at a monthly interest rate of 1%. During the first year, you make monthly payments of $1,000 each. However, due to a drastic change in your consulting business, you negotiate with the bank to change your second-year monthly payments to $X per month. At the beginning of the third year, there is another drastic change in your business. This time, you negotiate with the bank to reduce your remaining monthly payments to $X/2 per month. Find what the value of X should be in order to have the loan totally paid off at the end of the fourth year.

5-10. The chief engineer of a major corporation is evaluating alternatives to supply electricity to the company. Under present conditions, it is anticipated that the company will pay $3 million at the end of this year for electricity purchased from a utility company. It is estimated that this cost will increase by $300,000 per year. The engineer needs to decide if the company should build a 4,000-kilowatt power plant to generate its own electricity. If a power plant is built, the operating costs (excluding cost of fuel) are estimated to be $130,000 per year. Two alternate power plants are under consideration:

a) Coal power plant: Installed cost of the coal power plant is $1,200 per kilowatt. Coal fuel consumption will be 30,000 tons per year. The cost of coal fuel for the first year is $20 per ton and is estimated to increase at a rate of $2 per ton per year. The plant will have no salvage value.

b) Oil fuel power plant: Installed cost of the oil-based power plant is $1,000 per kilowatt. Oil consumption will be 46,000 barrels per year. The cost of oil fuel for the first year is $34 per barrel and is estimated to increase at $1 per barrel per year. The plant will have no salvage value.

If the interest rate is 12% per year and the planning horizon is 10 years, use the equivalent annual cost (EAC) method to determine which alternative the engineer should recommend to the company. Assume that the "do-nothing" alternative is feasible.

CHAPTER 6

LEARNING CURVE ANALYSIS
FOR PROJECT CONTROL

Learning curve analysis is one method through which project control can be achieved in terms of cost and performance control. This chapter presents learning models for productivity and performance analysis in project planning and control. *Learning*, in the context of project planning and control, refers to the improved efficiency obtained from repetition of a task. Workers learn and improve by repeating operations. Research studies have confirmed that human performance improves with reinforcement or frequent repetition. J. Smith (1989) gives excellent examples of using learning curves for cost control. Badiru (1992b) presents a computational survey of univariate and multivariate learning curves. Other references that cover various aspects of learning curves include Belkaoui (1986), Nanda (1979), Pegels (1976), Richardson (1978), Towill (1978), Womer (1984), Camm et al. (1987), Liao (1979), McIntyre (1977), Smunt (1986), Sule (1978), and Yelle (1976, 1979, 1983).

Reductions in task times achieved through learning curve effects can directly translate to project cost savings and improved project performance. Learning curves are essential for setting project goals, establishing schedules, and monitoring progress. Learning curves present the relationship between cost (or time) and level of activity on the basis of the effect of learning. An early study by Wright (1936) disclosed the "80 percent learning" effect, which indicates that a given operation is subject to a 20 percent productivity improvement each time the activity level or production volume doubles. A learning curve can serve as a predictive tool for obtaining time estimates for tasks that are repeated within a project life cycle. A new learning curve does not necessarily commence each time a new operation is started, since workers can sometimes transfer previous skills to new operations. The point at which the learning curve begins to flatten depends on the degree of similarity of the new operation to previously performed operations. Typical learning rates that have been encountered in practice range from 70 percent to 95 percent. Several terms have been used to describe the learning phenomenon. Some of the terms are: *progress function, cost-quantity relationship, cost curve, product acceleration curve, improvement curve, performance curve, experience curve,* and *efficiency curve.*

UNIVARIATE LEARNING CURVES

Several alternate models of learning curves have been presented in the literature. Some of the most notable models are the *log-linear model,* the *S-curve,* the *Stanford-B model, DeJong's learning formula, Levy's adaptation function, Glover's learning formula, Pegels' exponential function, Knecht's upturn model,* and *Yelle's product model.* The univariate learning curve expresses a dependent variable (e.g., production cost) in terms of some independent variable (e.g., cumulative production). the log-linear model is by far the most popular and most used of all the learning curve models.

The Log-Linear Model

The log-linear model states that the improvement in productivity is constant (i.e., it has a constant slope) as output increases. There are two basic forms of the log-linear model: The average cost function and the unit cost function.

AVERAGE COST MODEL

The average cost model is used more than the unit cost model. It specifies the relationship between the cumulative average cost per unit and cumulative production. The relationship indicates that cumulative cost per unit will decrease by a constant percentage as the cumulative production volume doubles. The model is expressed as:

$$C_x = C_1 x^b,$$

where:
C_x = cumulative average cost of producing x units
C_1 = cost of the first unit
x = cumulative production count
b = the learning curve exponent (i.e., constant slope of on log-log paper).
        The relationship between the learning curve exponent, b, and the learning rate percentage, p, is given by:

$$b = \frac{\log p}{\log 2} \quad \text{or} \quad p = 2^b.$$

The derivation of the above relationship can be seen by considering two production levels where one level is double the other, as shown below.

Let Level I = x_1 and Level II = $x_2 = 2x_1$. Then,

$$C_{x_1} = C_1(x_1)^b \quad \text{and} \quad C_{x_2} = C_1(2x_1)^b.$$

The percent productivity gain is then computed as:

$$p = \frac{C_1(2x_1)^b}{C_1(x_1)^b} = 2^b.$$

When linear graph paper is used, the log-linear learning curve is a hyperbola of the form shown in Figure 6-1. On log-log paper, the model is represented by the following straight line equation:

$$\log C_x = \log C_1 + b \log x,$$

where b is the constant slope of the line. It is from this straight line that the name *log-linear* was derived.

Figure 6-1. The Log-Linear Learning Curve

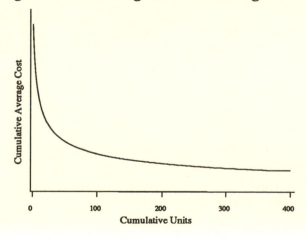

Example

Assume that 50 units of an item are produced at a cumulative average cost of $20 per unit. Suppose we want to compute the learning percentage when 100 units are produced at a cumulative average cost of $15 per unit. The learning curve analysis would proceed as follows:

Initial production level = 50 units; average cost = $20.
Double production level = 100 units; Ccost = $15.

Using the log relationship, we obtain the following equations:

$$\log 20 \;=\; \log C_1 \;+\; b \log 50$$
$$\log 15 \;=\; \log C_1 \;+\; b \log 100.$$

Solving the equations simultaneously yields:

$$b \;=\; \frac{\log 20 - \log 15}{\log 50 - \log 100} \;=\; -0.415.$$

Thus,

$$p \;=\; (2)^{-0.415} \;=\; 0.75.$$

That is 75% learning rate. In general, the learning curve exponent, b, may be calculated directly from actual data or computed analytically. That is:

$$b \;=\; \frac{\log C_{x_1} - \log C_{x_2}}{\log x_1 - \log x_2}$$

or

$$b \;=\; \frac{\ln(p)}{\ln(2)} \;,$$

where
x_1 = first production level
x_2 = second production level
C_{x1} = cumulative average cost per unit at the first production level
C_{x2} = cumulative average cost per unit at the second production level
p = learning rate percentage.

Expression for Total Cost: Using the basic cumulative average cost function, the total cost of producing x units is computed as:

$$TC_x \;=\; (x)C_x \;=\; (x)C_1 x^b \;=\; C_1 x^{(b+1)}.$$

Expression for Unit Cost: The unit cost of producing the xth unit is given by:

$$UC_x = C_1 x^{(b+1)} - C_1 (x-1)^{(b+1)}$$

$$= C_1 [x^{(b+1)} - (x-1)^{(b+1)}].$$

Expression for Marginal Cost: The marginal cost of producing the xth unit is given by:

$$MC_x = \frac{d[TC_x]}{dx} = (b+1)C_1 x^b.$$

Example
Suppose in a production run of a certain product it is observed that the cumulative hours required to produce 100 units is 100,000 hours with a learning curve effect of 85%. For project planning purposes, an analyst needs to calculate the number of hours spent in producing the fiftieth unit. Following the notation used previously, we have the following information:

$p = 0.85$
$X = 100$ units
$C_X = 100,000$ hours/100 units $= 1,000$ hours/unit.

Now,
$0.85 = 2^b$
Therefore, $b = -0.2345$.

Also,
$1000 = C_1(100)^b$.
Therefore, $C_1 = 2,944.42$ hours

Thus,
$C_{50} = C_1(50)^b$
       $= 1,176.50$ hours.
That is, the cumulative average hours for 50 units is 1,176.50 hours. Therefore, cumulative total hours for 50 units $= 58,824.91$ hours.

Similarly,
$C_{49} = C_1(49)^b$
       $= 1,182.09$ hours.
That is, the cumulative average hours for 49 units is 1,182.09 hours. Therefore, cumulative total hours for 49 units $= 57,922.17$ hours. Consequently, the number of hours for the fiftieth unit is given by:

$C_{50} - C_{49}$ = 58,824.91 hours - 57,922.17 hours
= 902.74 hours.

UNIT COST MODEL

The unit cost model is expressed in terms of the specific cost of producing the xth unit. The unit cost formula specifies that the individual cost per unit will decrease by a constant percentage as cumulative production doubles. The functional form of the unit cost model is the same as for the average cost model except that the interpretations of the terms are different. It is expressed as:

$$UC_x = C_1 x^b,$$

where:
UC_x = cost of producing the xth unit
C_1 = cost of the first unit
x = cumulative production count
b = the learning curve exponent = $(\log p)/(\log 2)$
p = learning rate percent = 2^b.

From the unit cost formula, we can derive expressions for the other cost basis. For the case of discrete product units, the total cost of producing x units is given by:

$$TC_x = \sum_{i=1}^{x} UC_i = C_1 \sum_{i=1}^{x} (i)^b.$$

The cumulative average cost per unit is given by:

$$Y_x = \frac{TC_x}{x} = \frac{1}{x} \sum_{i=1}^{x} UC_i = \frac{C_1}{x} \sum_{i=1}^{x} (i)^b.$$

The marginal cost is found as follows:

$$MC_x = \frac{d[TC_x]}{dx} = \frac{d\left[C_1 \sum_{i=1}^{x} (i)^b\right]}{dx}.$$

For the case of continuous product volume (e.g., chemical processes), we have the following corresponding expressions:

$$TC_x = \int_0^x UC(z)dz = C_1 \int_0^x z^b dz = \frac{C_1 x^{(b+1)}}{b+1}$$

$$Y_x = \left(\frac{1}{x}\right)\frac{C_1 x^{(b+1)}}{b+1}$$

$$MC_x = \frac{d[TC_x]}{dx} = \frac{d\left[\frac{C_1 x^{(b+1)}}{b+1}\right]}{dx} = C_1 x^b.$$

Graphical Modeling of Learning Curve

For another example of cost analysis with learning curves, suppose an observation of the cumulative hours required to produce a unit of an item was recorded at irregular intervals during a production cycle. The recorded observations are presented in Table 6-1.

Table 6-1. Learning Curve Observations

Cumulative Units Produced (X)	Cumulative Average Hours (C_x)
10	92.5
15	71.2
25	50.0
40	35.0
50	26.2
60	20.0
85	11.3
115	10.0
165	7.5
190	6.3

The project analyst would like to perform the following computational analyses:

1. Calculate the learning curve percentage when cumulative production doubles from 10 to 20 units.

2. Calculate learning curve percentage when cumulative production doubles from 20 units to 40 units.

3. Calculate the learning curve percentage when cumulative production doubles from 40 units to 80 units.

4. Calculate the learning curve percentage when cumulative production doubles from 80 units to 160 units.

5. Compute average learning curve percentage for the given operation.

6. Estimate a standard time for performing the given operation if the steady production level per cycle is 200 units.

A plot of the recorded data is shown in Figure 6-2. A regression model fitted to the data is also shown in the figure. The fitted model is expressed mathematically as:

$$C_x = 634.22x^{-0.8206},$$

with an R^2 value of 98.6%. Thus, we have a highly significant model fit. The fitted model can be used for estimation and planning purposes. Time requirements for the operation at different production levels can be estimated from the model. From the model, we have an estimated cost of the first unit as:

$C_1 = 634.22$

$b = -0.8206$

$p = 2^{(-0.8206)} = 56.62\%$ learning rate.

Figure 6-2. Graphical Analysis of Empirical Learning Curve

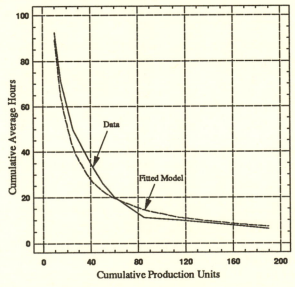

By using linear interpolation for the recorded data, we can estimate the percent improvement from one production level to another. For example, when production doubles from 10 to 20 units, we obtain an estimated cumulative average hours of 60.6 hours by interpolating between 71.2 hours and 50 hours. Similarly, cumulative average hours of 13.04 hours was obtained for the production level of 80 units, and cumulative average hours of 7.75 hours was obtained for the production level of 160 units. Now, these average hours are used to compute the percent improvement over the various production levels. For example, the percent improvement when production doubles from 10 units to 20 units is obtained as $p = 60.6/92.5 = 60.6\%$. The calculated percent improvement levels are presented in Table 6-2. The average percent is found to be 53.76%. This compares favorably with the 56.62% suggested by the fitted regression model.

Table 6-2. Learning Curve Percentage Analysis

Initial Production Level	Doubled Production Level	Learning Percentage
10	20	60.60%
20	40	57.76%
40	80	37.26%
80	160	59.43%
	Average	53.76%

Using the fitted model, the estimated cumulative average hours per unit when 200 units are produced is estimated as:

$$C_x = 634.22(200)^{-0.8206}$$

$$= 8.20 \quad \text{hours.}$$

Since this estimate represents an extrapolation beyond the range of the data used to fit the model, it can be expected that there will be some inaccuracy associated with the estimated value. Minor adjustment may thus be needed when using such estimates to make project planning decisions.

MULTIVARIATE LEARNING CURVES

Extensions of the univariate learning curve are important for realistic analysis of productivity gain. In project operations, several quantitative and qualitative factors intermingle to compound performance analysis. Heuristic decision making, in particular, requires a careful consideration of qualitative factors. There are numerous factors that can influence how fast, how far, and how well a worker learns within a given time span. Multivariate models are useful for performance analysis in project planning and control. One form of multivariate learning curve is defined as:

$$C_x = K \prod_{i=1}^{n} c_i x_i^{b_i},$$

where C_x = cumulative average cost per unit, K = cost of first unit of the product, x = vector of specific values of independent variables, x_i = specific value of the ith factor, n = number of factors in the model, c_i = coefficient for the ith factor, and b_i = learning exponent for the ith factor. A bivariate form of the model is presented below:

$$C = \beta_0 x_1^{\beta_1} x_2^{\beta_2},$$

where C is a measure of cost and x_1 and x_2 are independent variables of interest. Some of the multivariate models that have been reported in the literature are discussed briefly below.

Alchian (1963) modeled learning curves that estimate direct labor per pound of airframe needed to manufacture the Nth airframe in a cumulative production of N planes based on World War II data. He studied the alternate functions presented below to describe the relationships between *direct labor* per pound of airframe *(m)*, *cumulative production (N)*, *time (T)*, and *rate of production* per month *(DN)*:

1. $\log m = a_2 + b_2 T$
2. $\log m = a_3 + b_3 T + b_4 DN$
3. $\log m = a_4 + b_5(\log T) + b_6(\log DN)$
4. $\log m = a_5 + b_7 T + b_8 (\log DN)$
5. $\log m = a_6 + b_9 T + b_{10} (\log N)$
6. $\log m = a_7 + b_{11}(\log N) + b_{12}(\log DN)$

The multiplicative power function, often referred to as the Cobb-Douglas function, was investigated by Goldberger (1968) as a model for the learning curve. The model is of the general form below:

$$C = b_0 x_1^{b_1} x_2^{b_2} ... x_n^{b_n} \varepsilon,$$

where C = estimated cost, b_0 = model coefficient, x_i = ith independent variable ($i=1, 2,..., n$), b_i = exponent of the ith variable, and ε = error term. For parametric cost analysis, Waller and Dwyer (1981) studied an additive model of the form:

$$C = c_1 x_1^{b_1} + c_2 x_2^{b_2} + ... + c_n x_n^{b_n} + \varepsilon,$$

where c_i (i=1, 2,..., n) is the coefficient of the ith independent variable. The model was reported to have been fitted successfully for missile tooling and equipment cost. A variation of the power model was used by Bemis (1981) to study weapon system production. Cox and Gansler (1981) discuss the use of a bivariate model for the assessment of the costs and benefits of a single source versus multiple source production decision with variations in quantity and production rate in major DOD (Department of Defense) programs. A similar study by Camm, Evans, and Womer (1987) also uses the multiplicative power model to express program costs in terms of cumulative quantity and production rate in order to evaluate contractor behavior.

McIntyre (1977) introduced a nonlinear cost-volume-profit model for learning curve analysis. The nonlinearity in the model is effected by incorporating a nonlinear cost function that expresses the effects of employee learning. The profit equation for the initial period of production for a product subject to the usual learning function is expressed as:

$$P = px - c(ax^{b+1}) - f,$$

where P = profit, p = price per unit, x = cumulative production, c = labor cost per unit time, f = fixed cost per period, and b = index of learning. The profit function for the initial period of production with n production processes operating simultaneously is given as:

$$P = px - nca\left(\frac{x}{n}\right)^{b+1} - f,$$

where x is the number of units produced by n labor teams consisting of one or more employees each. Each team is assumed to produce x/n units. This model indicates that when additional production teams are included, more units are produced over a given time period. However, the average time for a given number of units increases because more employees are producing while they are still learning. That is, more employees with low (but improving) productivity are engaged in production at the same time. The preceding model is extended to the case where employees with different skill levels produce different learning parameters between production runs. This is modeled as:

$$P = p \sum_{i=1}^{n} x_i - c \sum_{i=1}^{n} a_i x_i^{b_i+1} - f,$$

where a_i and b_i denote the parameters applicable to the average skill level of the ith production run, and x_i represents the output of the ith run in a given time period. This model could be useful for manufacturing systems that call for concurrent engineering. Womer (1979) presents a multivariate model that incorporates cumulative production, production rate, and program cost. His approach involves a production function that relates output rate to a set of inputs with variable utilization rates as presented below:

$$q(t) = AQ^\delta(t)x^{1/\gamma}(t),$$

where, A = constant, $q(t)$ = program output rate at time t, $Q(T)$ = cumulative production at time T, δ = learning parameter, $1/\gamma$ = returns to scale parameter, and $x(t)$ = rate of variable resource utilization at time t. To optimize the discounted program cost, the cost function is defined as:

$$C = \int_0^T x(t)e^{-pt}dt,$$

where p is the discount rate and T is the time horizon for the analysis. If V is defined as the planned cumulative production at time T (i.e., $Q(T) = V$), then the problem can be formulated as the following optimization problem:

Minimize $\displaystyle\int_0^T x(t)e^{-pt}dt$

Subject to: $q(t) = AQ^\delta(t)x^{1/\gamma}(t),$

$x(t) \geq 0, \quad Q(0) = 0, \quad Q(T) = V,$

whose solution yields the estimated cost at time t, given V and T:

$$C(t|V,T) = [p/(\gamma-1)]^{\gamma-1}(1-\delta)^{-\gamma}A^{-\gamma}V^{\gamma(1-\delta)}[e^{pT/(\gamma-1)} - 1]^{-\gamma}[e^{pt/(\gamma-1)} - 1].$$

A Bivariate Model

A bivariate model is used here to illustrate the nature and modeling approach for general multivariate models. An experiment presented by Badiru (1992b) models a learning curve containing two independent variables: *cumulative production* (x_1) and *cumulative training time* (x_2). The following hypothesized model was chosen for illustrative purposes:

$$C_{x_1x_2} = Kc_1x_1^{b_1}c_2x_2^{b_2},$$

where C_x = cumulative average cost per unit for a given set, X, of factor values, K = intrinsic constant, x_1 = specific value of first factor, x_2 = specific value of second factor, c_i = coefficient for the ith factor, and b_i = learning exponent for the ith factor. The set of test data used for the modeling is shown in Table 6-3.

Table 6-3. Data for Modeling Bivariate Learning Curve

Treatment Number	Observation Number	Cumulative Average Cost ($)	Cumulative Production (Units)	Cumulative Training Time (Hours)
1	1	120	10	11
	2	140	10	8
2	3	95	20	54
	4	125	20	25
3	5	80	40	100
	6	75	40	80
4	7	65	80	220
	8	50	80	150
5	9	55	160	410
	10	40	160	500
6	11	40	320	660
	12	38	320	600
7	13	32	640	810
	14	36	640	750
8	15	25	1280	890
	16	25	1280	800
9	17	20	2560	990
	18	24	2560	900
10	19	19	5120	1155
	20	25	5120	1000

Two data replicates are used for each of the ten combinations of cost and time values. Observations are recorded for the number of units representing double production volumes. The model is transformed to the logarithmic form below:

$$\log C_x = [\log K + \log(c_1 c_2)] + b_1 \log x_1 + b_2 \log x_2$$

$$= \log a + b_1 \log x_1 + b_2 \log x_2,$$

where a represents the combined constant in the model such that $a = (K)(c_1)(c_2)$. A regression approach yielded the fitted model below:

$$\log C_x = 5.70 - 0.21(\log x_1) - 0.13(\log x_2),$$

$$C_x = 298.88x_1^{-0.21}x_2^{-0.13},$$

with an R^2 value of 96.7%. The variables in the model are explained as follows:
$\log(a) = 5.70$ (i.e., $a = 298.88$)
x_1 = cumulative production units
x_2 = cumulative training time in hours.

Figure 6-3 shows the response surface for the fitted model. As in the univariate case, the bivariate model indicates that the cumulative average cost decreases as cumulative production and training time increase. For a production level of 1,750 units and a cumulative training time of 600 hours, the fitted model indicates an estimated cumulative average cost per unit shown below:

$$C_{(1750,600)} = (298.88)(1750^{-0.21})(600^{-0.13}) = 27.12.$$

Similarly, a production level of 3500 units and training time of 950 hours yield the following cumulative average cost per unit:

$$C_{(3500,950)} = (298.88)(3500^{-0.21})(950^{-0.13}) = 22.08.$$

Figure 6-3. Bivariate Learning Curve Model

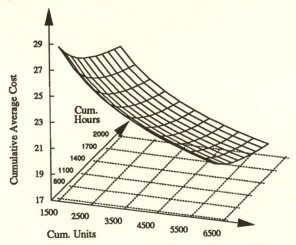

APPLICATION EXAMPLE

For a numerical application of the fitted model, consider the following problem: Given that the standards department of a manufacturing plant has set a target average cost per unit of $12.75 to be achieved after 1,000 hours of training, find the cumulative units that must be produced in order to achieve the target cost. Using the fitted model, the following relationship is obtained:

$$\$12.75 = (298.88)(X^{-0.21})(1000^{-0.13}),$$

which yields a required cumulative production units of: $X = 46,444$ units.

On the basis of the large number of cumulative production units required to achieve the expected standard cost, the standards department may want to review the cost standard. The standard of $12.75 may not be achievable if there is a limited market demand (i.e., demand is much less than 46,444 units) for the particular product being considered. The relatively flat surface of the learning curve model as units and training time increase implies that more units will need to be produced in order to achieve any additional significant cost improvements. Thus, even though an average cost of $22.08 can be obtained at a cumulative production level of 3,500 units, it takes several thousands of additional units to bring the average cost down to $12.75 per unit.

LEARN-FORGET MODELS

Learning improves performance, while forgetting reduces performance. Learning and forgetting are natural phenomena that directly affect productivity and performance. While extensive literature abounds on the subject of learning, very few studies of forgetting have been done. A major factor that has not been adequately addressed in the learning curve is the fact that workers also forget during the process of learning. Sule (1978) presents a study of alternate periods of learning and forgetting using a univariate learning curve. Here, we consider an extension of the univariate learn-forget model to multivariate models. This approach accounts for alternate periods of learning and forgetting. Multivariate analysis facilitates the inclusion of additional important factors in project productivity analysis. The consideration of a forget model creates a realistic representation of operations that are subject to interruption in the learning process (J. Smith, 1989). This is contrary to the conclusion by Womer (1984) that production breaks do not necessarily induce a loss of learning. Here, it is suggested that production breaks can, indeed, cause a loss in learning if during the breaks workers are involved in noncomplementary operations, the learning process of which counteracts the preceding learning process. For example, shifting from learning one computer programming syntax to another can lead to loss of learning.

Retention rate and retention capacity of different workers will influence the modeling of forget functions. Whenever interruption occurs in the learning process, it results in some forgetting. The resulting drop in performance rate depends on the initial level of performance and the length of the interruption. There are three potential cases for the occurrence of forgetting:

Case 1: Forgetting occurs continuously throughout the learning process.
Case 2: Forgetting occurs only over a bounded time interval.
Case 3: Forgetting occurs over intermittent time intervals where the time of occurrence and the duration of forgetting are described by some probability distributions.

Univariate Learn-Forget Model

Any operation that is subject to interruption in the learning process is suitable for the application of forget functions. Sule (1978) postulated that the forget model can be represented as:

$$Y_f = X_f R_f^{B_f},$$

where Y_f = number of units that could be produced on Rth day, X_f = equivalent production on the first day of the forget curve, R_f = cumulative number of days in the forget cycle, and B_f = forgetting rate. This forget model is of the same form as the standard progress function, except that the forgetting rate will be negative where the learning rate is positive and vice versa. Possible forms of univariate forget functions are shown in Figure 6-4. Model (a) shows a case where the worker forgets rapidly from an initial performance level but with a residual retention level. Model (b) shows a case where forgetting occurs more slowly in a concave fashion but with no residual retention. Under this model, the worker will eventually forget everything that has been learned. Model (c) shows a case where the rate of forgetting temporarily slows down after an initial period of rapid forgetting. Forgetting then picks up at a rate similar to that of model (b).

Figure 6-4. Possible Modes of Forgetting

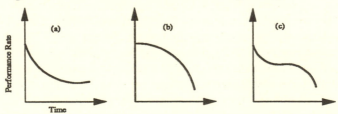

The combination of the learning and forgetting models will present a more realistic picture of what actually occurs in a learning process. The combination is not as simple as resolving two curves to obtain a resultant curve. The resolution is particularly complex in the case of intermittent periods of forgetting. Figure 6-5 presents a representation of some periods where forgetting takes place and the resultant learn-forget curve.

Figure 6-5. Intermittent Periods of Learning Decay

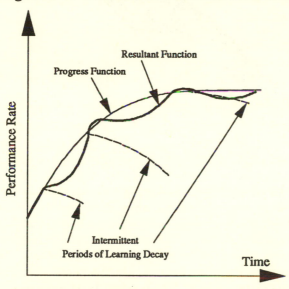

Bivariate Learn-Forget Model

Hypothetical examples of bivariate learning function, *l(t,u)*, and forget function, *f(t,u)*, are shown respectively below:

$$l(t,u) \;=\; 20t^{0.09} \;+\; u^{-0.05},$$

$$f(t,u) \;=\; t^{-0.20}u^{-0.30},$$

for $100 \le t \le 3000$ and $100 \le u \le 1000$, where *t* represents time and *u* represents production units. Figure 6-6 shows the learning function, while Figure 6-7 shows the forgetting function. In multivariate cases, we will be referring to performance surfaces rather than performance curves. The positive effect of learning is represented in terms of performance rate. Thus, in Figure 6-6, performance rate increases with time.

Figure 6-6. Bivariate Model of Increasing Performance

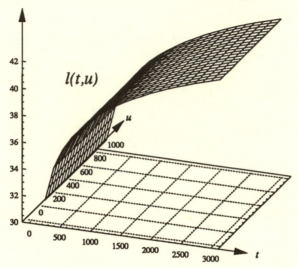

Figure 6-7. Bivariate Model of Decreasing Performance

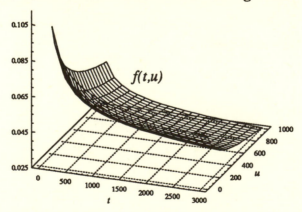

The forgetting function may be viewed as the model of what the performance level would be if no additional learning occurs. Thus, if learning terminates at a particular performance level, the effect of forgetting will gradually reduce that initial performance level in accordance with the functional form of the forgetting model. Due to the effect of forgetting, the performance level tends to decrease with time. An approach to resolving the surfaces is presented below.

CASE OF CONTINUOUS FORGETTING

If learning and forgetting start at a particular performance level, the resultant performance function, $r(t,u)$, may be modeled as:

$$r(t,u) = l(t,u) - \frac{[l(t,u) - f(t,u)]}{2}$$

$$= \frac{l(t,u) + f(t,u)}{2}.$$

This is simply the point-by-point average of the learning and forgetting functions. The justification for using the above approach for resolving the two functions can be seen by considering the univariate curves in Figure 6-8. In the figure, the learn function, $l(t)$, is above the forget function, $f(t)$. The forget function will create a downward pull on the learn function. This creates the resultant function, $r(t)$. The resolution of the two functions is applicable only for the time periods over which forgetting actually occurs.

Figure 6-8. Resolution of Learning and Forgetting Curves

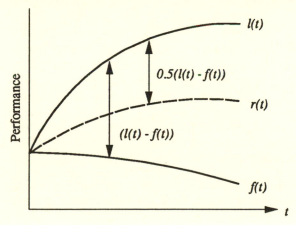

Using the resolution approach in Figure 6-8 for $l(t,u)$ and $f(t,u)$, we obtain the following resultant function for the case of continuous forgetting:

$$r(t,u) \;=\; 20t^{0.09} \;+\; u^{-0.05} \;-\; \frac{[20t^{0.09} \;+\; u^{-0.05} \;-\; t^{-0.20}u^{-0.30}]}{2}$$

$$=\; 10t^{0.09} \;+\; 0.5u^{-0.05} \;+\; 0.5t^{-0.2}u^{-0.3}.$$

A plot of the resultant performance surface, $r(t,u)$, is presented in Figure 6-9, which shows that the effect of forgetting has reduced the resultant performance levels.

Figure 6-9. Resultant Performance Curve

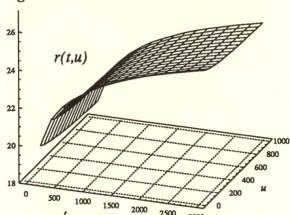

Note that $l(t,u)$ and $f(t,u)$ do not really start at the same performance level, since the expected performance at $t=0$ for $l(t,u)$ is much higher than the expected performance at $t=0$ for $f(t,u)$. Thus, alternate resolution approaches need to be investigated for this type of function. This leads us to an important definition:

Coincident Learning and Forgetting Functions: A learning function and a forgetting function are said to be *coincident* if both functions originate at the same performance level.

For noncoincident functions, alternate resolution approaches may be considered whereby the starting point of the forget function is incorporated into the resolution procedure. For example, an integer multiple of the learning function may be used (relative to the forget function) during the resolution process. In a specific case, the learning function may be given N times as much weight as the forget function in obtaining the point-by-point average of the functions. Another approach is to define the forget function as a *relative* function based directly on the level of decrement it creates in the overall performance. In this case, the two functions may be added directly to obtain the resultant performance function.

It is noted that the forget function in the above example is defined as an *absolute* function that starts at low performance levels. The low starting levels result in net performance levels that are about half the original performance level without the effect of forgetting.

Bounded Interval of Forgetting
    Suppose forgetting only occurs over the bounded time interval $500 \leq t \leq 1500$ in the preceding example. Figure 6-10 shows the bounded portions of the learning, forgetting, and resultant functions. In this case the resolution of the curves is done over only a bounded time interval.

Figure 6-10. Bounded Intervals of Learning and Forgetting

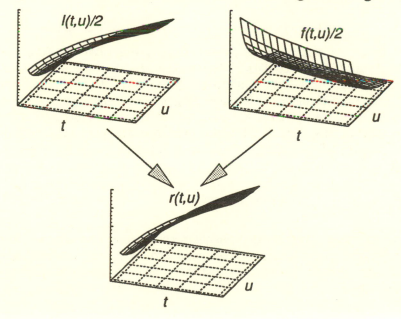

CASE OF INTERMITTENT FORGETTING

In this case, forgetting occurs in an intermittent fashion. Each occurrence is described by the prevailing forgetting function. It is also possible to have alternate periods of learning and forgetting. The plot of the resultant bivariate model for this case will exhibit a "wave-like" form.

Incipient Performance Level

It was noted earlier that the functions used in the illustrative example were not coincident. Coincidence can be achieved by shifting up the forgetting function by a scaling constant in such a way that its highest point coincides with the lowest point of the learning function. This common point will be referred to as the *incipient* performance level, P_i. For our example, this approach yields a shifted function, $f_s(t,u)$, and an adjusted resultant function, $r_a(t,u)$, defined as follows:

$$f_s(t,u) = 31.0 + t^{-0.20}u^{-0.30},$$

$$r_a(t,u) = 15.5 + 10t^{0.09} + 0.5u^{-0.05} + 0.5t^{-0.2}u^{-0.3},$$

for $100 \leq t \leq 3000$ and $100 \leq u \leq 1000$. The resultant function can be used for various practical applications. An example is the evaluation of production standards as illustrated below.

Application Problem

Let the units of performance expressed by $r_a(t,u)$ be in terms of hundreds of assembly components produced per cycle, while u represents cumulative units of completed assemblies; and let t represent cumulative hours of operation. Given that the standards department of a manufacturing plant has set a target production rate of 4,000 (i.e., $r = 40.00$) components per cycle to be achieved after 2000 hours (i.e. $t = 2,000$) of operation and 670 cumulative production units (i.e., $u = 670$), determine the feasibility of the target performance. Using the fitted model of $r_a(t,u)$, we have:

$$r_a(2000, 670) = 15.5 + 10(2000)^{0.09} + 0.5(670)^{-0.05} + 0.5(2000)^{-0.2}(670)^{-0.3},$$

which yields a performance rate of 3,570 components per cycle, as seen in Table 6-4. On the basis of this result, it can be determined that the target performance is not feasible. Note that without the effect of forgetting, the performance rate is computed to be:

$$l(2000, 670) = 20(2000)^{0.09} + (670)^{-0.05} = 40.36.$$

That is, 4,036 components per production cycle, which exceeds the target performance level. Thus, under regular learning without the effect of forgetting, it is possible to achieve higher performance levels. With the detrimental effect of forgetting, actual performance may not be as high as we might normally expect. This example illustrates the importance of considering the effect of forgetting when evaluating performance on the basis of learning curves. Table 6-4 presents a sample of the tabulation of values of $r_a(t,u)$ for various combinations of values of t and u.

Table 6-4. Tabulated Values of $r_a(t,u)$

t	u	$r_a(t,u)$	t	u	$r_a(t,u)$
100	100	3108	1600	550	3531
200	130	3204	1700	580	3541
300	160	3263	1800	610	3551
400	190	3306	1900	640	3561
500	220	3341	2000	670	3570
600	250	3369	2100	700	3578
700	280	3393	2200	730	3586
800	310	3415	2300	760	3594
900	340	3434	2400	790	3602
1000	370	3451	2500	820	3609
1100	400	3467	2600	850	3616
1200	430	3482	2700	880	3623
1300	460	3495	2800	910	3630
1400	490	3508	2900	940	3636
1500	520	3520	3000	970	3642

J. Smith (1989) accounts for the effect of interruption in the learning process by developing what he calls a *manufacturing interruption ratio*. The ratio considers the learning decay that occurs when a learning process is interrupted. He presents the following expression:

$$Z = (C_1 - C_x)\frac{(t - 1)}{11},$$

where:

Z = per-product loss of learning costs due to manufacturing interruption
t = 1, 2, . . ., 11 (months of interruption from one month to twelve months)
C_1 = cost of the first unit of the product
C_x = cost of the last unit produced before a production interruption.

Thus, the unit cost of the first unit produced after production begins again is given by:

$$C_{(x+1)} = C_x + Z$$

$$= C_x + (C_1 - C_x)\frac{(t - 1)}{11}.$$

In any practical situation, an allowance must be made for the potential impacts that forgetting may have on performance. Potential applications of the combined learning and forgetting models include design of training programs, manufacturing economic analysis, manpower scheduling, production planning, labor estimation, budgeting, and resource allocation.

EXERCISES

6-1.   In a certain project operation, it was noted that a total assembly cost of $2,000 was incurred for the production of 50 units of a product. Suppose an additional 100 units were produced at a cost of $1,000. Determine the learning curve percentage for the operation.

6-2.   Suppose an operation is known to exhibit a learning curve rate of 85 percent. Production was interrupted for three months after 100 units have been produced. If the cost of the very first unit is $50, find the unit cost of the first unit produced after production begins again.

6-3.   For the operation described in Question 6-2, determine the cost of unit 150 of the product assuming no further production interruptions occur.

6-4.   Suppose the first 20-unit batch of a product has an average cost of $72 per unit; the next 30-unit batch has an average cost of $60 per unit; and the next 50-unit batch has an average cost of $50 per unit. Based on this cost history, determine the appropriate learning curve percent to recommend for this operation.

6-5.   The first performance of a task requires eight hours. The twentieth performance of the task requires only two hours. If this task is subject to a conventional learning process, determine the learning rate associated with the task.

6-6.   For the task in Question 6-5, determine how many hours it will take to perform the task the twelfth time.

6-7.   Suppose unit 190 of a product requires 45 hours to produce under a learning curve rate of 80 percent. Determine the number of hours required by the first unit of the product and the number of hours required by unit 250.

6-8.   The first 50-unit order of a job shop costs $1,500. It is believed that the shop experiences a 75 percent learning curve rate. Determine a reasonable price quote for the next 80-unit order of the same job.

6-9.   Suppose the sixtieth unit of a product produced under a learning rate of 80 percent is $30. If the production standard is $20 per unit, determine how many more units must be produced before the standard can be reached.

6-10.   Suggest other appropriate approaches for resolving learning and forgetting curves for tasks that are subject to both learning and forgetting processes.

CHAPTER 7

STATISTICAL DATA ANALYSIS FOR PROJECT PLANNING AND CONTROL

The word *statistics* can have several meanings in terms of project analysis. In some cases, *statistics* refers simply to the collection of numerical data. This is the connotation that most people encounter in day-to-day activities. In more specialized cases, *statistics* refers more specifically to the processes of collecting, organizing, analyzing, interpreting, and presenting data. Another connotation of *statistics* involves the method of drawing inferences based on known or assumed characteristics of a process. In project planning and control, all the possible connotations of *statistics* can come into play. This chapter presents some important data analysis and statistical techniques useful for project planning and control.

BASIC DATA ANALYSIS

The way in which project data is analyzed and presented can affect how the information content is perceived by a project analyst. In many cases, data is presented in response to direct questions such as: When is the project deadline? Who are the people assigned to the first task? How many resource units are available? Answers to these types of questions constitute data of different forms or expressed on different scales. The resulting data may be qualitative or quantitative. Different techniques are available for analyzing different types of data. This section discusses some of the basic techniques for data analysis. The data presented in Table 7-1 is used to illustrate the data analysis techniques.

Raw Data

Raw data consists of ordinary observations recorded for a decision variable or factor. Examples of factors for which data may be collected for decision making are revenue, cost, personnel productivity, task duration, project completion time, product quality, and resource availability. Raw data should be organized into a format suitable for visual review and computational analysis. Our sample data represents the quarterly revenues from four projects: Projects A, B, C, and D. For example, the data for quarter number one indicates that Project C yielded the highest revenue of $4,500,000, while Project B yielded the lowest revenue of $1,200,000. Figure 7-1 presents the raw data of project revenue as a line graph. The same information is presented as a multiple bar chart in Figure 7-2.

Table 7-1. Quarterly Revenues from Four Projects (in $1,000s)

Project	Quarter 1	Quarter 2	Quarter 3	Quarter 4	Row Total
A	3000	3200	3400	2800	12,400
B	1200	1900	2500	2400	8,000
C	4500	3400	4600	4200	16,700
D	2000	2500	3200	2600	10,300
Column Total	10,700	11,000	13,700	12,000	47,400

Figure 7-1. Line Graph of Quarterly Project Revenues

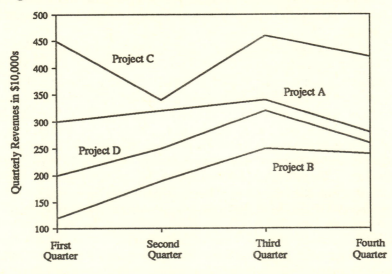

Figure 7-2. Multiple Bar Chart of Quarterly Revenues

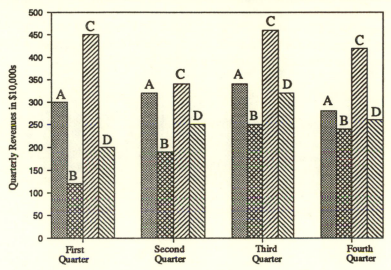

Total Revenue

The total or sum indicates the magnitude of a particular variable. If X_1, X_2, X_3, . . . , X_n represent a set of n observations (e.g., revenues), then the total is computed as:

$$T = \sum_{i=1}^{n} X_i.$$

For the data in Table 7-1, the total revenues indicate that Project C has the largest total revenue over the four quarters, while Project B produced the lowest total revenue. The last row of the table shows the total revenue for each quarter. The totals reveal that the largest revenues occur in the third quarter. The first quarter brought in the lowest total revenue. The grand total revenue for the four projects over the four quarters is shown as $47,400,000 in the last cell in the table. Figure 7-3 presents the quarterly total revenues as stacked bar charts. Each segment in a stack of bars represents the revenue contribution from a particular project. The percentage of the overall revenue contributed by each project is also shown in the pie chart in Figure 7-4.

Figure 7-3. Stacked Bar Graph of Quarterly Total Revenues

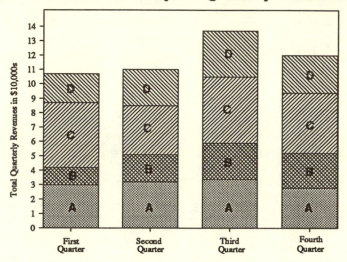

Figure 7-4. Pie Chart of Total Revenue per Project

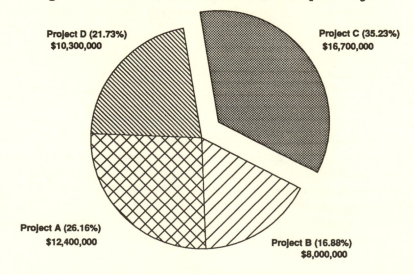

Average Revenue

The average is one of the most frequently used measures in data analysis. Given n observations (e.g., revenues), $X_1, X_2, X_3, \ldots, X_n$, the average of the observations is computed as:

$$\overline{X} \;=\; \frac{\sum\limits_{i=1}^{n} X_i}{n} \;=\; \frac{T}{n}.$$

For the sample data, the average quarterly revenues for the four projects are:

$$\overline{X}_A \;=\; \frac{(3000 + 3200 + 3400 + 2800)(\$1,000)}{4}$$

$$=\; \$3,100,000.$$

$$\overline{X}_B \;=\; \frac{(1200 + 1900 + 2500 + 2400)(\$1,000)}{4}$$

$$=\; \$2,000,000.$$

$$\overline{X}_C \;=\; \frac{(4500 + 3400 + 4600 + 4200)(\$1,000)}{4}$$

$$=\; \$4,175,000.$$

$$\overline{X}_D \;=\; \frac{(2000 + 2500 + 3200 + 2600)(\$1,000)}{4}$$

$$=\; \$2,575,000.$$

Similarly, the expected average revenue per project for the four quarters are as presented below:

$$\overline{X}_1 \;=\; \frac{(3000 + 1200 + 4500 + 2000)(\$1,000)}{4}$$

$$=\; \$2,675,000.$$

$$\overline{X}_2 \;=\; \frac{(3200 + 1900 + 3400 + 2500)(\$1,000)}{4}$$

$$=\; \$2,750,000.$$

$$\overline{X}_3 = \frac{(3400 + 2500 + 4600 + 3200)(\$1,000)}{4}$$

$$= \$3,425,000.$$

$$\overline{X}_4 = \frac{(2800 + 2400 + 4200 + 2600)(\$1,000)}{4}$$

$$= \$3,000,000.$$

The above values are shown in a bar chart in Figure 7-5. The average revenue from any of the four projects at any given quarter is calculated as the sum of all the observations divided by the number of observations. That is,

$$\overline{X} = \frac{\sum\limits_{i=1}^{N}\sum\limits_{j=1}^{M} X_{ij}}{K},$$

where
N = number of projects
M = number of quarters
K = total number of observations ($K = NM$).

Figure 7-5. Average Revenue per Project for Each Quarter

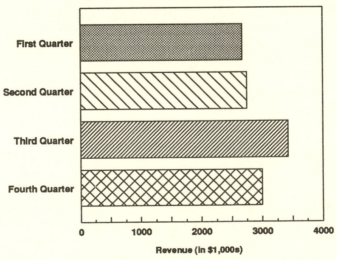

Referring again to the sample data, overall average revenue per project per quarter is:

$$\overline{X} = \frac{\$47,400,00}{16} = \$2,962,500.$$

As a cross-check, the sum of the quarterly averages should be equal to the sum of the project revenue averages, which is equal to the grand total divided by four. That is,

$$(2675 + 2750 + 3425 + 3000)(\$1,000) = (3100 + 2000 + 4175 + 2575)(\$1,000)$$

$$= \$11,800,000$$

$$= \$47,400,000/4.$$

The cross-check procedure above works because we have a balanced table of observations. That is, we have four projects and four quarters. If there were only three projects, for example, the sum of the quarterly averages would not be equal to the sum of the project averages.

Median Revenue

The median is the value that falls in the middle of a group of observations arranged in order of magnitude. One half of the observations are above the median and the other half are below the median. The method of determining the median depends on whether or not the observations are organized into a frequency distribution. For unorganized data, it is necessary to arrange the data in an increasing or decreasing order before finding the median. Given K observations (e.g., revenues), $X_1, X_2, X_3, \ldots, X_K$, arranged in increasing or decreasing order, the median is identified as the value in position $(K+1)/2$ in the data arrangement if K is an odd number. If K is an even number, then the average of the two middle values is considered to be the median. If our sample data are arranged in increasing order, we get the following:

1200, 1900, 2000, 2400, 2500, 2500, 2600, 2800, 3000, 3200, 3200, 3400, 3400, 4200, 4500, 4600.

The median is then calculated as: $(2800+3000)/2 = 2900$. Thus, half of the recorded revenues are expected to be above \$2,900,000, while half are expected to be below that amount. Figure 7-6 presents a bar chart of the revenue data arranged in increasing order. The median is somewhere between the eighth and ninth values in the ordered data above.

Figure 7-6. Bar Chart of Ordered Data

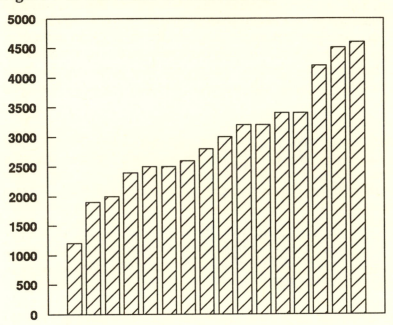

Quartiles and Percentiles

The median discussed above is a position measure because its value is based on its position in a set of observations. Other measures of position are *quartiles* and *percentiles*. There are three quartiles which divide a set of data into four equal categories. The first quartile, denoted Q1, is the value below which one fourth of all the observations in the data set will fall. The second quartile, denoted Q2, is the value below which two fourths or one half of all the observations in the data set fall. The third quartile, denoted Q3, is the value below which three fourths of the observations fall. The second quartile is identical to the median. It is technically incorrect to refer to the "fourth quartile," because this implies that there is a point within the data set below which all the data points fall: a contradiction! A data point cannot lie within the range of the observations and at the same time exceed all the observations, including itself.

The concept of percentiles is similar to the concept of quartiles except that reference is made to percentage points. There are 99 percentiles that divide a set of observations into 100 equal parts. The Xth percentile is the value below which

X percent of the data fall. Thus, the 99th percentile refers to the point below which 99% of the observations fall. The three quartiles discussed previously are regarded as the 25th, 50th, and 75th percentiles. As was explained above, it would be technically incorrect to refer to the "100th percentile." In performance ratings, such as on an examination or product quality level, the higher the percentile of an individual or product, the better. In many cases, recorded data are classified into categories that are not indexed to numerical measures. In such cases, other measures of central tendency or position will be needed. An example of such a measure is the mode.

The Mode

The mode is defined as the value that has the highest frequency in a set of observations. When the recorded observations can only be classified into categories, the mode can be particularly helpful in describing the data. Given a set of K observations (e.g., revenues), $X_1, X_2, X_3, \ldots, X_K$, the mode is identified as the value that occurs more than any other value in the set. Sometimes, the mode is not unique in a set of observations. For our sample data, the values 2500, 3200, and 3400 have the same number of occurrences. Thus, each of them is a mode of the set of revenue observations. If there is a unique mode in a set of observations, then the data is said to be unimodal. The mode is very useful in expressing the central tendency for observations with nonnumeric characteristics such as color, marital status, or state of origin. The three modes in the raw data can be identified in Figure 7-6.

Range of Revenue

The range is determined by the two extreme values in a set of observations. Given K observations (e.g., revenues), $X_1, X_2, X_3, \ldots, X_K$, the range of the observations is the difference between the lowest and the highest observations. The range of revenues in our sample data is $4,600,000 - $1,200,000 = $3,400,000. Because of its dependency on only two values, the range tends to increase as the sample size increases. Furthermore, it does not provide a measurement of the variability of the observations relative to the center of the distribution.

The variability of a distribution is generally expressed in terms of the deviation of each observed value from the sample average. If the deviations are small, the set of data is said to have low variability. The deviations provide information about the degree of dispersion in a set of observations. Unfortunately, a general formula to evaluate the variability of data cannot be based on the deviations. This is because some of the deviations are negative while some are positive and the sum of all the deviations is equal to zero. One possible solution to this probelm is to compute the average deviation.

Average Deviation

The average deviation is the average of the absolute values of the deviations from the sample average. Table 7-2 shows how the average deviation is computed for the sample data. Given K observations (e.g., revenues), $X_1, X_2, X_3, \ldots, X_K$, the average deviation of the data is computed as:

$$\overline{D} = \frac{\sum_{i=1}^{K} |X_i - \overline{X}|}{K}.$$

Table 7-2. Tabulation of Sample Statistics

Observation Number (i)	Recorded Observation X_i	Deviation from Average $X_i - \overline{X}$	Absolute Value $\|X_i - \overline{X}\|$	Square of Deviation $(X_i - \overline{X})^2$
1	3000	37.5	37.5	1406.25
2	1200	-1762.5	1762.5	3106406.30
3	4500	1537.5	1537.5	2363906.30
4	2000	-962.5	962.5	926406.25
5	3200	237.5	237.5	56406.25
6	1900	-1062.5	1062.5	1128906.30
7	3400	437.5	437.5	191406.25
8	2500	-462.5	462.5	213906.25
9	3400	437.5	437.5	191406.25
10	2500	-462.5	462.5	213906.25
11	4600	1637.5	1637.5	2681406.30
12	3200	237.5	237.5	56406.25
13	2800	-162.5	162.5	26406.25
14	2400	-562.5	562.5	316406.25
15	4200	1237.5	1237.5	1531406.30
16	2600	-362.5	362.5	131406.25
Total	47,400.0	0.0	11,600.0	13,137,500.25
Average	2,962.5	0.0	725.0	821,093.77
Square Root				906.14

One of the disadvantages of the average deviation measure is that it ignores the sign associated with each deviation. Despite this shortcoming, its simplicity and ease of computation makes it useful for basic statitical analysis. A knowledge of the average deviation helps in understanding the standard deviation, which is the most frequently used measure of dispersion.

Sample Variance

Sample variance is the average of the squared deviations computed from a set of observations. Variance conveys the level of variability inherent in a set of observations. Given K observations (e.g., revenues), $X_1, X_2, X_3, \ldots, X_K$, the sample variance of the data is computed as:

$$s^2 = \frac{\sum_{i=1}^{K}(X_i - \overline{X})^2}{K-1}.$$

The variance can also be computed by the following alternate formulas:

$$s^2 = \frac{\sum_{i=1}^{K} X_i^2 - \left(\frac{1}{K}\right)\left[\sum_{i=1}^{K} X_i\right]^2}{K-1}.$$

$$s^2 = \frac{\sum_{i=1}^{K} X_i^2 - K(\overline{X})^2}{K-1}.$$

Using the first formula, the sample variance of our sample data is calculated as:

$$s^2 = \frac{13,137,500.25}{16-1} = 875,833.33.$$

Note that the average calculated in the last column of Table 7-2 is obtained by dividing the total for that column by 16 instead of 16-1 = 15. Thus, that average is not the correct value of the sample variance. However, as the number of observations gets very large, the average as computed in Table 7-2 will become a close estimate for the correct sample variance. The average calculated by the procedure in Table 7-2 is referred to as the population variance when K is very large. The average calculated by the formulas above is referred to as the sample variance, particularly when K is small. For our example, the population variance is given by:

$$\sigma^2 = \frac{\sum_{i=1}^{K}(X_i - \overline{X})^2}{K} = \frac{13,137,500.25}{16} = 821,093.77,$$

while the sample variance, as shown previously, is given by:

$$s^2 = \frac{\sum\limits_{i=1}^{K}(X_i - \overline{X})^2}{K-1} = \frac{13,137,500.25}{(16-1)} = 875,833.33.$$

Standard Deviation

The sample standard deviation of a set of observations is the positive square root of the sample variance. Standard deviation gives a more direct measure of variability than variance, because it is expressed in the original units of the data being analyzed. Given K observations, $X_1, X_2, X_3, \ldots, X_K$, the sample standard deviation of the data is computed as:

$$s = \sqrt{\frac{\sum\limits_{i=1}^{K}(X_i - \overline{X})^2}{K-1}}.$$

The sample standard deviation can also be computed by the following alternate formulas:

$$s = \sqrt{\frac{\sum\limits_{i=1}^{K} X_i^2 - \left(\frac{1}{K}\right)\left[\sum\limits_{i=1}^{K} X_i\right]^2}{K-1}}.$$

$$s = \sqrt{\frac{\sum\limits_{i=1}^{K} X_i^2 - K(\overline{X})^2}{K-1}}.$$

Using the first formula, the sample standard deviation of our sample data is calculated as:

$$s = \sqrt{\frac{13,137,500.25}{16-1}} = \sqrt{875,833.33} = 935.8597.$$

The population standard deviation is given by:

$$\sigma = \sqrt{\frac{\sum\limits_{i=1}^{K}(X_i - \overline{X})^2}{K}} = \sqrt{\frac{13,137,500.25}{16}} = 906.1423,$$

while the sample standard deviation is given by:

$$ s \;=\; \sqrt{\frac{\sum\limits_{i=1}^{K}(X_i - \overline{X})^2}{K-1}} \;=\; \sqrt{\frac{13,137,500.25}{(16-1)}} \;=\; 935.8597. $$

DESCRIPTIVE AND INFERENTIAL STATISTICS

Descriptive statistics refers to analyses that are performed in order to describe the characteristics of a process. The analyses presented in the preceding section fall under the category of *descriptive statistics* because they are concerned with summary calculations and graphical display of observations.

Inferential statistics refers to the process of drawing inferences about a process based on a limited observation of the process. The techniques presented in this section fall under the category of *inferential statistics*. Inferential statistics is of more interest to many practitioners because it is more dynamic and provides generalizations about a population by investigating only a portion of the population. The portion of the population investigated is referred to as a *sample*. For example, the expected duration of a proposed task can be inferred from several previous observations of the durations of identical tasks.

DEDUCTIVE AND INDUCTIVE STATISTICS

Deductive statistics involves assigning properties to a specific item in a set on the basis of the properties of a general class covering the set. For example, if it is known that 20% of projects in a given organization fail, then deduction can be used to assign a probability of 0.20 to the event that a specific project in the organization will fail.

Inductive statistics involves drawing general conclusions from specific facts. That is, inferences about populations are drawn from samples. For example, if 95% of a sample of 100 people surveyed in a 5,000-person organization favor a particular project, then induction can be used to conclude that 95% of the personnel in the organization favor the project. The different types of statistics play important roles in project management. Frequently, inferences must be made about factors such as expected task duration, weather conditions, resource availability, and equipment failures.

SAMPLE SPACE AND SAMPLING

A *sample space* of an experiment is the set of all possible distinct outcomes of the experiment. An *experiment* is some process that generates distinct sets of observations. The simplest and most common example is the experiment of tossing a coin to observe whether heads or tails will show up. An *outcome* is a distinct observation resulting from a single trial of an experiment. In the experiment of tossing a coin, "heads" and "tails" are the two possible outcomes. Thus, the sample space consists of only two items.

An experiment may involve checking to see whether it rains or not on a given day. Another experiment may involve counting how many tasks fall behind schedule during a project life cycle. Another example of an experiment may involve recording how long it takes to perform a given activity in each of several selected projects. The outcome of any experiment is frequently referred to as a *random event* because the outcomes of the experiment occur in a random fashion. We cannot predict with certainty what the outcome of a particular trial of the experiment will be.

Sample
A sample is a subset of a population that is selected for observation and statistical analysis. Inferences are drawn about the population on the basis of the results of the analysis of the sample. The reasons for using sampling rather than complete population enumeration are:

1. It is more economical to work with a sample.
2. There is a time advantage to using a sample.
3. Populations are typically too large to work with.
4. A sample is more accessible than the whole population.
5. In some cases, the sample may have to be destroyed during the analysis.

There are three primary types of samples: convenience sample, judgment sample, and random sample. They differ in the manner in which their elementary units are chosen.

Convenience Sample: A convenience sample is a sample that is selected on the basis of how convenient certain elements of the population are for observation.

Judgment Sample: A judgment sample is one that is obtained on the basis of the discretion of someone familiar with the relevant characteristics of the population.

Random Sample: A random sample is a sample in which the elements of the sample are chosen at random. This is the most important type of sample for statistical analysis. In random sampling, all the items in the population have an equal chance of being selected to be included in the sample.

Since a sample is a collection of observations representing only a portion of the population, the way in which the sample is chosen can significantly affect the adequacy and reliability of the sample. Even after the sample is chosen, the manner in which specific observations are obtained may still affect the validity of the results. The possible bias and errors in the sampling process are discussed below:

Sampling Error: A sampling error is the difference between a sample mean and the population mean that is due solely to the particular sample elements that are selected for observation.

Nonsampling Error: A nonsampling error is an error that is due solely to the manner in which the observation is made.

Sampling Bias: Sampling bias is the tendency to favor the selection of certain sample elements having specific characteristics. For example, a sampling bias may occur if a sample of the personnel is selected from only the engineering department in a survey addressing the implementation of high technology projects.

Stratified Sampling: Stratified sampling involves dividing the population into classes, or groups, called strata. The items contained in each stratum are expected to be homogeneous with respect to the characteristics to be studied. A random subsample is taken from each stratum. The subsamples from all the strata are then combined to form the desired overall sample. Stratified sampling is typically used for heterogeneous populations such as data on employee productivity in an organization. By stratification groups of employee are set up so that the individuals within each stratum are mostly homogeneous and the strata are different from one another. For another example, a survey of project managers on some important issue of personnel management may be conducted by forming strata on the basis of the types of projects they manage. There may be one stratum for technical projects, one for construction projects, and one for manufacturing projects.

A *proportionate stratified sampling* results if the units in the sample are allocated among the strata in proportion to the relative number of units in each stratum in the population. That is, equal sampling ratio is assigned to all strata in a proportionate stratified sampling. In *disproportionate stratified sampling*, the sampling ratio for each stratum is inversely related to the level of homogeneity of the units in the stratum. The more homogeneous the stratum, the smaller its proportion included in the overall sample. The rationale for using disproportionate stratified sampling is that when the units in a stratum are more homogeneous, a smaller subsample is needed to ensure good representation. The smaller subsample helps to reduce sampling cost.

Cluster Sampling: Cluster sampling involves the selection of random clusters, or groups, from the population. The desired overall sample is made up of the units in each cluster. Cluster sampling is different from stratified sampling in that differences between clusters are usually small. In addition, the units within each cluster are generally more heterogeneous. Each cluster, also known as a *primary sampling unit*, is a expected to be a scaled-down model that gives a good representation of the characteristics of the population.

All the units in each cluster may be included in the overall sample, or a subsample of the units in each cluster may be used. If all the units of the selected clusters are included in the overall sample, the procedure is referred to as a *single-stage sampling*. If a subsample is taken at random from each selected cluster and all units of each subsample are included in the overall sample, then the sampling procedure is called a *two-stage sampling*. If the sampling procedure involves more than two stages of subsampling, then the procedure is referred to as a *multistage sampling*. Cluster sampling is typically less expensive to implement than stratified sampling. For example, the cost of taking a random sample of 2,000 managers from different industry types may be reduced by first selecting a sample, or cluster, of 25 industries and then selecting 80 managers from each of the 25 industries. This represents a two-stage sampling that will be considerably cheaper than trying to survey 2,000 individuals in several industries in a single-stage procedure.

FREQUENCY DISTRIBUTION

Once a sample has been drawn and observations of all the items in the sample are recorded, the task of data collection is completed. The next task involves organizing the raw data into a meaningful format. In addition to the various methods discussed earlier in this chapter, frequency distribution is another tool for organizing data. Frequency distribution involves the arrangement of observations into classes so as to show the frequency of occurrences in each class. An appropriate class interval must be selected for the construction of the frequency distribution. The guidelines for selecting the class interval are:

1. The number of classes should not be too small or too large for the true nature of the underlying distribution to be identified. Generally, the number of classes should be between 6 and 20.

2. The interval length of each class should be the same. The interval length should be selected so that every observation falls within some class.

3. The difference between midpoints of adjacent classes should be constant and equal to the length of each interval.

Example

Suppose a set of data was collected about project costs in an organization. Twenty projects are selected for the study. The observations below are recorded in thousands of dollars:

$3,000	$1,100	$4,200	$800	$3,000
$1,800	$2,500	$2,500	$1,700	$3,000
$2,900	$2,100	$2,300	$2,500	$1,500
$3,500	$2,600	$1,300	$2,100	$3,600

Table 7-3 shows the tabulation of the cost data as a frequency distribution. Note how the end points of the class intervals are selected in such a way that no recorded data point falls at an end point of a class.

Table 7-3. Frequency Distribution of Cost Data

Cost Interval	Midpoint	Frequency	Cum. Frequency
750 - 1250	1000	2	2
1250 - 1750	1500	3	5
1750 - 2250	2000	3	8
2250 - 2750	2500	5	13
2750 - 3250	3000	4	17
3250 - 3750	3500	2	19
3750 - 4250	4000	1	20
Total		20	

Seven class intervals seem to be the most appropriate size for this particular set of observations. Each class interval has a spread of $500, which is an approximation obtained from the following expression.

$$W = \frac{X_{max} - X_{min}}{N}$$

$$= \frac{4200 - 800}{7}$$

$$= 485.71 \approx 500.$$

Table 7-4 shows the relative frequency distribution. The relative frequency of any class is the proportion of the total observations that fall into that class. It is obtained by dividing the frequency of the class by the total number of observations. The relative frequencies of all the classes should add up to 1. From the relative frequency table, it is seen that 25 percent of the observed project costs fall within the range of $2,250 to $2,750. Only 15 percent (0.10 + 0.05) of the observed project costs fall in the upper two intervals of project costs. Figure 7-7 shows the histogram of the frequency distribution for the project cost data. Figure 7-8 presents a plot of the cumulative relative frequency of the project cost data.

Table 7-4. Data for Relative Frequency Distribution

Cost Interval	Midpoint	Relative Frequency	Relative Cum. Frequency
750 - 1250	1000	0.10	0.10
1250 - 1750	1500	0.15	0.25
1750 - 2250	2000	0.15	0.40
2250 - 2750	2500	0.25	0.65
2750 - 3250	3000	0.20	0.85
3250 - 3750	3500	0.10	0.95
3750 - 4250	4000	0.05	1.00
Total		1.00	

Figure 7-7. Histogram of Project Cost Distribution Data

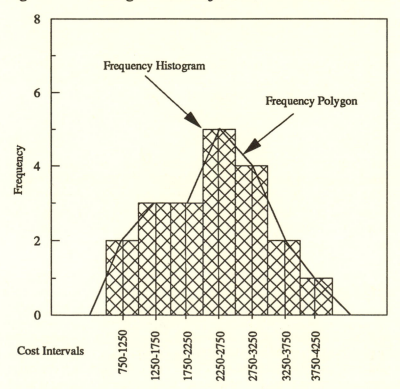

Figure 7-8. Plot of Cumulative Relative Frequency

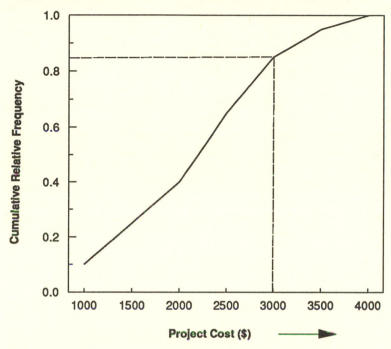

The plot of the cumulative relative frequency is superimposed on the relative frequency plot. The relative frequency of the observations in each class represents the probability that a project cost will fall within that range of costs. The corresponding cumulative relative frequency gives the probability that project cost will fall below the midpoint of that class interval. For example, 85 percent of project costs in this example are expected to fall below or equal to $3,000.

PROBABILITY CONCEPTS

Probability is something that we deal with in everyday life. A manager of a construction project may reschedule available manpower on the basis of weather forecasts, which are based on probability. People may adjust their life-styles on the basis of reports that make statements such as, "The probability of dying of heart disease in the West is 65%."

Probability refers to the chances of occurrence of an event out of several possible events in a sample space. For example, if a coin is tossed a large number of times, say several million times, the proportion of heads tends to be one-half of the total number of tosses. In that case, the number, one half, is referred to as the *probability* that heads will occur on one toss of the coin. For another example, if ten items with different colors are placed in a jar and one item is pulled out of the jar at random, the probability of pulling out one specific color is one-tenth.

The assignment of probabilities to physical events does not require a great deal of mathematical training. In the real world, experienced practitioners assign intuitive probabilities to events on the basis of experience and familiarity with previous occurrences of the event. Questions such as "What percentage of your project work force would show up on a rainy day?" or "What is the daily absenteeism rate?" can easily be answered by experienced managers without any mathematical reasoning. Thus, experienced managers can generate probabilities subconsciously. These probability values can be very valuable to project analysts in making inferences about events in a project environment.

NORMAL PROBABILITY DENSITY FUNCTION

A *probability density function* is a mathematical function that describes the random behaviors of events in a sample space. Probability density functions are associated with continuous sample spaces where there is an infinite number of possible events. If the number of elements in a sample space is ifinite or countably infinite, then the behavior of the events in the sample space is described by a discrete probability distribution rather than a continuous probability density function. Countably infinite means that there is an unending sequence with as many elements as there are whole numbers. Thus, probability distributions refer to discrete sample spaces, while probability density functions refer to continuous sample spaces.

In most practical problems, continuous random variables represent measured data, such as all possible distances a car can travel, weights, temperatures, and task duration, while discrete random variables represent counted data, such as the number of absent employees on a given day, the number of late jobs in a project, and the amount of dollars available for a particular project. Examples of discrete probability distributions are the binomial distribution, the geometric distribution, and the Poisson distribution. This section presents some of the basic properties of the normal probability density function. Other examples of probability density functions are the exponential probability density function, gamma probability density function, chi-square probability density function, and Weibull probability density function.

The normal probability density function is the most important continuous probability density function in statistics. It is often referred to as the normal distribution, normal curve, bell-shaped curve, or Gaussian distribution. It has been found that this distribution fits many of the physical events in nature. Hence its popularity and wide appeal. The normal distribution is characterized by the following expression:

$$f(x) = \frac{1}{\sqrt{2\pi}\sigma} e^{-\frac{1}{2}\left(\frac{x-\mu}{\sigma}\right)^2}, \quad -\infty < x < \infty,$$

where
μ = mean of the distribution
σ = standard deviation of the distribution
e = 2.71828..... (a natural constant)
π = 3.14159..... (a natural constant).

The bell-shaped appearance of the normal distribution is shown in Figure 7-9. The values of μ and σ are the parameters that determine the specific appearance (fat, thin, long, short, narrow, or wide) of the normal distribution. Theoretically, the tails of the curve trail on to infinity.

Figure 7-9. The Normal Curve

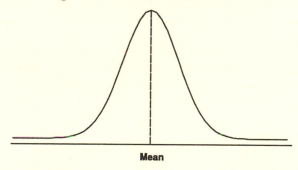

Mean

When $\mu = 0$ and $\sigma = 1$, the normal distribution is referred to as the *standard normal distribution*. It is the values of the standard normal distribution that are widely tabulated in books. Because of the variety and complexity of working with the general normal distribution, practically all analyses with the normal curve are based on the standard normal distribution. This is done by using the transformation given below:

$$Z = \frac{X - \mu}{\sigma},$$

where Z is the standard normal random variable and X is the general normal random variable with a mean of μ and standard deviation of σ. The variable Z is often referred to as the *normal deviate*. One important aspect of the normal distribution relates to the percent of observations within one, two, or three standard deviations from the mean. Approximately 68.27 percent of observations following a normal distribution lie within plus and minus one standard deviation from the mean. Approximately 95.27 percent of the observations lie within plus or minus two standard deviations from the mean, and approximately 99.73 percent of the observations lie within plus or minus three standard deviations from the mean. These percentages are shown graphically in Figure 7-10.

Figure 7-10. Areas under the Normal Curve

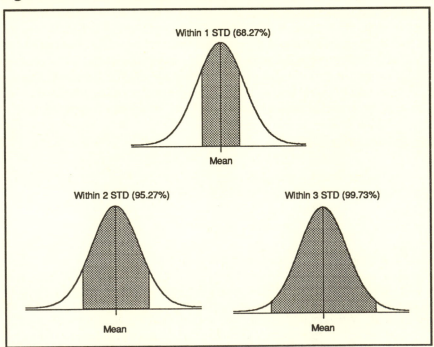

PERIODIC DISTRIBUTION TIME SERIES

There are numerous applications of statistical distributions to practical, real-world problems. Several distributions have been developed and successfully utilized for a large variety of problems. Despite the large number of distributions available, it is often confusing to determine which distribution is applicable to which real-world random variable. In many applications, the choices are limited to a few familiar distributions due either to a lack of better knowledge or computational ease. Such familiar distributions include the *normal, exponential,* and *uniform* distributions. To accommodate cases where the familiar distributions do not adequately represent the variable of interest, some special purpose distributions have been developed. Examples of such special distributions are *Pareto, Rayleigh, log-normal,* and *Cauchy* distributions. Another special case that may be of interest involves random variables that are governed by periodic or cyclic processes.

This section introduces the development of a *periodic probability density function* suitable for use when analyzing project time series. A time series is a collection of observations that are drawn from a periodic or cyclic process. Example of project time series are monthly cost, quarterly revenue, and seasonal energy consumption. The standard periodic *pdf* is a continuous wave-form periodic function defined on the interval $[0, 2\pi]$. The standard function is transformed into a general periodic function defined over any time series interval $[a, b]$. One possible application of the periodic distribution is the estimation of time-to-failure for components or equipment that undergo periodic maintenance. Another application may be in the statistical analysis of the peak levels in a time series process.

Modeling Approach

The trigonometric sine function provides the basis for the periodic distribution. The basic sine function is given by:

$$y = \sin\theta, \quad -\infty < \theta < \infty,$$

where θ is in radians. The sine function is shown in Figure 7-11. The function is periodic with period 2π. The sine function has its maxima and minima (1 and -1 respectively) at the points $\theta = \pm n\pi/2$, where n is an odd positive integer. The function also satisfies the relationship:

$$\sin(\theta + 2n\pi) = \sin\theta,$$

for any integer n. In general, any function $f(x)$ satisfying the relationship

$$f(x + nT) = f(x),$$

is said to be periodic with period T, where T is a positive constant and n is an integer. A graph of $f(x)$ truncated to an interval $[a, a+T]$ or $(a, a+T]$ is called one cycle of the function.

Figure 7-11. Basic Sine Function

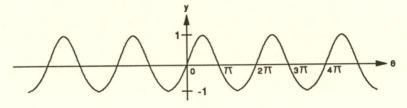

Standard Periodic Pdf

The periodic probability density function *(pdf)* is defined as:

$$f(x) = \begin{cases} \dfrac{1}{\pi}\sin^2 mx, & 0 \le x \le 2\pi, \quad m = 1,2,3,\dots \\ 0, & \text{otherwise,} \end{cases}$$

where x is in radians and m (positive integer) is the number of peaks (or modes) associated with the function on the interval $[0, \pi]$, which is half of the period. Thus, $f(x)$ represents a multi-modal distribution. A graph of the standard periodic *pdf* is presented in Figure 7-12.

Figure 7-12. Standard Periodic Distribution for *m=2*

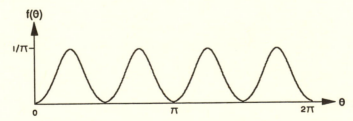

To be a legitimate *pdf*, $f(x)$ must satisfy the following conditions:

1. $f(x) \geq 0$ for all x in $[0, 2\pi]$.

2. $\int_0^{2\pi} f(x)dx = 1$.

3. $P(x_1 < X < x_2) = \int_{x_1}^{x_2} f(x)dx$.

The first condition can be seen to be true by inspection. Each value of x yields a probability value equal to or greater than zero. The second condition can be verified by examining the definite integral below:

$$\int_0^{2\pi} f(x)dx = \frac{1}{\pi}\int_0^{2\pi} \sin^2(mx)dx$$

$$= \frac{1}{\pi}\left[\frac{x}{2} - \frac{\sin(2mx)}{4m}\right]_0^{2\pi}$$

$$= \frac{1}{\pi}\left[\pi - \frac{\sin(4m\pi)}{4m}\right]$$

$$= 1.$$

The third condition is easily verified by computing the probability that X will fall between x_1 and x_2 as the area under the curve for $f(x)$ from x_1 to x_2.

EXPECTED VALUE

The expected value of X is given by:

$$E[X] = \int_0^{2\pi} xf(x)dx$$

$$= \frac{1}{\pi}\int_0^{2\pi} x\sin^2(mx)dx$$

$$= \frac{1}{\pi}\left[\frac{x^2}{4} - \frac{x\sin(2mx)}{4m} - \frac{\cos(2mx)}{8m^2}\right]_0^{2\pi}$$

$$= \pi.$$

VARIANCE

The variance of X is calculated from the theoretical definition of variance, which makes use of the definite integral from 0 to 2π. This is given by:

$$V[X] = \int_0^{2\pi} x^2 f(x)dx - \{E[X]\}^2$$

$$= \frac{1}{\pi}\int_0^{2\pi} x^2 \sin^2(mx)dx - \pi^2$$

$$= \frac{1}{\pi}\left[\frac{x^3}{6} - \left(\frac{x^2}{4m} - \frac{1}{8m^3}\right)\sin(2mx) - \frac{x\cos(2mx)}{4m^2}\right]_0^{2\pi} - \pi^2$$

$$= \frac{1}{3}\pi^2.$$

CUMULATIVE DISTRIBUTION FUNCTION

The cumulative distribution function of $f(x)$ is given by:

$$F(x) = \int_0^x f(r)dr$$

$$= \int_0^x \frac{1}{\pi}\sin^2(mr)dr$$

$$= \frac{2mx - \sin(2mx)}{4m\pi}.$$

General Periodic *pdf*

For practical applications, a general form of the periodic *pdf* defined over any real interval [a, b] will be of more interest. This general form is given by:

$$f(r) = \begin{cases} \frac{1}{\pi}\sin^2 mr, & 0 \le r \le 2\pi, \quad m = 1,2,3,\ldots \\ 0, & \text{otherwise,} \end{cases}$$

where
m = half of the number of peaks expected over the interval [a, b]
r = radian equivalent of the real number x in the interval [a, b].

The transformations from real units to radians and vice versa are accomplished by the expression below:

$$r = 2\pi\frac{(x - a)}{(b - a)}, \quad 0 \le r \le 2\pi; \quad a \le x \le b.$$

$$x = a + (r)\frac{(b - a)}{2\pi}, \quad 0 \le r \le 2\pi; \quad a \le x \le b.$$

Using the above transformation relationships and the expressions derived previously for the standard periodic random variable, the mean and variance of the general periodic random variable are derived to be:

$$E[X] = a + \frac{(b - a)}{2\pi}(E[r])$$

$$= a + \frac{(b - a)}{2\pi}(\pi)$$

$$= \frac{(a + b)}{2}.$$

$$V[X] = 0 + \left(\frac{b - a}{2\pi}\right)^2 V[r]$$

$$= \frac{(b - a)^2}{4\pi^2}\left(\frac{\pi^2}{3}\right)$$

$$= \frac{(b - a)^2}{12}.$$

Note that these expressions are identical to the expressions for the mean and variance of the uniform distribution.

APPLICATION EXAMPLES

Let us suppose that a system contains a certain type of component that undergoes periodic maintenance. The periodic distribution will be an appropriate model for the time-to-failure analysis for the system. Assume that the useful life of the component is estimated to be four years. The component will undergo maintenance three times during the four-year period. The failure times of the component after its first installation and between maintenance will have identical bell shapes. This is represented graphically in Figure 7-13. Now, suppose we are interested in the probability that the component will fail no later than 2.8 years after its first installation. The calculations, using the periodic *pdf*, will proceed as follow:

$a = 0$, $b = 4$, $m = 2$, $x = 2.8$.
$r = (2\pi)(2.8 - 0)/(4 - 0) = 1.4\pi = 4.3982$ radians
$P(0 \le X \le 2.8) = P(0 \le r \le 4.3982) = \int_0^{4.3982} \frac{1}{\pi}\sin^2(2r)dr = 0.7378.$

Figure 7-13. Periodic Distribution for Component Time-to-Failure

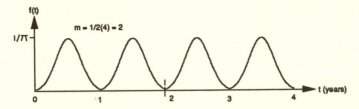

For another example, suppose we are interested in analyzing the peak points in the distribution of monthly energy consumption. Suppose the times of occurrence of consumption peaks are periodically distributed and evenly spaced from month to month. The peak times are modeled as shown in Figure 7-14. The graphical representation shows that on a month-to-month basis, the most likely peak point is the middle of the month. Any other peak point (e.g., end of the month) can be accommodated by shifting the time reference to the distribution.

Figure 7-14. Periodic Distribution for Peak Occurrence Times

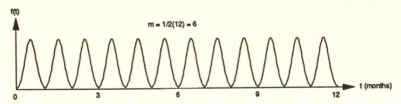

Now, suppose we are interested in the probability that there will be a peak between $t = 1$ and $t = 4.1$ months. The analysis will be done as follows:

$a = 0$, $b = 12$, $m = 6$, $x_1 = 1.0$; $x_2 = 4.1$
$r_1 = 2\pi/12 = 0.1667\pi$
$r_2 = 2\pi/12 \ (4.1) = 0.6833\pi$

$$P(1 \leq X \leq 4.1) = P(0.1667\pi \leq r \leq 0.6833\pi)$$

$$= \int_{0.1667\pi}^{0.6833\pi} \frac{1}{\pi} \sin^2(6r)dr$$

$$= F(0.6833\pi) - F(0.1667\pi)$$

$$= 0.2506.$$

The periodic distribution can be modeled for cyclic time series data collected for project parameters that fit the assumptions and requirements of the distribution. The analysis performed with the periodic distribution can complement analyses performed with other distribution types.

EXERCISES

7-1. Given the data for the three projects below, perform the complete data analysis as was done in Table 7-1.

Project	January	February	March	April	Total	Average
A	3000	3200	3400	2800		
B	1200	1900	2500	2400		
C	4500	3400	4600	4200		
Total						
Average						XXX

7-2. Discuss examples of descriptive and inferential statistics in the context of project planning and control.

7-3. The employees selected to work on a project are surveyed to select the type of organization structure suitable for the project. Which measure of central tendency would be the most appropriate to determine the preference by the greatest number of employees?

7-4. Use the data in Exercise 7-1 to verify that $\Sigma(X - \overline{X}) = 0$.

7-5. Use a software tool, such as a spreadsheet program, to compute the average deviation, standard deviation and variance for the data in Exercise 7-1.

7-6. What types of data would you recommend to be collected for a project involving the construction of a new recreational center in a small community? Discuss why and how.

7-7. List at least ten of the factors that should be included in the documentation of data requirements for a project involving the launching of a satellite.

7-8.   How would the data requirements in Exercise 7-7 be different from the data requirements involving the launching of a space shuttle?

7-9.   The duration of a certain program is known to be normally distributed with a mean of 9 months and a standard deviation of 2 months. Find the following:

   a)   The probability that the program can be completed in exactly 7 months.

   b)   The probability that the program can be completed in less than 9 months.

   c)   The probability that the program will require more than 10 months to complete.

7-10.   Verify the expressions presented in this chapter for the mean and variance of the periodic probability density function.

7-11.   Suppose a general random variable between 15 and 28 time units is known to have a periodic distribution with $m = 8$. Plot a graphical representation of the distribution of the random variable. Find the probability that the variable will have a value greater than 22 time units.

7-12.   Compare and contrast the periodic distribution and the uniform distribution. Consider the mean and variance of each distribution in your discussion.

CHAPTER 8

PROJECT ANALYSIS
AND SELECTION TECHNIQUES

Project success starts with proper project selection. In an environment of critical resource shortage, the right project must be undertaken at the right time. Project analysis and selection should be a major aspect of project planning and control. The significance of project selection strategies for project success has been addressed by several authors, including Hess (1962), Baker and Pound (1964), Schwartz and Vertinsky (1977), C. A. Nelson (1986), Liberatore (1987), Khorramshahgol et al. (1988), Bidanda (1989), Oral et al. (1991), Mustafa and Al-Bahar (1991), and Gupta et al. (1992). These numerous publications attest to the importance of the topic. Projects may be selected on the basis of a combination of several criteria. Some of these criteria are:

- Technical merit
- Management desire
- Schedule efficiency
- Cost-benefit ratio
- Resource availability
- Critical need
- Availability of sponsors
- Potential for user acceptance

Many aspects of project selection cannot be expressed in quantitative terms. For this reason, project analysis and selection must be addressed by techniques that permit the incorporation of both quantitative and qualitative factors. This chapter presents project analysis and selection techniques that facilitate the marriage of quantitative and qualitative considerations in the project decision process. Other techniques such as net present value, profit ratio, equity break even point, and learning curves presented in the preceding chapters are also applicable to project analysis and selection strategies. The analytic hierarchy process (AHP) and computer simulation are two of the techniques presented in this chapter.

ANALYTIC HIERARCHY PROCESS

The analytic hierarchy process (Saaty, 1980) is a practical approach to solving complex decision problems involving the comparisons of alternatives. The technique, popularly known as AHP, has been used extensively in practice to solve many decision problems.   AHP enables decision makers to represent the hierarchical interaction of factors, attributes, characteristics, or alternatives. Figure 8-1 presents an example of a decision hierarchy for project alternatives.

Figure 8-1. AHP for Project Alternatives

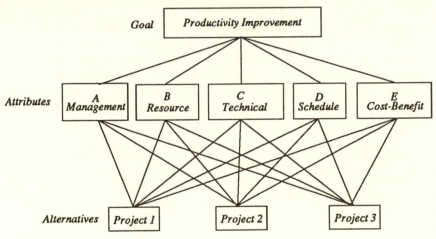

In a AHP hierarchy, the top level reflects the overall objective of the decision problem. The factors or attributes on which the final objective is dependent are listed at intermediate levels in the hierarchy. The lowest level in the hierarchy contains the competing alternatives through which the final objective might be achieved. After the hierarchy has been constructed, the decision maker must undertake a subjective prioritization procedure to determine the weight of each element at each level of the hierarchy. Pairwise comparisons are performed at each level to determine the relative importance of each element at that level with respect to each element at the next higher level in the hierarchy. In Figure 8-1, three alternate projects are to be considered. The projects are to be compared on the basis of the following five project attributes:

- Management support
- Resource requirements
- Technical merit
- Schedule effectiveness
- Cost-benefit ratio

The first step in the AHP procedure involves the relative weighting of the attributes with respect to the overall goal. The attributes are compared pairwise with respect to their respective importance to the goal. The pairwise comparison is done through subjective and/or quantitative evaluation by the decision maker(s). The matrix below shows the general layout for pairwise comparisons.

$$\mathbf{F} = \begin{bmatrix} r_{11} & r_{12} & \cdots & r_{1n} \\ r_{21} & r_{22} & \cdots & r_{2n} \\ \cdot & \cdot & \cdots & \cdot \\ \cdot & \cdot & \cdots & \cdot \\ \cdot & \cdot & \cdots & \cdot \\ r_{n1} & r_{n2} & \cdots & r_{nn} \end{bmatrix},$$

where
$\mathbf{F}$ = matrix of pairwise comparisons
r_{ij} = relative preference of the decision maker for i to j
$r_{ij} = 1/r_{ji}$
$r_{ii} = 1$.

If $r_{ik}/r_{ij} = r_{jk}$ for all i, j, k, then matrix $\mathbf{F}$ is said to be perfectly consistent. In order words, the transitivity of the preference orders is preserved. Thus, if factor A is preferred to factor B by a scale of 2 and factor A is preferred to factor C by a scale of 6, then factor B will be preferred to factor C by a factor of 3. That is:
$A = 2B$
$A = 6C$
Then, $2B = 6C \implies B = 3C$.

In practical situations, one cannot expect all pairwise comparison matrices to be perfectly consistent. Thus, a tolerance level for consistency was developed by Saaty. The tolerance level, referred to as consistency ratio, is acceptable if it is less then 0.10 (10%). Readers should refer to Saaty (1980) for further details on the procedure for computing the consistency ratio. If a consistency ratio is greater than 10%, the decision maker has the option of going back to reconstruct the comparison matrix or proceeding with the analysis with the recognition that he accepts the potential bias that may exist in the final decision. Once the pairwise comparisons matrix is complete, the relative weights of the factors included in the matrix are obtained from the estimate of the maximum eigenvector of the matrix. This is done by the expression below:

$$\hat{F}\hat{W} = \lambda_{max}\hat{W}$$

where:
F = estimation of the matrix of pairwise comparisons
λ_{max} = maximum eigenvector of F
$\hat{W}$ = estimation of W, vector of relative weights.

For the example in Figure 8-1, Table 8-1 shows the tabulation of the pairwise comparison of the project attributes.

Table 8-1. Pairwise Comparisons of Project Attributes

Attributes	Management	Resource	Technical	Schedule	Cost-Benefit
Management	1	1/3	5	6	5
Resource	3	1	6	7	6
Technical	1/5	1/6	1	3	1
Schedule	1/6	1/7	1/3	1	1/4
Cost-Benefit	1/5	1/6	1	4	1

Each of the attributes listed along the rows of the table is compared against each of the attributes listed in the columns. Each number in the body of the table indicates the degree of preference or importance of one attribute over the other on a scale of 1 to 9. A typical question that may be used to arrive at the relative rating is the following:

"With respect to the goal of improving productivity, do you consider project resource requirements to be more important than technical merit?"
"If so, how much more important is it on a scale of 1 to 9?"

Similar questions are asked iteratively until each attribute has been compared with each of the other attributes. For example, in Table 8-1, attribute B (resource requirements) is considered to be more important than attribute C (technical merit) with a degree of 6. In general, the numbers indicating the relative importance of the attributes are based on the following weight scales:

1: Equally important.
3: Weakly more important.
5: Strongly more important.
7: Very strongly more important.
9: Absolutely more important.

Intermediate ratings are used as appropriate to indicate intermediate levels of importance. If the comparison order is reversed (e.g., B versus A rather than A versus B), then the reciprocal of the importance rating is entered in the pairwise comparison table. The relative evaluation ratings in the table are converted to the matrix of pairwise comparisons shown in Table 8-2.

Table 8-2. Pairwise Comparisons of Project Attributes

Attributes	A	B	C	D	E
A	1.000	0.333	5.000	6.000	5.000
B	3.000	1.000	6.000	7.000	6.000
C	0.200	0.167	1.000	3.000	1.000
D	0.167	0.143	0.333	1.000	0.250
E	0.200	0.167	1.000	4.000	1.000
Column Sum	4.567	1.810	13.333	21.000	13.250

The entries in Table 8-2 are normalized to obtain Table 8-3. The normalization is done by dividing each entry in a column by the sum of all the entries in the column. For example, the first cell in Table 8-3 (i.e., 0.219) is obtained by dividing 1.000 by 4.567. Note that the sum of the normalized values in each attribute column is one.

Table 8-3. Normalized Matrix of Pairwise Comparisons

Attributes	A	B	C	D	E	Sum	Average
A: Management support	0.219	0.184	0.375	0.286	0.377	1.441	0.288
B: Resource reqmt.	0.656	0.551	0.450	0.333	0.454	2.444	0.489
C: Technical merit	0.044	0.094	0.075	0.143	0.075	0.431	0.086
D: Schedule effectiveness	0.037	0.077	0.025	0.048	0.019	0.206	0.041
E: Cost-Benefit ratio	0.044	0.094	0.075	0.190	0.075	0.478	0.096
Column Sum	1.000	1.000	1.000	1.000	1.000		1.000

The last column in Table 8-3 shows the normalized average rating associated with each attribute. This column represents the estimated maximum eigenvector of the matrix of pairwise comparisons. The first entry in the column (0.288) is obtained by dividing 1.441 by 5, which is the number of attributes. The averages represent the relative weights (between 0.0 and 1.0) of the attributes that are being evaluated. The relative weights show that attribute B (resource requirements) has the highest importance rating of 0.489. Thus, for this example, resource consideration is seen to be the most important factor in the selection of one of the three alternate projects. It should be emphasized that these attribute weights are valid only for the particular goal specified in the AHP model for the problem. If another goal is specified, the attributes would need to be reevaluated with respect to that new goal.

After the relative weights of the attributes are obtained, the next step is to evaluate the alternatives on the basis of the attributes. In this step, relative evaluation rating is obtained for each alternative with respect to each attribute. The procedure for the pairwise comparison of the alternatives is similar to the procedure for comparing the attributes. Table 8-4 presents the tabulation of the pairwise comparisons of the three alternatives with respect to attribute A (management support).

The table shows that Project 1 and Project 3 have the same level of management support. Examples of questions that may be used in obtaining the pairwise ratings of the alternatives are:

"Is Project 1 preferred to Project 2 with respect to management support?"
"What is the level of preference on a scale of 1 to 9?"

Table 8-4. Project Ratings Based on Management Support

Alternatives	Project 1	Project 2	Project 3
Project 1	1	1/3	1
Project 2	3	1	2
Project 3	1	1/2	1

It should be noted that the comparisons shown in Table 8-4 are valid only when management support of the projects is being considered. Separate pairwise comparisons of the project must be done whenever another attribute is being considered. Consequently, for our example, we would have five separate matrices of pairwise comparisons of the alternatives; one matrix for each attribute. Table 8-4 is the first of the five matrices. The other four are not shown. The normalization of the entries in Table 8-4 yields the following relative weights of the projects with respect to management support: Project 1 (0.21), Project 2 (0.55), and Project 3 (0.24). Table 8-5 shows a summary of the normalized relative ratings of the three projects with respect to each of the five attributes.

Table 8-5. Project Weights Based on Attributes

	Attributes				
	Management Support	Resource Requirements	Technical Merit	Schedule Effectiveness	C/B Ratio
Project 1	0.21	0.12	0.50	0.63	0.62
Project 2	0.55	0.55	0.25	0.30	0.24
Project 3	0.24	0.33	0.25	0.07	0.14

The attribute weights shown in Table 8-4 are combined with the weights in Table 8-5 to obtain the overall relative weights of the projects as shown below:

$$\alpha_j = \sum_i (w_i k_{ij}),$$

where:

α_j = *overall* weight for Project j

w_i = relative weight for attribute i

k_{ij} = rating (local weight) for Project j with respect to attribute i

$w_i k_{ij}$ = *global* weight of alternative j with respect to attribute i.

Table 8-6 shows the summary of the final AHP analysis for the example. The summary shows that Project 2 should be selected, since it has the highest overall weight of 0.484. Some commercial computer programs are available for AHP. *Expert Choice* and *NEWTECH* from Expert Choice, Inc., are two examples.

Table 8-6. Summary of AHP Evaluation of Three Projects

	Attributes					
	A $i{=}1$	B $i{=}2$	C $i{=}3$	D $i{=}4$	E $i{=}5$	
$w_i \Rightarrow$	0.288	0.489	0.086	0.041	0.096	
Project j			k_{ij}			α_j
Project 1	0.21	0.12	0.50	0.63	0.62	0.248
Project 2	0.55	0.55	0.25	0.30	0.24	0.484
Project 3	0.24	0.33	0.25	0.07	0.14	0.268
Column Sum	1.000	1.000	1.000	1.000	1.000	1.000

UTILITY APPROACH TO PROJECT SELECTION

The overall utility of a project can be measured in terms of both quantitative and qualitative factors. The vast body of literature available on utility theory makes the utility approach to project selection very appealing. This section presents an approach to project selection based on utility models. The approach fits an empirical utility function to each factor to be included in a multi-attribute selection model. The specific utility values (weights) that are obtained from the utility functions are used as the basis for selecting a project.

Utility Models

Utility theory is a branch of decision analysis that involves the building of mathematical models to describe the behavior of a decision maker when faced with making a choice among alternatives in the presence of risk. Several utility models are available in the literature (Keeney and Raiffa, 1976). In its simplest form, the utility of a composite set of outcomes of n decision factors is expressed in the general form below:

$$U(x) = U(x_1, x_2, ..., x_n),$$

where x_i = specific outcome of attribute X_i, $i = 1,2,...,n$ and $U(x)$ is the utility of the set of outcomes to the decision maker. The basic assumption of utility theory is that people make decisions with the objective of maximizing their *expected utility*. Drawing on an example presented by Park and Sharp-Bette (1990), we may consider a decision maker whose utility function with respect to project selection is represented by:

$$u(x) = 1 - e^{-0.0001x},$$

where x represents a measure of the benefit derived from a project. Benefit, in this sense, may be a combination of several factors (e.g., quality improvement, cost reduction, productivity improvement) that can be represented in dollar terms. Suppose this decision maker is faced with a choice between two project alternatives with benefits as specified below:

Project I: Probabilistic levels of project benefits

Benefit, x	-$10,000	$0	$10,000	$20,000	$30,000
Probability, $P(x)$	0.2	0.2	0.2	0.2	0.2

Project II: A definite benefit of $5,000

Assuming an initial benefit of zero and identical levels of required investment, the decision maker is required to choose between the two projects. For Project I, the expected utility is computed as shown below:

$$E[u(x)] = \sum u(x)\{P(x)\}.$$

Benefit, x	Utility, $u(x)$	$P(x)$	$u(x)P(x)$
-$10,000	-1.7183	0.2	-0.3437
$0	0	0.2	0
$10,000	0.6321	0.2	0.1264
$20,000	0.8647	0.2	0.1729
$30,000	0.9502	0.2	0.1900
		Sum	0.1456

Thus, $E[u(x)_1] = 0.1456$. For Project II, we have $u(x)_2 = u(\$5000) = 0.3935$. Consequently, the project providing the certain amount of \$5,000 is preferred to the more risky Project I even though Project I has a higher expected benefit of $\sum xP(x) = \$10,000$. A plot of the utility function used in the above example is presented in Figure 8-2.

Figure 8-2. Utility Function Illustrating Certainty Equivalent

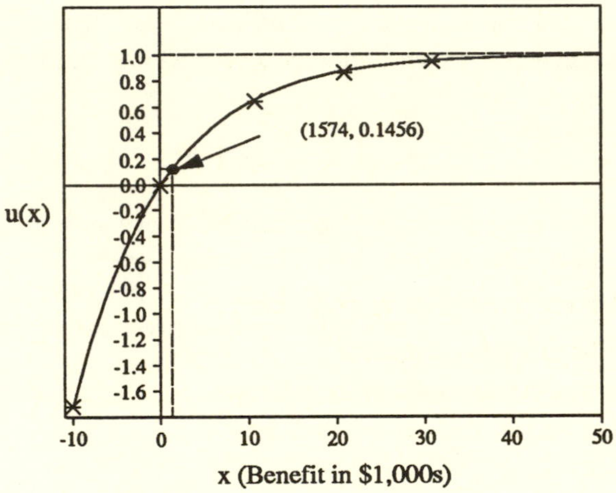

If the expected utility of 0.1456 is set equal to the decision maker's utility function, we obtain:

$$0.1456 = 1 - e^{-0.0001x^*},$$

which yields $x^* = \$1,574$, which is referred to as the *certainty equivalent (CE)* of Project I $(CE_I = 1574)$. The certainty equivalent of an alternative with variable outcomes is a *certain amount (CA)*, which a decision maker will consider to be desirable to the same degree as the variable outcomes of the alternative. In general, if *CA* represents the certain amount of benefit that can be obtained from Project II, then the criteria for making a choice between the two projects can be summarized as follows:

IF *CA* < \$1,754, select Project I
If *CA* = \$1,754, select either project
If *CA* > \$1,574, select Project II.

The key point in using utility theory for project selection is the proper choice of utility models. The sections that follow present two simple but widely used utility models: the *additive utility model* and the *multiplicative utility model*.

Additive Utility Model

The additive utility of a combination of outcomes of n factors $(X_1, X_2, \ldots, X_{n1})$ is expressed as:

$$U(x) = \sum_{i=1}^{n} U(x_i, \overline{x}_i^0)$$

$$= \sum_{i=1}^{n} k_i U_i(x_i),$$

where:

x_i = measured or observed outcome of attribute i

n = number of factors to be compared

x = combination of the outcomes of the n factors

$U_i(x_i)$ = utility of the outcome, x_i, for attribute i

$U(x)$ = combined utility of the set of outcomes, x

k_i = weight or scaling factor for attribute i $(0 < k_i < 1)$

X_i = variable notation for attribute i

x_i^0 = worst outcome of attribute i

x_i^* = best outcome of attribute i

$\overline{x}_i^0$ = set of worst outcomes for the complement of x_i.

$U(x_i, \overline{x}_i^0)$ = utility of the outcome of attribute i and the set of worst outcomes for
        the complement of attribute i

$k_i = U(x_i^*, \overline{x}_i^0)$

$\sum_{i=1}^{n} k_i = 1.0$ (required for the additive model).

For example, let A be a collection of four project attributes defined as: A = {Profit, Flexibility, Quality, Productivity}. Now, define X = {Profit, Flexibility} as a subset of A. Then, $\overline{X}$ is the complement of X defined as $\overline{X}$ = {Quality, Productivity}. An example of the comparison of two projects under the additive utility model is summarized in Table 8-7, which yields the following results:

$$U(x)_A = \sum_{i=1}^{n} k_i U_i(x_i) = .4(.95) + .2(.45) + .3(.35) + .1(.75) = 0.650$$

$$U(x)_B = \sum_{i=1}^{n} k_i U_i(x_i) = .4(.90) + .2(.98) + .3(.20) + .1(.10) = 0.626.$$

Since $U(x)_A > U(x)_B$, Project A is selected.

Table 8-7. Example for Additive Utility Model

Attribute (i)	k_i	Project A $U_i(x_i)$	Project B $U_i(x_i)$
Profitability	0.4	0.95	0.90
Flexibility	0.2	0.45	0.98
Quality	0.3	0.35	0.20
Throughput	0.1	0.75	0.10
	1.00		

Multiplicative Utility Model

Under the multiplicative utility model, the utility of a combination of outcomes of n factors $(X_1, X_2, \ldots, X_{nl})$ is expressed as:

$$U(x) = \frac{1}{C}\left[\prod_{i=1}^{n}(Ck_iU_i(x_i)+1) - 1\right],$$

where C and k_i are scaling constants satisfying the following conditions:

$$\prod_{i=1}^{n}(1+Ck_i) - C = 1.0$$

$$-1.0 < C < 0.0$$
$$0 < k_i < 1.$$

The other variables are as defined previously for the additive model. Using the multiplicative model for the data in Table 8-7 yields $U(x)_A = 0.682$ and $U(x)_B = 0.676$. Thus, Project A is selected.

Modeling of Project Utility Functions

An approach presented in this section for multi-attribute project selection is to fit an empirical utility function to each factor to be considered in the selection process. The specific utility values (weights) that are obtained from the utility functions may then be used in any of the available justification methodologies discussed by Canada and Sullivan (1989). One way to develop an empirical utility function for a project attribute is to plot the "best" and the "worst" outcomes expected from the attribute and then fit a reasonable approximation of the utility function using concave, convex, linear, S-shaped, or any other logical functional form.

Alternately, if an appropriate probability density function can be assumed for the outcomes of the attribute, then the associated cumulative distribution function may yield a reasonable approximation of the utility values between 0 and 1 for corresponding outcomes of the attribute. In that case, the cumulative distribution function gives an estimate of the cumulative utility associated with increasing levels of attribute outcome. Simulation experiments, histogram plotting, and goodness-of-fit tests may be used to determine the most appropriate density function for the outcomes of a given attribute. For example, the following five attributes are used to illustrate how utility values may be developed for a set of project attributes. The attributes are return on investment (ROI), productivity improvement, quality improvement, idle time reduction, and safety improvement.

Suppose we have historical data on the return on investment (ROI) for investing in a particular project. Assume that the recorded ROI values range from 0% to 40%. Thus, worst outcome is 0% and best outcome is 40%. A frequency distribution of the observed ROI values is developed and an appropriate probability density function (*pdf*) is fitted to the data. For our example, suppose the ROI is found to be exponentially distributed with a mean of 12.1%. That is,

$$f(x) = \begin{cases} \dfrac{1}{\beta}e^{-x/\beta}, & \text{if } x \geq 0 \\ 0, & \text{otherwise} \end{cases}$$

$$F(x) = \begin{cases} 1 - e^{-x/\beta}, & \text{if } x \geq 0 \\ 0, & \text{otherwise} \end{cases}$$

$$\approx U(x),$$

where $\beta = 12.1$. The probability density function and cumulative distribution function are shown graphically in Figure 8-3. The utility of any observed ROI within the applicable range may be read directly from the cumulative distribution function.

Figure 8-3. Estimated Utility Function for Project ROI

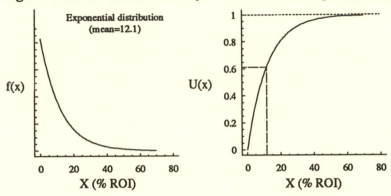

For the productivity improvement attribute, suppose it is found (based on historical data analysis) that the level of improvement is normally distributed with a mean of 10% and a standard deviation of 5%. That is,

$$f(x) \;=\; \frac{1}{\sqrt{2\pi\sigma}} e^{-\frac{1}{2}\left(\frac{x-\mu}{\sigma}\right)^2}, \quad -\infty < x < \infty,$$

where $\mu = 10$ and $\sigma = 5$. Since the normal distribution does not have a closed form expression for $F(x)$, $U(x)$ is estimated by plotting representative values based on the standard normal table. Figure 8-4 shows $f(x)$ and the estimated utility function for productivity improvement. The utility of productivity improvement may also be evaluated on the basis of cost reduction.

Suppose quality improvement is subjectively assumed to follow a beta distribution with shape parameters $\alpha = 1.0$ and $\beta = 2.9$. That is,

$$f(x) \;=\; \frac{\Gamma(\alpha+\beta)}{\Gamma(\alpha)\Gamma(\beta)} \cdot \frac{1}{(b-a)^{\alpha+\beta-1}} \cdot (x-a)^{\alpha-1} (b-x)^{\beta-1} \;,$$

for $a \le x \le b$ and $\alpha > 0$, $\beta > 0$.

where:
a = lower limit for the distribution
b = upper limit for the distribution
α, β are the shape parameters for the distribution.

As with the normal distribution, there is no closed form expression for $F(x)$ for the beta distribution. However, if either of the shape parameters is a positive integer, then a binomial expansion can be used to obtain $F(x)$. Figure 8-5 shows a plot of $f(x)$ and the estimated $U(x)$ for quality improvement due to the proposed project.

Figure 8-4. Utility Function for Productivity Improvement

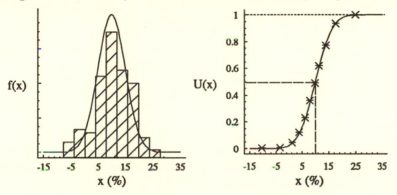

Figure 8-5. Utility Function for Quality Improvement

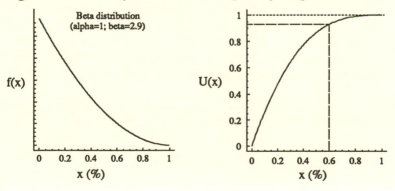

Based on work study observations, suppose idle time reduction is found to be best described by a lognormal distribution with a mean of 10% and standard deviation of 5%. This is represented as:

$$f(x) = \frac{1}{x\sqrt{2\pi\sigma^2}}e^{\left[\frac{-(\ln x - \mu)^2}{2\sigma^2}\right]} , \quad x > 0.$$

There is no closed form expression for $F(x)$. Figure 8-6 shows $f(x)$ and the estimated $U(x)$ for idle time reduction due to the project.

Figure 8-6. Utility Function for Idle Time Reduction

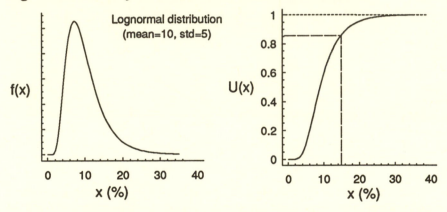

For the example, suppose safety improvement is assumed to have a previously known utility function defined as:

$$U_p(x) = 30 - \sqrt{400 - x^2} ,$$

where x represents percent improvement in safety. For the expression, the unscaled utility values range from 10 (for 0% improvement) to 30 (for 20% improvement). To express any particular outcome of an attribute i, x_i, on a scale of 0.0 to 1.0, it is expressed as a proportion of the range of best to worst outcomes as shown below:

$$X = \frac{x_i - x_i^0}{x_i^* - x_i^0} ,$$

where X = outcome expressed on a scale of 0.0 to 1.0

x_i = measured or observed raw outcome of attribute i

x_i^0 = worst raw outcome of attribute i

x_i^* = best raw outcome of attribute i.

The utility of the outcome may then be represented as $U(X)$ and read off the empirical utility curve. Using the above scaling approach, the utility function for safety improvement is scaled from 0.0 to 1.0. This is shown in Figure 8-7. The numbers within parentheses represent the scaled values.

Figure 8-7. Utility Function for Safety Improvement

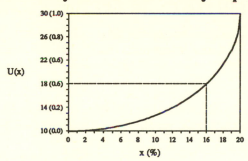

The respective utility values for the five attributes may be viewed as relative weights for comparing project alternatives. The utility values obtained from the modeled functions can be used in the additive and multiplicative utility models discussed earlier. For example, Table 8-8 shows a composite utility profile for a proposed project.

Table 8-8. Composite Utility for a Proposed Project

Attribute (i)	k_i	Value	$U_i(x_i)$
Return on Investment	0.30	12.1%	0.61
Productivity Improvement	0.20	10.0%	0.49
Quality Improvement	0.25	60.0%	0.93
Idle Time Reduction	0.15	15.0%	0.86
Safety Improvement	0.10	15.0%	0.40
	1.00		

Using the additive utility model, the *composite utility (CU)* of the project, based on the five attributes, is given by:

$$U(X) = \sum_{i=1}^{n} k_i U_i(x_i)$$

$$= .30(.61) + .20(.49) + .25(.93) + .15(.86) + .10(.40) = 0.6825.$$

This composite utility value may then be compared with the utilities of other projects. On the other hand, a single project may be evaluated independently on the basis of some minimum acceptable level of utility (MALU) desired by the decision maker. The criteria for evaluating a project based on MALU may be expressed by the following rule:

Project j is acceptable if its composite utility, U(X)ⱼ, is greater than MALU.
Project j is not acceptable if its composite utility, U(X)ⱼ, is less than MALU.

The utility of a project may be evaluated on the basis of its economic, operational, or strategic importance to a company. Utility functions can be incorporated into existing justification methodologies. For example, in the analytic hierarchy process, utility functions can be used to generate values that are used to evaluate the relative preference levels of attributes and alternatives. Utility functions can be used to derive component weights when comparing overall effectiveness of projects. Utility functions can generate descriptive levels of project performance as well as indicate the limits of project effectiveness, as shown by the *S-Curve* in Figure 8-8.

Figure 8-8. S-Curve Model Showing Limit of Project Utility

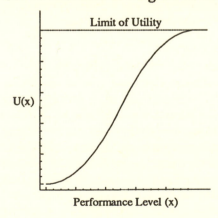

Performance Level (x)

SIMULATION APPROACH TO PROJECT ANALYSIS

Computer simulation is a tool that can be effectively utilized to enhance project planning, scheduling, and control. At any given time, only a small segment of a project network will be available for direct observation and analysis. The major portion of the project either will have been in the past or will be expected in the future. Such unobservable portions of the project can best be studied by simulation.

Using the historical information from previous segments of a project and the prevailing events in the project environment, projections can be made about future expectations of the project. Outputs of simulation can alert management to real and potential problems. The information provided by simulation can be very helpful in project selection decisions. Simulation-based project analysis may involve the following components:

- Activity time modeling
- Simulation of project schedule
- What-if analysis and statistical modeling
- Management decisions and sensitivity analysis

Project Schedule Simulation

Schedule simulation is the most obvious avenue for the application of simulation to project analysis. A computer program, named STARC (Badiru, 1991c), is used in this section to illustrate schedule simulation and analysis. STARC is a project planning aid. It simulates project networks and performs what-if analysis of projects involving probabilistic activity times and resource constraints. The output of STARC can serve as a decision aid for project selection. The effects of different activity time estimates and resource allocation options can be studied with STARC prior to actual project commitments.

ACTIVITY TIME MODELING

The true distribution of activity times will rarely be known. Even when known, the distribution may change from one type to another depending on who is performing the activity, where the activity is performed, and when the activity is performed. Simulation permits a project analyst to experiment with different activity time distributions. Commonly used activity time distributions are beta, normal, uniform, and triangular distributions. The results of simulation experiments can guide the analyst in developing definite action plans. Using the three PERT estimates *a* (optimistic time), *m* (most likely time), and *b* (pessimistic time), a beta distribution with appropriate shape parameters was modeled for each activity time. The details of the methodology for activity time modeling are presented by Badiru (1991c).

DURATION RISK COVERAGE FACTOR

This is a percentage factor (q) which provides a risk coverage for the potential inaccuracies in activity time estimates. A risk factor of 10% ($q=0.10$), for example, extends the range [a,b] of an activity's duration by 10% over the specified PERT time interval. An example of the extension of the activity duration interval is shown in Figure 8-9.

Figure 8-9. Risk Coverage Adjustment for Activity Time

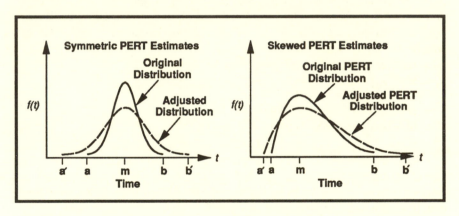

The extension of the range ensures that there is some probability (greater than zero) of generating activity times below the optimistic estimate or above the pessimistic estimate. Further details of the procedure for the PERT interval extension can be found in Badiru and Whitehouse (1989). If a risk coverage of 0% is specified, there is no interval extension and no adjustments are made to the PERT estimates. By comparison, a risk coverage of 100% yields an extended interval that is twice as wide as the original PERT interval. While a large extension of the PERT interval may be desirable for more simulation flexibility, it does result in a high variance for activity times.

RESOURCE ALLOCATION HEURISTIC

During a simulation run, STARC uses the composite allocation factor (CAF) presented by Badiru (1988a) to prioritize activities for resource allocation. The resource allocation process takes into account both the resource requirements and the variabilities in activity times. Activities with higher values of CAF are given priority during the resource allocation process.

Composite Allocation Factor (CAF)

For each activity i, CAF is a weighted and scaled sum of two components: RAF (resource allocation factor) and SAF (stochastic activity duration factor). It is computed as:

$$\text{CAF}_i = (w)\text{RAF}_i + (1-w)\text{SAF}_i,$$

where w is a weight between 0 and 1. RAF is defined for each activity i as:

$$\text{RAF}_i = \frac{1}{t_i}\sum_{j=1}^{N}\frac{r_{ij}}{R_j},$$

where
r_{ij} = number of resource type j units required by activity i
R_j = $\underset{j}{\text{Max}}\{r_{ij}\}$, maximum units of resource type j required

t_i = expected duration of activity i
N = number of resource types.

RAF is a measure of the expected resource consumption per unit time. In the case of multiple resource types, the different resource units are scaled to unit-less values by the y_j component in the formula for RAF. To eliminate the time-based unit, the following scaling method is used:

$$\text{scaled RAF}_i = \frac{\text{RAF}_i}{\text{Max}\{\text{RAF}_i\}}(100).$$

This yields unit-less values of RAF between 0 and 100. Resource-intensive activities will have larger magnitudes of RAF and, as such, will require a higher priority in the scheduling process. To incorporate the stochastic nature of activity times in a project schedule, SAF is defined for each activity i as:

$$\text{SAF}_i = t_i + \frac{s_i}{t_i},$$

where
t_i = expected duration for activity i
s_i = standard deviation of duration for activity i
s_i/t_i = coefficient of variation of the duration of activity i.

It should be noted that the formula for SAF has one component (t_i) with units of time and one component (s_i/t_i) with no units. It is, thus, necessary to scale each component as shown below:

$$\text{scaled} \quad t_i \quad = \quad \frac{t_i}{\text{Max}\{t_i\}}(50)$$

$$\text{scaled} \quad (s_i/t_i) \quad = \quad \frac{(s_i/t_i)}{\text{Max}\{s_i/t_i\}}(50).$$

When the above scaled components are plugged into the formula for SAF, we obtain unit-less scaled SAF values that are on a scale of 0 to 100. However, the 100 weight will be observed only if the same activity has the highest scaled t_i value and the highest scaled s_i/t_i value at the same time. Similarly, the 0 weight will be observed only if the same activity has the lowest scaled t_i value and the lowest scaled s_i/t_i value at the same time. The scaled values of SAF and RAF are now inserted in the formula for CAF as shown below:

$$\text{CAF}_i \quad = \quad (w)\{\text{scaled RAF}_i\} \quad + \quad (1-w)\{\text{scaled SAF}_i\}.$$

To ensure that the resulting CAF values range from 0 to 100, the following final scaling approach is applied:

$$\text{scaled CAF}_i \quad = \quad \frac{\text{CAF}_i}{\text{Max}\{\text{CAF}_i\}}(100) \, .$$

The above computations and scaling are done internally by STARC. It is on the basis of the magnitudes of CAF that an activity is assigned a priority for resource allocation in the project schedule.   Activities with larger values of CAF have higher priorities for resource allocation.   An activity that lasts longer, consumes more resources, and varies more in duration will have a larger magnitude of CAF. Such an activity is given priority for resources during the scheduling process. The weighting factor, w, is used to vary the relative weights assigned to the RAF and SAF components of CAF. Thus, the project planner has the option of assigning more weight to the resource requirement aspects of a project and less to the probabilistic time aspects and vice versa. The purpose of the analysis presented in this paper is to investigate the effects of different combinations of w and q on project duration.

CASE OF SINGLE RESOURCE CONSTRAINT

The sample project presented in Table 8-9 is used to illustrate project network simulation analysis using STARC. The project network is shown in Figure 8-10. The sample project consists of seven activities and one resource type. There are ten units of the resource available.

Table 8-9. Sample Project Data with Resource Constraint

Activity ID	Activity No.	Preceding Activities	*a, m, b* (in Months)	Resource Units Required
A	1	-	1, 2, 4	3
B	2	-	5, 6, 7	5
C	3	-	2, 4, 5	4
D	4	A	1, 3, 4	2
E	5	C	4, 5, 7	4
F	6	A	3, 4, 5	2
G	7	B, D, E	1, 2, 3	6

Figure 8-10. Project Network for Simulation Analysis

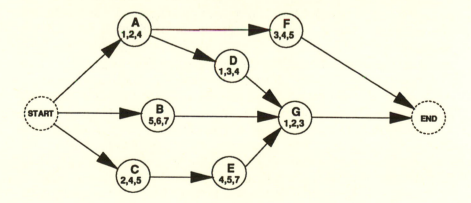

Simulation runs were made with $w = 0.5$ and $q = 0.15$. Figure 8-11 shows the output of the unconstrained PERT analysis. The expected duration (DUR), earliest start (ES), earliest completion (EC), latest start (LS), latest completion (LC), total slack (TS), free slack (FS), and critical path indicator (CRIT) are presented for each activity. The output shows that the PERT time without resource constraints is 11 months. Activities 3, 5, and 7 are on the critical path.

Figure 8-12 shows the simulated sample averages for the network parameters. The average project duration is 13.23 months (based on a simulation sample size of 100). With the resource constraints, the criticality indices for activities 1 through 7 are 0.97, 0.0, 0.03, 0.84, 0.03, 0.13, and 0.87, respectively. The criticality index of an activity is the probability that the activity will fall on the critical path. The simulation indicates that activity 1 is critical most of the time (probability of 0.97), whereas activity 2 is never on the critical path. It should be noted that the average ES, EC, LS, LC, TS, and FS will not necessarily match conventional PERT network calculations. Thus, we cannot draw a PERT network based on the sample averages. This is because each average value (e.g., MEAN EC) is computed from the results of several independent simulation runs. However, for each separate simulation run, the simulated outputs will fit conventional PERT network calculations.

Figure 8-13 shows a deadline analysis for a set of selected project deadlines. The second column in the figure presents the probabilities calculated analytically on the basis of the *central limit theorem*. The third column presents the sample probabilities based on simulation observations. The larger the number of simulation runs, the closer the analytical and sample probabilities will be. Suppose we are considering a contract deadline of 13 months; we might like to know the probability of being able to finish the project within that time frame. The simulation output indicates a simulated probability of 0.42 for completion within 13 months. So, the chances of finishing the project in 13 months are not so good. There is a very low probability (0.0114) of finishing the project in 11 months, which is the unconstrained PERT duration. A 15-month deadline (with a probability of 0.97) seems quite achievable for this project.

Figure 8-11. Unconstrained PERT Analysis

```
                    UNCONSTRAINED PERT SCHEDULE
  ACT.   DUR.     ES      EC      LS       LC      TS      FS    CRIT
-----------------------------------------------------------------------
   1     2.17    0.00    2.17    4.00     6.17    4.00    0.00  0.000
   2     6.00    0.00    6.00    3.00     9.00    3.00    3.00  0.000
   3     3.83    0.00    3.83    0.00     3.83    0.00    0.00  1.000
   4     2.83    2.17    5.00    6.17     9.00    4.00    4.00  0.000
   5     5.17    3.83    9.00    3.83     9.00    0.00    0.00  1.000
   6     4.00    2.17    6.17    7.00    11.00    4.83    0.00  0.000
   7     2.00    9.00   11.00    9.00    11.00    0.00    0.00  1.000
UNCONSTRAINED PERT PROJECT COMPLETION TIME =  11.00
```

Figure 8-12. Simulated Sample Averages

```
                       SIMULATED SAMPLE AVERAGES
  ACT.   MEAN    MEAN    MEAN    MEAN     MEAN     MEAN    MEAN   CRIT.
   #     DUR.    ES      EC      LS       LC       TS      FS    INDEX
-----------------------------------------------------------------------
   1     2.28    6.04    8.32    6.04     8.32    0.06    0.00   0.970
   2     6.04    0.00    6.04    5.17    11.21    5.17    5.11   0.000
   3     3.78    0.00    3.78    2.25     6.05    2.25    0.00   0.030
   4     2.81    8.32   11.13    8.40    11.21    0.14    0.08   0.840
   5     5.16    3.78    8.94    6.05    11.21    2.25    2.19   0.030
   6     4.01    8.32   12.33    9.22    13.23    0.91    0.00   0.130
   7     2.01   11.16   13.17   11.22    13.23    0.06    0.00   0.870
AVERAGE PROJECT DURATION =  13.23
```

Figure 8-13. Project Deadline Analysis

```
                      PROJECT DEADLINE ANALYSIS
    DEADLINE    CALCULATED PROBABILITY    OBSERVED PROBABILITY
    -------------------------------------------------------------
     10.00          0.0000                    0.0000
     11.00          0.0062                    0.0000
     12.00          0.0836                    0.0700
     13.00          0.3969                    0.4200
     14.00          0.8048                    0.7900
     15.00          0.9761                    0.9700
     16.00          0.9990                    1.0000
     17.00          1.0000                    1.0000
     18.00          1.0000                    1.0000
     19.00          1.0000                    1.0000
```

Figure 8-14 shows the simulation output with the shortest project duration of 11.07 months. If plotted on a Gantt chart, this schedule can serve as an operational schedule for the project, provided the simulated activity durations are realistic. It should be recalled, however, that 11 months has a low probability of being achieved.

Figure 8-14. Best Simulated Project Schedule

```
                    SHORTEST SIMULATED SCHEDULED
    ACT.  DUR.    ES      EC      LS      LC      TS      FS     CRIT
    ----------------------------------------------------------------------
     1    1.14   5.47    6.61    5.47    6.61    0.00    0.00   1.000
     2    5.47   0.00    5.47    4.31    9.78    4.31    4.16   0.000
     3    4.37   0.00    4.37    0.15    4.52    0.15    0.00   0.000
     4    2.04   6.61    8.65    7.74    9.78    1.13    0.98   0.000
     5    5.26   4.37    9.63    4.52    9.78    0.15    0.00   0.000
     6    4.46   6.61   11.07    6.61   11.07    0.00    0.00   1.000
     7    1.30   9.63   10.92    9.78   11.07    0.15    0.00   0.000
    SHORTEST SIMULATED PROJECT DURATION = 11.07
```

The project network data as organized by STARC are shown in Figure 8-15. The scaled CAF measures for the activities are presented in the last column. Activity 2 has the highest priority (100.0) for resource allocation when activities compete for resources. Activity 4 has the lowest priority (54.0).

Figure 8-15. Project Simulation Data

```
                PROJECT ACTIVITIES DATA
ACTIVITY        A      M      B     MEAN  VAR. RANGE  CAF
----------------------------------------------------------
   1           1.0    2.0    4.0    2.2   0.3   3.0   55.4
   2           5.0    6.0    7.0    6.0   0.1   2.0  100.0
   3           2.0    4.0    5.0    3.8   0.3   3.0   72.6
   4           1.0    3.0    4.0    2.8   0.3   3.0   54.0
   5           4.0    5.0    7.0    5.2   0.3   3.0   88.0
   6           3.0    4.0    5.0    4.0   0.1   2.0   66.6
   7           1.0    2.0    3.0    2.0   0.1   2.0   75.3
```

A frequency distribution histogram for the project duration based on the simulated sample is presented in Figure 8-16. As expected, the average project duration appears to be approximately normally distributed.

Figure 8-16. Histogram of Project Duration

```
FREQUENCY DISTRIBUTION HISTOGRAM FOR PROJECT DURATION
------------------------------------------------------
CLASS       INTERVAL        ELEMENTS
------------------------------------------------------
  1      11.01 to  11.24    3  *********
  2      11.24 to  11.46    0
  3      11.46 to  11.68    5  **************
  4      11.68 to  11.90    4  ************
  5      11.90 to  12.12    3  *********
  6      12.12 to  12.35    7  *********************
  7      12.35 to  12.57    9  ****************************
  8      12.57 to  12.79   11  **********************************
  9      12.79 to  13.01   14  ******************************************
 10      13.01 to  13.23    7  *********************
 11      13.23 to  13.46   11  **********************************
 12      13.46 to  13.68    8  ************************
 13      13.68 to  13.90    6  ******************
 14      13.90 to  14.12    4  ************
 15      14.12 to  14.35    1  ***
 16      14.35 to  14.57    2  ******
 17      14.57 to  14.79    2  ******
 18      14.79 to  15.01    2  ******
 19      15.01 to  15.23    0
 20      15.23 to  15.46    1  ***
```

Other portions of the simulation output (not shown) present the sample duration variances, sample duration ranges, and the parameters of the fitted beta distributions for the activity durations. The variances and sample ranges are useful for statistical or analytical purposes such as control charts for activity durations and resource loading diagrams.

What-If Analysis

In the safe environment of simulation, the parameters involved in developing project planning strategies may be varied to determine the resulting effects on the overall project structure. Resource allocation is a major area where simulation-based what-if analysis can be useful. For example, the project analyst can determine the lower and upper bounds for resource allocation in order to achieve the specified project goal. Statistical modeling techniques, such as regression analysis, may be employed to analyze simulation data and study the relationships between factors in the project. The effectiveness of different resource allocation heuristics can be tested in the simulation environment.

A review of the simulation output may indicate what type of what-if analysis may be performed. For example, a change was made in the sample project data. The number of available units of resource was increased from 10 to 15. With the additional resource units available, the average project duration was reduced from 13.23 months to 11.09 months. The deadline analysis revealed that the probability of finishing the project in 13 months increased from 0.42 to 0.9895 after the additional resource allocation.

Another revision of the project data was also analyzed. In this revision, the resource availability was decreased from 10 units to 7 units. It turns out that decreasing the resource availability by 3 units caused the average project duration to increase from 13.23 to 17.56 months. With the decreased resource availability, even a generous deadline of 17 months has a low probability (0.25) of being achieved. Using the revised simulation outputs, management can make better-informed decisions about resource allocation.

Sensitivity Analysis

Management decisions based on a simulation analysis will exhibit more validity than decisions based on absolute subjective reasoning. Simulation simplifies sensitivity analysis so that a project analyst can quickly determine what changes in project parameters will necessitate a change in management decisions. For example, with the information obtained from simulation, we can study the sensitivity of project completion times to changes in resource availability. The potential effects of decisions can be studied prior to making actual resource and time commitments.

MULTIPLE RESOURCE CONSTRAINTS

One additional resource type was added to the sample project data. Table 8-10 presents the revised project data. The simulation outputs for the revised project data are used for the statistical modeling presented later. Several simulation runs of the project network were made. Several combinations of w and q were investigated, and the average project durations were recorded for simulation sample size of 100. Table 8-11 presents a tabulation of the average project durations based on alternate values of w and q. Values of w range from 0.0 to 1.0, while values of q are 0, 0.1, 0.15, and 0.2.

Figure 8-17 shows a plot of the simulation output. Note that there is not much difference between the results for risk coverage levels (q) of 0%, 10%, 15%, and 20%. Thus, the project duration appears to be insensitive to risk coverage levels less than or equal to 20%. This preliminary conclusion was confirmed by a formal statistical test. There appear to be differences between the results for different levels of w between 0.0 and 1.0. The increase in the project durations for values of w greater than 0.9 are particularly significant. Thus, the project duration appears to be sensitive to changes in w. This observation was also confirmed by a formal statistical test.

Table 8-10. Project Data with Multiple Resource Constraints

Activity	Predecessor	a, m, b	Resources r_{i1}, r_{i2}
A	-	1, 2, 4	3, 0
B	-	5, 6, 7	5, 4
C	-	2, 4, 5	4, 1
D	A	1, 3, 4	2, 0
E	C	4, 5, 7	4, 3
F	A	3, 4, 5	2, 7
G	B, D, E	1, 2, 3	6, 2

Units of resource type 1 available = 10
Units of resource type 2 available = 15

Table 8-11. Simulation Output for Project Durations

w	Average Project Duration			
	q=0.0	q=0.1	q=0.15	q=0.2
0.0	12.98	13.06	13.12	12.60
0.1	13.56	12.88	13.33	13.05
0.2	13.56	12.96	13.03	13.30
0.3	13.48	13.18	12.90	13.03
0.4	13.33	13.08	13.13	13.02
0.5	12.69	13.34	12.51	13.63
0.6	12.76	13.12	13.11	12.91
0.7	13.33	12.10	12.65	12.50
0.8	13.01	13.09	13.45	13.19
0.9	13.25	13.42	13.04	13.23
1.0	16.89	16.77	16.71	17.03

w	q	f(w, q)	w	q	f(w, q)	w	q	f(w, q)	w	q	f(w, q)
0.0	0.0	12.98	0.0	0.1	13.06	0.0	0.15	13.12	0.0	0.20	12.60
0.1	0.0	13.56	0.1	0.1	12.88	0.1	0.15	13.33	0.1	0.20	13.05
0.2	0.0	13.56	0.2	0.1	12.96	0.2	0.15	13.03	0.2	0.20	13.30
0.3	0.0	13.48	0.3	0.1	13.18	0.3	0.15	12.90	0.3	0.20	13.03
0.4	0.0	13.33	0.4	0.1	13.08	0.4	0.15	13.13	0.4	0.20	13.02
0.5	0.0	12.69	0.5	0.1	13.34	0.5	0.15	12.51	0.5	0.20	13.63
0.6	0.0	12.76	0.6	0.1	13.12	0.6	0.15	13.11	0.6	0.20	12.91
0.7	0.0	13.33	0.7	0.1	12.10	0.7	0.15	12.65	0.7	0.20	12.50
0.8	0.0	13.01	0.8	0.1	13.09	0.8	0.15	13.45	0.8	0.20	13.19
0.9	0.0	13.25	0.9	0.1	13.42	0.9	0.15	13.04	0.9	0.20	13.23
1.0	0.0	16.89	1.0	0.1	16.77	1.0	0.15	16.71	1.0	0.20	17.03

Figure 8-17. Plot of Simulated Average Project Duration

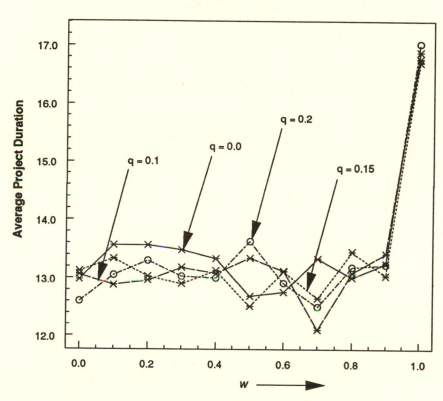

Regression Models

A multifactor analysis of variance (ANOVA) of the simulation results was conducted with STATGRAPHICS software. Two replicates of the simulation experiment were used in the analysis. The data shown in Table 8-11 is for the first replicate. The ANOVA results show that the effect of w on the project duration is significant at the 95% confidence level ($\alpha = 0.05$), while the effect of q is not significant. This confirms graphical observation in Figure 8-17. It was also found that the interaction effect of w and q is significant at the 95% confidence level. Even though q does not seem to have a direct effect on the project duration, it interacts with w to contribute to the observed differences in the project duration.

There is no significant difference between the levels of q for this particular project. There are, however, significant differences between the levels of w. Thus, for this illustrative project, more attention should be directed at the resource constraints. Since $w=1.0$ yielded the longest average project duration, it is concluded that the duration of this project is likely to increase when emphasis is placed on the resource considerations alone. Thus, variabilities in activity time durations should also be considered in the decision process. A simple linear regression model fitted to the data in Table 8-11 is presented below. The model gives a relationship between the average project duration, D, and w for the case when $q = 0.15$:

$$D_{(q=0.15)} \quad = \quad 12.565 \quad + \quad 1.5936w.$$

The R-squared value of 21.40% is very low. It is concluded that the simple linear model does not significantly account for variabilities in the project duration. A multiple linear regression model fitted to the data is presented below:

$$f(w, q) \quad = \quad 12.66 \quad + \quad 1.67w \quad - \quad 0.69q,$$

with a low R^2 value of 18.46%. The model is shown graphically in Figure 8-18. It is concluded that a multiple linear regression model also does not adequately represent the simulated data.

Figure 8-18. Plot of Multiple Linear Regression Model

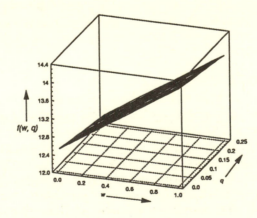

MULTIPLE NONLINEAR REGRESSION MODEL

A multiple nonlinear regression model is the next logical option in the analysis of the simulation output. We will investigate a multiple nonlinear regression model of the form:

$$f(w, q) = \beta_0 + \beta_1 w^{\alpha_1} + \beta_2 q^{\alpha_2} + \varepsilon,$$

where β_i and α_i are appropriate model parameters and ε is the error term. The simulated data in Table 8-11 is once again used for the modeling. The following nonlinear model was obtained:

$$f(w, q) = 13.17 + 3.80w^{28.37} - 0.20q^{-0.37},$$

with a high R^2 value of 93.34%. Most of the variabilities in average project duration are explained by the terms in the nonlinear model. A plot of the response surface for the fitted model is shown in Figure 8-19. Note that w accounts for most of the fit in this particular nonlinear model. This confirms the visual assessment obtained earlier from the plot of the simulated data. Alternate nonlinear models were investigated. The alternate models were of the forms presented below:

$$f(w, q) = \beta_0 + \beta_1 w^{\alpha_1} + \beta_2 q^{\alpha_2} + \beta_3 w^{\alpha_3} q^{\alpha_4} + \varepsilon$$

$$f(w, q) = \beta_0 + \beta_1 w + \beta_2 q + \beta_3 w^{\alpha_1} + \beta_4 q^{\alpha_2} + \beta_5 w^{\alpha_3} q^{\alpha_4} + \varepsilon.$$

These did not yield any feasible model fit. Besides, these alternate models contain too many parameters. Since the objective is to keep the fitted model as parsimonious in parameters as possible, the alternate models were rejected without further investigation. For practical applications, a model must be simple enough to appeal to decision makers.

APPLICATION OF THE REGRESSION MODEL

Now that the nonlinear model has been fitted and validated, the next step is the application of the model to project decision analysis. Suppose the ABC classification under a Pareto distribution analysis has been used to determine the relative effects of different factors on the complexity of resource allocation in a large project. Two factors have been identified for analysis. The first factor (factor A) is defined as the "rate of multiple resource consumption per unit time." The second factor (factor B) is defined as "variabilities in task durations." Using the ABC classification, management has assigned a weight of 80% to factor A and 20% to factor B. These relative weights will be used to make resource allocation plans for the project. A project analyst has been asked to analyze the potential

Figure 8-19. Multiple Nonlinear Regression Model

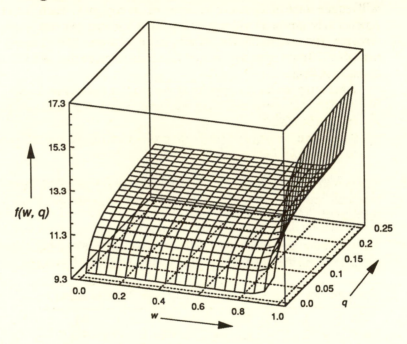

effects of the relative weights on the expected number of months it will take to complete the project. Using the fitted model, the analyst would set $w = 0.8$ and $q = 0.20$ and estimate the expected project duration as:

$$E[\text{Duration}] \quad = \quad 13.17 \quad + \quad 3.80(0.8)^{28.37} \quad - \quad 0.20(0.20)^{-0.37}$$

$$= \quad 12.81 \quad \text{months.}$$

Management would then review this information and probably incorporate it with other qualitative considerations before making final resource allocation decisions. The analyst may try alternate combinations of the values of w and q before making a recommendation to management. If properly used for project planning and control, simulation can yield significant benefits involving better product quality, improved resource utilization, higher project productivity, and increased probability of meeting due dates.

EXERCISES

8-1. A multinational company is considering a new manufacturing project which will require some of the scarce resources of the company. Each unit of the product to be produced will require 3 units of resource type one, 4 units of resource type two, and 5 units of resource type three. The company has available 120 units of resource one, 152 units of resource two, and 150 units of resource three.
   a) What is the maximum quantity of this product that can be made?
   b) If a $5 profit is expected from each unit, what is the maximum profit that can be made?
   c) If the cost of tooling up to make the product is $100, should this project be selected for funding by the company? Explain.

8-2. Develop an analytic hierarchy process model for the goal of selecting an industrial development project. List and justify the important factors to be considered.

8-3. The following are evaluation ratings of how well each of three project alternatives satisfies each of four attributes on a scale of 0 to 100.

Attribute	Rank	Alternative 1	Alternative 2	Alternative 3
A	1	25	55	80
B	2	15	73	70
C	3	70	10	70
D	4	85	62	24

Use the information presented to determine which of the projects should be selected.

8-4. Discuss how you might use simulation analysis to evaluate project alternatives.

8-5. Using a quantitative example, show how a project analyst might use learning curve analysis as a decision aid for project selection.

8-6. Discuss the differences between project feasibility analysis and project selection analysis.

8-7. If you have access to an appropriate simulation software package, construct and run a simulation experiment to verify the results of the simulation analysis presented in this chapter.

8-8. Develop an approach to using quantitative parameters to generate the pairwise ratings in an AHP comparison matrix. The objective here is to use quantitative measures rather than subjective ratings to compare the factors and alternatives involved in the analysis.

8-9. Discuss why it is not prudent to select a project on the basis of economic measures alone.

8-10. Using an appropriate mathematical procedure, find the eigenvector of the matrix below and compare your result to the vector of attribute weights presented in Table 8-3.

$$
\begin{vmatrix}
1.000 & 0.333 & 5.000 & 6.000 & 5.000 \\
3.000 & 1.000 & 6.000 & 7.000 & 6.000 \\
0.200 & 0.167 & 1.000 & 3.000 & 1.000 \\
0.167 & 0.143 & 0.333 & 1.000 & 0.250 \\
0.200 & 0.167 & 1.000 & 4.000 & 1.000
\end{vmatrix}
$$

APPENDIX
STANDARD NORMAL TABLE

z	.00	.01	.02	.03	.04	.05	.06	.07	.08	.09
.0	.5000	.5040	.5080	.5120	.5160	.5199	.5239	.5279	.5319	.5359
.1	.5398	.5438	.5478	.5517	.5557	.5596	.5636	.5675	.5714	.5753
.2	.5793	.5832	.5871	.5910	.5948	.5987	.6026	.6064	.6103	.6141
.3	.6179	.6217	.6255	.6293	.6331	.6368	.6406	.6443	.6480	.6517
.4	.6554	.6591	.6628	.6664	.6700	.6736	.6772	.6808	.6844	.6879
.5	.6915	.6950	.6985	.7019	.7054	.7088	.7123	.7157	.7190	.7224
.6	.7257	.7291	.7324	.7357	.7389	.7422	.7454	.7486	.7517	.7549
.7	.7580	.7611	.7642	.7673	.7704	.7734	.7764	.7794	.7823	.7852
.8	.7881	.7910	.7939	.7967	.7995	.8023	.8051	.8078	.8106	.8133
.9	.8159	.8186	.8212	.8238	.8264	.8289	.8315	.8340	.8365	.8389
1.0	.8413	.8438	.8461	.8485	.8508	.8531	.8554	.8577	.8599	.8621
1.1	.8643	.8665	.8686	.8708	.8729	.8749	.8770	.8790	.8810	.8830
1.2	.8849	.8869	.8888	.8907	.8925	.8944	.8962	.8980	.8997	.9015
1.3	.9032	.9049	.9066	.9082	.9099	.9115	.9131	.9147	.9162	.9177
1.4	.9192	.9207	.9222	.9236	.9251	.9265	.9279	.9292	.9306	.9319
1.5	.9332	.9345	.9357	.9370	.9382	.9394	.9406	.9418	.9429	.9441
1.6	.9452	.9463	.9474	.9484	.9495	.9505	.9515	.9525	.9535	.9545
1.7	.9554	.9564	.9573	.9582	.9591	.9599	.9608	.9616	.9625	.9633
1.8	.9641	.9649	.9656	.9664	.9671	.9678	.9686	.9693	.9699	.9706
1.9	.9713	.9719	.9726	.9732	.9738	.9744	.9750	.9756	.9761	.9767
2.0	.9772	.9778	.9783	.9788	.9793	.9798	.9803	.9808	.9812	.9817
2.1	.9821	.9826	.9830	.9834	.9838	.9842	.9846	.9850	.9854	.9857
2.2	.9861	.9864	.9868	.9871	.9875	.9878	.9881	.9884	.9887	.9890
2.3	.9893	.9896	.9898	.9901	.9904	.9906	.9909	.9911	.9913	.9916
2.4	.9918	.9920	.9922	.9925	.9927	.9929	.9931	.9932	.9934	.9936
2.5	.9938	.9940	.9941	.9943	.9945	.9946	.9948	.9949	.9951	.9952
2.6	.9953	.9955	.9956	.9957	.9959	.9960	.9961	.9962	.9963	.9964
2.7	.9965	.9966	.9967	.9968	.9969	.9970	.9971	.9972	.9973	.9974
2.8	.9974	.9975	.9976	.9977	.9977	.9978	.9979	.9979	.9980	.9981
2.9	.9981	.9982	.9982	.9983	.9984	.9984	.9985	.9985	.9986	.9986
3.0	.9987	.9987	.9987	.9988	.9988	.9989	.9989	.9989	.9990	.9990
3.1	.9990	.9991	.9991	.9991	.9992	.9992	.9992	.9992	.9993	.9993
3.2	.9993	.9993	.9994	.9994	.9994	.9994	.9994	.9995	.9995	.9995
3.3	.9995	.9995	.9995	.9996	.9996	.9996	.9996	.9996	.9996	.9997
3.4	.9997	.9997	.9997	.9997	.9997	.9997	.9997	.9997	.9997	.9998

BIBLIOGRAPHY

Adrian, James J., *Quantitative Methods in Construction Management*, Elsevier Publishing Co., New York, 1973.

Afiesimama, Boma T., "Aggregate Manpower Requirements for Strategic Project Planning," *Computers and Industrial Engineering*, Vol. 12, No. 4, 1987, pp. 249-262.

Akao, Y. and T. Asaka, eds., *Quality Function Deployment*, Productivity, Inc., Cambridge, MA, 1990.

Alchian, Armen, "Reliability of Progress Curves in Airframe Production," *Econometrica*, Vol. 31, No. 4, 1963, pp. 679-693.

Anthonisse, J. M., K. M. Van Hee, and J. K. Lenstra, "Resource-Constrained Project Scheduling: An International Exercise in DSS Development," *Decision Support Systems*, Vol. 4, No. 2, 1988, pp. 249-257.

Aquilano, N. J. and D. E. Smith, "A Formal Set of Algorithms for Project Scheduling with Critical Path Method - Material Requirements Planning," *Journal of Operations Management*, Vol. 1, No. 2, 1980, pp. 57-67.

Arinze, Bay and F. Y. Partovi, "A Knowledge-Based Decision Support System for Project Management," *Computers and Operations Research*, Vol. 19, No. 5, 1992, pp. 321-334.

Assad, A. A. and E. A. Wasil, "Project Management Using A Microcomputer," *Computers and Operations Research*, Vol. 13, No. 2/3, 1986, pp. 231-260.

Assad, Michael G. and G. P. J. Pelser, "Project Management: A Goal-Directed Approach," *Project Management Quarterly*, June 1983, pp. 49-58.

Badiru, Adedeji B., *Expert Systems Applications in Engineering and Manufacturing*, Prentice-Hall, Englewood Cliffs, NJ, 1992a.

Badiru, Adedeji B., "Computational Survey of Univariate and Multivariate Learning Curve Models," *IEEE Transactions on Engineering Management*, Vol. 39, No. 2, May 1992b, pp. 176-188.

Badiru, Adedeji B., *Project Management Tools for Engineering and Management Professionals*, Industrial Engineering and Management Press, Norcross, GA, 1991a.

Badiru, Adedeji B., "Manufacturing Cost Estimation: A Multivariate Learning Curve Approach," *Journal of Manufacturing Systems*, Vol. 10, No. 6, 1991b, pp. 431-441.

Badiru, Adedeji B., "A Simulation Approach to PERT Network Analysis," *Simulation*, Vol. 57, No. 4, October 1991c, pp. 245-255.

Badiru, Adedeji B., "STARC 2.0: An Improved PERT Network Simulation Tool," *Computers and Industrial Engineering*, Vol. 20, No. 3, 1991d, pp. 389-400.

Badiru, Adedeji B., "A Management Guide to Automation Cost Justification," *Industrial Engineering*, Vol. 22, No. 2, Feb. 1990a, pp. 26-30.

Badiru, Adedeji B., "A Systems Approach to Total Quality Management," *Industrial Engineering*, Vol. 22, No. 3, March 1990b, pp. 33-36.

Badiru, Adedeji B., *Project Management in Manufacturing and High Technology Operations*, John Wiley & Sons, New York, 1988a.

Badiru, Adedeji B., "Cost-Integrated Network Planning Using Expert Systems," *Project Management Journal*, Vol. 19, No. 2, April 1988b, pp. 59-62.

Badiru, Adedeji B., "Towards the Standardization of Performance Measures for Project Scheduling Heuristics," *IEEE Transactions on Engineering Management*, Vol. 35, No. 2, May 1988c, pp. 82-89.

Badiru, Adedeji B., "Graphic Evaluation of Amortization Schedules," *Industrial Engineering*, Vol. 20, No. 9, September 1988d, pp. 18-22.

Badiru, Adedeji B., "Communication, Cooperation, Coordination: The Triple C of Project Management," in *Proceedings of 1987 IIE Spring Conference*, Washington, DC, May 1987, pp. 401-404.

Badiru, Adedeji B., "Process Capability Analysis on a Microcomputer," *Softcover Software*, Industrial Engineering and Management Press, Norcross, GA, 1985, pp. 7-14.

Badiru, Adedeji B. and David Russell, "Minimum Annual Project Revenue Requirement Analysis," *Computers and Industrial Engineering*, Vol. 13, Nos. 1-4, 1987, pp. 366-370.

Badiru, Adedeji B. and James R. Smith, "Setting Tolerances by Computer Simulation," *Proceedings of IIE Fall Conference*, Cincinnati, OH, November 1982, pp. 284-288.

Badiru, Adedeji B. and Gary E. Whitehouse, *Computer Tools, Models, and Techniques for Project Management*, TAB Books, Inc., Blue Ridge Summit, PA, 1989.

Baker, N. R. and W. H. Pound, "Project Selection: Where We Stand," *IEEE Transactions on Engineering Management*, Vol. EM-11, 1964, pp. 124-134.

Banerjee, B. P., "Single Facility Sequencing with Random Execution Times," *Operations Research*, Vol. 13, May-June 1965, pp. 358-364.

Baran, Robert H., "A Case Study in the Allocation of Research Funds," *Systems and Decisions*, Vol. 1, No. 1, 1988, pp. 1-11.

Barber, T. J., J. T. Boardman, and N. Brown, "Practical Evaluation of an Intelligent Knowledge-Based Project Control System," *IEE Proceedings*, Vol. 137, Part A, No. 1, January 1990, pp. 35-51.

Batson, Robert G., "Critical Path Acceleration and Simulation in Aircraft Technology Planning," *IEEE Transactions of Engineering Management*, Vol. EM34, No. 4, 1987, pp. 244-251.

Bazaraa, Mokhtar S. and John J. Jarvis, *Linear Programming and Network Flows*, John Wiley & Sons, New York, 1977.

Bedworth, David D., *Industrial Systems: Planning, Analysis and Control*, The Ronald Press Co., New York, 1973.

Bedworth, D. D. and James E. Bailey, *Integrated Production Control Systems: Management, Analysis, Design*, John Wiley & Sons, New York, 1982.

Beimborn, E. A. and W. A. Garvey, "The Blob Chart," *Industrial Engineering*, December 1972, pp. 17-19.

Belkaoui, Ahmed, *The Learning Curve*, Quorum Books, Westport, CT, 1986.

Bell, Colin E., "Maintaining Project Networks in Automated Artificial Intelligence Planning," *Management Science*, Vol. 35, No. 10, 1989, pp. 1192-1214.

Bellmore, M. and G. L. Nemhauser, "The Travelling Salesman Problem: A Survey," *Operations Research*, Vol. 16, 1968, pp. 538-558.

Bemis, John C., "A Model for Examining the Cost Implications of Production Rate," *Concepts: The Journal of Defense Systems Acquisition Management*, Vol. 4, No. 2, 1981, pp. 84-94.

Bent, James A. and Albert Thumann, *Project Management for Engineering and Construction*, The Fairmont Press, Inc., Lilburn, GA, 1989.

Bergen, S. A., *RandD Management: Managing Projects and New Products*, Basil Blackwell, Inc., Cambridge, MA, 1990.

Berman, E. B., "Resource Allocation in a PERT Network Under Continuous Activity Time-Cost Functions," *Management Science*, Vol. 10, No. 4, July 1964, pp. 734-745.

Bey, Roger B., Robert H. Doersch, and James H. Patterson, "The Net Present Value Criterion: Its Impact on Project Scheduling," *Project Management Quarterly*, June 1981, pp. 223-233.

Bidanda, Bopaya, "Techniques to Assess Project Feasibility," *Project Management Journal*, Vol. 20, No. 2, June 1989, pp. 5-10.

Blanchard, Frederick L., *Engineering Project Management*, Marcel Dekker, New York, 1990.

Boctor, Fayez F., "Some Efficient Multi-Heuristic Procedures for Resource-Constrained Project Scheduling," *European Journal of Operational Research*, Vol. 49, 1990, pp. 3-13.

Brand, J. D., W. L. Meyer, and L. R. Shaffer, "The Resource Scheduling Method for Construction," *Civil Engineering Studies Report*, No. 5, University of Illinois, 1964.

Brooks, George H. and Charles R. White, "An Algorithm for Finding Optimal or Near Optimal Solutions to the Production Scheduling Problem," *Journal of Industrial Engineering*, January-February 1965, pp. 34-40.

Brown, Donald E. and A. R. Spillane, "A Knowledge-Based Design Aid for Superheaters Employing Pseudo-Random Search," *Journal of Operational Research Society*, Vol. 40, No. 6, 1989, pp. 539-550.

Browne, Jimmie, J. Harhen, and J. Shivnan, *Production Management Systems: A CIM Perspective*, Addison-Wesley Publishing Co., New York, 1988.

Buffa, E. S. and J. S. Dyer, *Management Science and Operations Research: Model Formulation and Solution Methods*, John Wiley, New York, 1977.

Burgess, A. R. and J. B. Killebrew, "Variation in Activity Level on a Cyclic Arrow Diagram," *Journal of Industrial Engineering*, March-April, 1962.

Bussey, Lynn E. and Ted G. Eschenbach, *The Economic Analysis of Industrial Projects*, 2ed, Prentice-Hall, Englewood Cliffs, NJ, 1992.

Camm, Jeffrey D., James R. Evans, and Norman K. Womer, "The Unit Learning Curve Approximation of Total Cost," *Computers and Industrial Engineering*, Vol. 12, No. 3, 1987, pp. 205-213.

Canada, John R. and William G. Sullivan, *Economic and Multiattribute Evaluation of Advanced Manufacturing Systems*, Prentice-Hall, Englewood Cliffs, NJ, 1989.

Carraway, Robert L. and R. L. Schmidt, "An Improved Discrete Dynamic Programming Algorithm for Allocating Resources Among Interdependent Projects," *Management Science*, Vol. 37, No. 9, 1991, pp. 1195-1200.

Chapman, C. B., "The Optimal Allocation of Resources to a Variable Timetable," *Operational Research Quarterly*, Vol. 21, No. 1, March 1970, pp. 81-90.

Chapman, C. B., D. F. Cooper, and M. J. Page, *Management for Engineers*, John Wiley & Sons, New York, 1987.

Charnes, A., W. W. Cooper, and G. L. Thompson, "Critical Path Analyses Via Chance Constrained and Stochastic Programming," *Operations Research*, Vol. 12, May-June 1964, pp. 460-470.

Chase, Richard B. and Nicholas J. Aquilano, *Production Operations Management*, Revised Edition, Richard D. Irwin, New York, 1977.

Chiang, Min K. and S. A. Zenios, "On the Use of Expert Systems in Network Optimization: With An Application to Matrix Balancing," *Annals of Operations Research*, Vol. 20, 1989, pp. 111-140.

Clark, C. E., "The Optimum Allocation of Resources Among the Activities of a Network," *Journal of Industrial Engineering*, Vol. 12, January-February 1961, pp. 11-17.

Cleland, David I. and W. R. King, *Systems Analysis and Project Management*, 3ed, McGraw-Hill, New York, 1983.

Cleland, David I. and W. R. King, eds., *Project Management Handbook*, Van Nostrand Reinhold Co., New York, 1983.

Cleland, David I., *Project Management: Strategic Design and Implementation*, TAB Professional and Reference Books, New York, 1990.

Cleland, David I., "Strategic Issues in Project Management," *Project Management Journal*, Vol. 20, No. 1, March 1989, pp. 31-39.

Cleland, David I. and Karen M. Bursic, *Strategic Technology Management*, American Management Association, New York, 1992.

Cleland, David I. and Dundar F. Kocaoglu, *Engineering Management*, McGraw-Hill, New York, 1981.

Cohen, William A., *High-Tech Management*, John Wiley & Sons, New York, 1986.

Cooper, D. F., "Heuristics for Scheduling Resource-Constrained Projects: An Experimental Investigation," *Management Science*, Vol. 22, July 1976, pp. 1186-1194.

Cooper, Dale and Chris Chapman, *Risk Analysis for Large Projects: Models, Methods, and Cases*, John Wiley, New York, 1987.

Cooper, Leon and David Steinberg, *Methods and Applications of Linear Programming*, W.B. Saunders Co., Philadelphia, 1974.

Cox, Larry W. and J. S. Gansler, "Evaluating the Impact of Quantity, Rate, and Competition," *Concepts: The Journal of Defense Systems Acquisition Management*, Vol. 4, No. 4, 1981, pp. 29-53.

Coyle, R. G., "A Systems Approach to the Management of a Hospital for Short-Term Patients," *Socio-Econ Planning Science*, Vol. 18, No. 4, 1984, pp. 219-226.

Crandall, Keith C., "Project Planning with Precedence Lead/Lag Factors," *Project Management Quarterly*, Vol. 4, No. 3, Sept. 1973, pp. 18-27.

Dallenback, H. and J. George, *Introduction to Operations Research Techniques*, Allyn and Bacon, Inc., Boston, 1978.

Dantzig, George B., *Linear Programming and Extensions*, Princeton University Press, Princeton, NJ, 1963.

Dar-El, E. M. and Yigal Tur, "A Multi-Resource Project Scheduling Algorithm," *AIIE Transactions*, Vol. 9, March 1977, pp. 44-52.

Davies, C., A. Demb, and R. Espejo, *Organization for Project Management*, John Wiley, New York, 1979.

Davies, E. M., "An Experimental Investigation of Resource Allocation in Multiactivity Projects," *Operational Research Quarterly*, Vol. 24, No. 4, 1974, pp. 587-591.

Davis, E. W. and J. W. Patterson, "A Comparison of Heuristic and Optimum Solutions in Resource-Constrained Project Scheduling," *Management Science*, Vol. 21, April 1975, pp. 944-955.

Davis, Edward W., "Project Network Summary Measures and Constrained-Resource Scheduling," *AIIE Transactions*, Vol. 7, No. 2, June 1975, pp. 132-142.

Davis, Edward W., "Resource Allocation in Project Network Models: A Survey," *Journal of Industrial Engineering*, April 1966, pp. 177-188.

Davis, Edward W., ed., *Project Management: Techniques, Applications, and Managerial Issues*, 2ed, Industrial Engineering and Management Press, Norcross, GA, 1983.

Davis, Edward W. and G. E. Heidorn, "An Algorithm for Optimal Project Scheduling Under Multiple Resource Constraints," *Management Science*, Vol. 17, No. 12, 1971, pp. B803-B814.

DeGarmo, E. Paul, William G. Sullivan, and James A. Bontadelli, *Engineering Economy*, 8ed, Macmillan, New York, 1988.

Dhillon, B. S., *Engineering Management: Concepts, Procedures and Models*, Technomic Publishing Co., Lancaster, PA, 1987.

Dinsmore, Paul, C., *Human Factors in Project Management*, rev. ed., American Management Association, New York, 1990.

DOE, *Cost and Schedule Control Systems: Criteria for Contract Performance Measurement: Work Breakdown Structure Guide*, U.S. Department of Energy, Office of Project and Facilities Management, Washington, DC, 1981.

Doersch, R. H. and J. H. Patterson, "Scheduling a Project to Maximize Its Present Value: A Zero-One Programming Approach," *Management Science*, Vol. 23, No. 8, 1977, pp. 882-889.

Donaldson, William A., "The Estimation of the Mean and Variance of A 'PERT' Activity Time," *Operations Research*, Vol. 13, 1965, pp. 383-387.

Dougherty, Edward R., *Probability and Statistics for the Engineering, Computing, and Physical Sciences*, Prentice-Hall, Englewood Cliffs, NJ, 1990.

Drexl, Andreas, "Scheduling of Project Networks by Job Assignment," *Management Science*, Vol. 37, No. 12, 1991, pp. 1590-1602.

Dreyfus, Stuart E., "An Appraisal of Some Shortest Path Algorithms," *Operations Research*, Vol. 17, 1969, 395-412.

Drigani, Fulvio, *Computerized Project Control*, Marcel Dekker, Inc., New York, 1989.

Dumbleton, J. H., *Management of High-Technology Research and Development*, Elsevier, New York, 1986.

East, E. William and Jeffrey G. Kirby, *A Guide to Computerized Project Scheduling*, Van Nostrand Reinhold, New York, 1989.

Eck, R., *Operations Research for Business*, Wadsworth, Belmont, CA, 1976.

Elmaghraby, Salah E., *Activity Networks: Project Planning and Control by Network Models*, John Wiley & Sons, New York, 1977.

Elmaghraby, Salah E. and Willy S. Herroelen, "On The Measurement of Complexity in Activity Networks," *European Journal of Operations Research*, Vol. 5, 1980, pp. 223-234.

Elmaghraby, Salah E. and P. S. Pulat, "Optimal Project Compression with Due-Dated Events," *Naval Research Logistics Quarterly*, Vol. 26, No. 2, 1979, pp. 331-348.

Elmaghraby, Salah E., "Project Bidding Under Deterministic and Probabilistic Activity Durations," *European Journal of Operational Research*, Vol. 49, 1990, pp. 14-34.

Elmaghraby, Salah E. and Willy S. Herroelen, "The Scheduling of Activities to Maximize the Net Present Value of Projects," *European Journal of Operational Research*, Vol. 49, 1990, pp. 35-49.

Elsayed, E. A., "Algorithms for Project Scheduling with Resource Constraints," *International Journal of Production Research*, Vol. 20, No. 1, 1982, pp. 95-103.

Fabrycky, Wolter J. and B. S. Blanchard, *Life-Cycle Cost and Economic Analysis*, Prentice-Hall, Englewood Cliffs, NJ, 1991.

Farid, Foad and R. Kangari, "A Knowledge-Based System for Selecting Project Management Microsoftware Packages," *Project Management Journal*, Vol. 22, No. 3, 1991, pp. 55-61.

Farnum, N. R. and L. W. Stanton, "Some Results Concerning the Estimation of Beta Distribution Parameters in PERT," *Journal of Operational Research Society*, Vol. 38, 1987, pp. 287-290.

Fendley, L. G., "Toward the Development of a Complete Multiproject Scheduling System," *Journal of Industrial Engineering*, Vol. 19, October 1968, pp. 505-515.

Fisher, Marshall L., "Worst-Case Analysis of Heuristic Algorithms," *Management Science*, Vol. 26, No. 1, 1980, pp. 1-17.

Fleischer, G. A., *Engineering Economy: Capital Allocation Theory*, Brooks/Cole Engineering Division, Monterey, CA, 1984.

Frame, J. Davidson, *Managing Projects in Organizations*, Jossey-Bass Publishers, San Francisco, 1987.

Gallagher, C., "A Note on PERT Assumptions," *Management Science*, Vol. 33, 1987, p. 1360.

Gessner, Robert A., *Manufacturing Information Systems: Implementation Planning*, John Wiley & Sons, New York, 1984.

Gibson, John E., *Modern Management of the High-Technology Enterprise*, Prentice-Hall, Englewood Cliffs, NJ, 1990.

Gilbreath, Robert D., *Winning At Project Management: What Works, What Fails, and Why*, John Wiley, New York, 1986.

Glasser, Alan, *Research and Development Management*, Prentice-Hall, Englewood Cliffs, NJ,, 1982.

Glover, J. H., "Manufacturing Progress Functions: An Alternative Model and Its Comparison with Existing Functions," *International Journal of Production Research*, Vol. 4, No. 4, 1966, pp. 279-300.

Goldberger, Arthur S., "The Interpretation and Estimation of Cobb-Douglas Functions," *Econometrica*, Vol. 35, No. 3-4, 1968, pp. 464-472.

Golden, Bruce L., Edward A. Wasil, and Patrick T. Harker, eds., *The Analytic Hierarchy Process: Applications and Studies*, Springer-Verlag, New York, 1989.

Golenko-Ginzburg, D., "A New Approach to the Activity-Time Distribution in PERT," *Journal of Operational Research Society*, Vol. 40, No. 4, 1989a, pp. 389-393.

Golenko-Ginzburg, D., "PERT Assumptions Revisited," *OMEGA*, Vol. 17, No. 4, 1989b, pp. 393-396.

Golenko-Ginzburg, D., "On the Distribution of Activity-Time in PERT," *Journal of Operational Research Society*, Vol. 39, 1988, pp. 767-771.

Gonen, Turan, *Engineering Economy for Engineering Managers with Computer Applications*, John Wiley & Sons, New York, 1990.

Goodman, D., "A Goal Programming Approach to Aggregate Planning of Production and Work Force," *Management Science*, Vol. 20, 1974, pp. 1569-1575.

Gordon, G. and I. Pressman, *Quantitative Decision-Making for Business*, Prentice-Hall, Englewood Cliffs, NJ, 1978.

Gorenstein, Samuel, "An Algorithm for Project (Job) Sequencing with Resource Constraints," *Operations Research*, Vol. 20, July-August 1972, pp. 835-850.

Graham, Robert J., *Project Management: Combining Technical and Behavioral Approaches for Effective Implementation*, Van Nostrand Reinhold, New York, 1985.

Grant, Eugene L., W. G. Ireson, and R. S. Leavenworth, *Principles of Engineering Economy*, 7ed, John Wiley & Sons, New York, 1982.

Grubbs, F. E. "Attempts to Validate Certain PERT Statistics or 'Picking on PERT'," *Operations Research*, 10, 1962, pp. 912-915.

Gulezian, R. C., *Statistics for Decision Making*, W. B. Saunders Company, Philadelphia, 1979.

Gulledge, T. R., Jr. and L. A. Litteral, eds., *Cost Analysis Applications of Economics and Operations Research*, Springer-Verlag, New York, 1989.

Gupta, Sushil K., J. Kyparisis and Chi-Ming Ip, "Project Selection and Sequencing to Maximize Net Present Value of the Total Return," *Management Science*, Vol. 38, No. 5, May 1992, pp. 751-752.

Gutierrez, Genaro J. and P. Kouvelis, "Parkinson's Law and Its Implications for Project Management, *Management Science*, Vol. 37, No. 8, 1991, pp. 990-1001.

Hajek, V. G., *Management of Engineering Projects*, McGraw-Hill, New York, 1977.

Hajek, Victor G., *Project Engineering: Profitable Technical Program Management*, McGraw-Hill, New York, 1965.

Hall, David L. and A. Nauda, "An Interactive Approach for Selecting R & D Projects," *IEEE Transactions on Engineering Management*, Vol. 37, No. 2, 1990, pp. 126-133.

Hammill, J., L. C. T. Sallabank, and P. B. Kelly, "Management of Large Projects," *IEE Proceedings*, Vol. 137, Part A, No. 1, January 1990, pp. 55-64.

Hannan, Edward L., "The Application of Goal Programming Techniques to the CPM Problem," *Socio-Economic Planning Science*, Vol. 12, 1978, pp. 267-270.

Harhalakis, G., "Special Features of Precedence Network Charts," *European Journal of Operational Research*, Vol. 49, 1990, pp. 50-59

Harrison, F. L. *Advanced Project Management*, 2ed, John Wiley & Sons, New York, 1985.

Healy, Thomas L., "Activity Subdivision and PERT Probability Statements," *Operations Research*, Vol. 9, 1962, pp. 341-348.

Hess, S. W., "A Dynamic Programming Approach to RandD Budgeting and Project Selection," *IEEE Transactions on Engineering Management*, EM-9, 1962, pp. 170-199.

Hicks, Philip E., *Introduction to Industrial Engineering and Management Science*, McGraw-Hill, New York, 1977.

Hillier, Frederick S. and Gerald J. Lieberman, *Operations Research*, 2ed, Holden-Day, San Francisco, 1974.

Hindelang, T. J. and J. F. Muth, "A Dynamic Programming Algorithm for Decision CPM Networks," *Operations Research*, Vol. 27, No. 2, 1979, pp. 225-241.

Hines, William W. and Douglas C. Montgomery, *Probability and Statistics in Engineering and Management Science*, 2ed, John Wiley & Sons, NY, 1980.

Hirshleifer, J., "Investment Decision under Uncertainty: Choice-Theoretic Approaches," *Quarterly Journal of Economics*, Vol. 79, No. 4, 1965, pp. 509-536.

Hoffman, Thomas R., *Production Management and Manufacturing Systems*, Wadsworth Publishing Co., Inc., Belmont, CA, 1967.

Hogg, Robert V. and J. Ledolter, *Applied Statistics for Engineers and Physical Scientists*, Macmillan Publishing Co., New York, 1992.

Holloway, C. A., R. T. Nelson, and V. Suraphongschai, "Comparison of a Multi-Pass Heuristic Decomposition Procedure with Other Resource-Constrained Project Scheduling Procedures," *Management Science*, Vol. 25, September 1979, pp. 862-872.

House, Ruth Sizemore, *The Human Side of Project Management*, Addison-Wesley, Reading, MA, 1988.

Howell, Sydney D., "Learning Curves for New Products," *Industrial Marketing Management*, Vol. 9, No. 2, 1980, pp. 97-99.

Hribar, John P., "Development of an Engineering Manager," *Journal of Management in Engineering*, Vol. 1, 1985, pp. 36-41.

Humphreys, Kenneth K., ed., *Project and Cost Engineer's Handbook*, 2ed, Marcel Dekker, Inc., 1984.

Ignizio, J. P., *Goal Programming and Extensions*, D. C. Heath and Company, Lexington, MA, 1976.

Izuchukwu, John I., "Shortening the Critical Path," *Mechanical Engineering*, February 1990, pp. 59-60.

Jelen, Frederic C. and James H. Black, *Cost and Optimization Engineering*, McGraw-Hill, New York, 1983.

Jennett, Eric, "Guidelines for Successful Project Management," *Chemical Engineering*, July 1973, pp. 70-82.

Jewell, William S., "A Generalized Framework for Learning Curve Reliability Growth Models," *Operations Research*, Vol. 32, No. 3, May-June, 1984, pp. 547-558.

Johnson, George A. and C. D. Schou, "Expediting Projects in PERT with Stochastic Time Estimates," *Project Management Journal*, Vol. 21, No. 2, 1990, pp. 29-34.

Johnson, James R., "Advanced Project Control," *Journal of Systems Management*, Vol. 28, No. 5, May 1977, pp. 24-27.

Johnson, L. A. and D. C. Montgomery, *Operations Research in Production, Scheduling, and Inventory Control*, John Wiley & Sons, New York, 1974.

Johnson, R. and P. Winn, *Quantitative Methods for Management*, Houghton Mifflin, Boston, 1976.

Johnson, R. A., F. E. Kast, and J. A. Rosenzweig, *The Theory and Management of Systems*, 2ed, McGraw-Hill, New York, 1967.

Johnson, T. J. R., *An Algorithm for the Resource-Constrained Project Scheduling Problem*, Ph.D. Thesis, MIT, 1967.

Juran, J. M. and Frank M. Gryna, Jr., *Quality Planning and Analysis*, 2ed, McGraw-Hill, New York, 1980.

Kaimann, R. A., "Coefficient of Network Complexity: Erratum," *Management Science*, Vol. 21, No. 10, 1975, pp. 1211-1212.

Kaimann, R. A., "Coefficient of Network Complexity," *Management Science*, Vol. 21, No. 2, 1974, pp. 172-177.

Keeney, R. L. and H. Raiffa, *Decisions with Multiple Objectives: Preferences and Value Tradeoffs*, John Wiley & Sons, New York, 1976.

Keller, Robert T., "Project Group Performance in Research and Development Organizations," *Academy of Management Proceedings*, San Diego, CA, Aug. 11-14, 1985, pp. 315-318.

Kelley, Albert J., ed., *New Dimensions of Project Management*, Lexington Books, Lexington, MA, 1982.

Kelley, James E., "Critical Path Planning and Scheduling: Mathematical Basis," *Operations Research*, Vol. 9, No. 3, 1961, pp. 296-320.

Kerridge, Arthur E. and Charles H. Vervalin, eds., *Engineering and Construction Project Management*, Gulf Publishing Company, Houston, TX, 1986.

Kerzner, Harold *Project Management: A Systems Approach to Planning, Scheduling, and Controlling*, 3ed, Van Nostrand Reinhold, New York, 1989.

Kerzner, Harold, *Project Management Operating Guidelines: Directives, Procedures, and Forms*, Van Nostrand Reinhold, New York, 1986.

Kezsbom, Deborah S., Donald L. Schilling, and Katherine A. Edward, *Dynamic Project Management: A Practical Guide for Managers and Engineers*, John Wiley & Sons, New York, 1989.

Khorramshahgol, Reza, H. Azani, and Y. Gousty, "An Integrated Approach to Project Evaluation and Selection," *IEEE Transactions on Engineering Management*, Vol. 35, No. 4, 1988, pp. 265-270.

Kim, C., *Quantitative Analysis for Managerial Decisions*, Addison-Wesley, Reading, MA, 1976.

Kimmons, Robert L. and James H. Loweree, *Project Management: A Reference for Professionals*, Marcel Dekker, New York, 1989.

Knutson, Joan and Ira Bitz, *Project Management: How to Plan and Manage Successful Projects*, American Management Association, New York, 1991.

Koenig, Michael H., "Management Guide to Resource Scheduling," *Journal of Systems Management*, Vol. 29, January 1978, pp. 24-29.

Koopmans, Tjalling C., ed., *Activity Analysis of Production and Allocation*, John Wiley & Sons, New York, 1951.

Kornbluth, J. S., "A Survey of Goal Programming," *Omega*, April 1973, pp. 193-206.

Kuhn, H. W., "Variants of the Hungarian Method for the Assignment Problem," *Naval Research Logistics Quarterly*, Vol. 3, 1956, pp. 253-258.

Kuhn, H. W., "The Hungarian Method for the Assignment Problem," *Naval Research Logistics Quarterly*, Vol. 2, 1955, pp. 83-97.

Kume, Hitoshi, *Statistical Methods for Quality Improvement*, Quality Resources, White Plains, NY, 1987.

Kurtulus, I. S. and E. W. Davis, "Multi-Project Scheduling: Categorization of Heuristic Rules Performace," *Management Science*, Vol. 28, February 1982, Vol. 161-172.

Lapin, L., *QuickQuant+: Decision Making Software*, Alamo Publishing Company, Pleasanton, CA, 1991.

Lapin, L., *Statistics for Modern Business Decisions*, 2ed, Harcourt Brace Jovanovich, New York, 1978.

Lapin, L., *Quantitative Management for Business Decisions*, Harcourt Brace Jovanovich, New York, 1976.

Lawrence, Kenneth D. and S. H. Zanakis, *Production Planning and Scheduling: Mathematical Programming Applications*, Industrial Engineering and Management Press, Norcross, GA, 1984.

Lee, Sang M., *Goal Programming Methods for Multiple Objective Integer Programs*, OR Monograph Series No. 2, Institute of Industrial Engineers, Norcross, GA, 1979.

Lee, Sang M., *Goal Programming for Decision Analysis*, Auerbach Publishers, Philadelphia, 1972.

Lee, Sang M. and E. R. Clayton, "A Goal Programming Model for Academic Resource Allocation," *Management Science*, Vol. 18, No. 8, 1972, pp. B395-B408.

Lee, Sang M. and H. B. Eom, "A Multi-Criteria Approach to Formulating International Project-Financing Strategies," *Journal of Operational Research Society*, Vol. 40, No. 6, 1989, pp. 519-528.

Levin, R. and C. Kirkpatrick, *Quantitative Approaches to Management*, 4ed, McGraw-Hill, New York, 1978.

Levine, Harvey A., *Project Management Using Microcomputers*, Osborne McGraw-Hill, New York, 1986.

Liao, W. M., "Effects of Learning on Resource Allocation Decisions," *Decision Sciences*, Vol. 10, 1979, pp. 116-125.

Liberatore, Matthew J., "An Extension of the Analytic Hierarchy Process for Industrial RandD Project Selection and Resource Allocation," *IEEE Transactions on Engineering Management*, Vol. EM34, No. 1, 1987, pp. 12-18.

Liepins, Gunar E. and V. R. R. Uppuluri, eds., *Data Quality Control*, Marcel Dekker, Inc., New York, 1990.

Lighthall, Frederick F., "Launching the Space Shuttle Challenger: Disciplinary Deficiencies in the Analysis of Engineering Data," *IEEE Transactions on Engineering Management*, Vol. 38, No. 1, 1991, pp. 63-74.

Lillrank, Paul and Noriaki Kano, *Continuous Improvement: Quality Control Circles in Japanese Industry*, Center for Japanese Studies, The University of Michigan, Ann Arbor, MI, 1989.

Little, J. D., G. Marty, D. W. Sweeney, and C. Karel, "An Algorithm for the Travelling Salesman Problem," *Operations Research*, Vol. 11, 1963, pp. 972-989.

Littlefield, T. K., Jr. and P. H. Randolph, "An Answer to Sasieni's Question on PERT Times," *Management Science*, Vol. 33, 1987, pp. 1357-1359.

Love, Sydney F., *Achieving Problem Free Project Management*, John Wiley & Sons, New York, 1989.

MacCrimmon, Kenneth R. and Charles A. Ryavec, "An Analytical Study of the PERT Assumptions," *Operations Research*, Vol. 12, 1964, pp. 16-21.

Machina, M. J., "Decision-Making in the Presence of Risk," *Science*, Vol. 236, May 1987, pp. 537-543.

Mackie, Dan, *Engineering Management of Capital Projects: A Practical Guide*, McGraw-Hill Ryerson Ltd., Toronto, 1984.

Malcomb, D. G., J. H. Roseboom, C. E. Clark, and W. Fazar, "Application of a Technique for Research and Development Program Evaluation," *Operations Research*, Vol. 7, No. 5, 1959, pp. 646-699.

Malstrom, Eric M., *What Every Engineer Should Know About Manufacturing Cost Estimating*, Marcel Dekker, Inc., New York, 1981.

Marshall, G., T. J. Barber, and J. T. Boardman, "Methodology for Modelling a Project Management Control Environment," *IEEE Proceeding-D: Control Theory and Applications*, Vol. 134, Part D, No. 4, July 1987, pp. 278-285.

McBride, William J. and Charles W. McClelland, "PERT and the Beta Distribution," *IEEE Transactions on Engineering Management*, Vol. EM-14, 1967, pp. 166-169.

McIntyre, E. V., "Cost-Volume-Profit Analysis Adjusted for Learning," *Management Science*, Vol. 24, No. 2, 1977, pp. 149-160.

Melcher, Bonita H. and Harold Kerzner, *Strategic Planning Development and Implementation*, TAB Professional and Reference Books, Blue Ridge Summit, PA, 1988.

Meredith, Jack R., ed., *Justifying New Manufacturing Technology*, Industrial Engineering and Management Press, Norcross, GA, 1986.

Meredith, Jack R. and Samuel L. Mantel, Jr., *Project Management: A Managerial Approach*, 2ed, John Wiley & Sons, New York, 1989.

Meredith, Jack R. and Nallan C. Suresh, "Justification Techniques for Advanced Manufacturing Technologies," *International Journal of Production Research*, September-October, Vol. 24, No. 5, 1986, pp. 1043-1058.

Merino, Donald N., "Developing Economic and Noneconomic Models Incentives to Select Among Technical Alternatives," *The Engineering Economist*, Vol. 34, No. 4, Summer 1989, pp. 275-290.

Metzger, Philip W., *Managing Programming People: A Personal View*, Prentice-Hall, Englewood Cliffs, NJ, 1987.

Michaels, Jack V. and William P. Wood, *Design to Cost*, John Wiley & Sons, New York, 1989.

Miller, David M. and J. W. Schmidt, *Industrial Engineering and Operations Research*, John Wiley & Sons, New York, 1984.

Miller, Irwin and John E. Freund, *Probability and Statistics for Engineers*, 2ed, Prentice-Hall, Englewood Cliffs, NJ, 1977.

Miller, Jule A. *From Idea To Profit: Managing Advanced Manufacturing Technology*, Van Nostrand Reinhold, 1986.

Mizuno, Shigeru, ed., *Management for Quality Improvement*, Quality Resources, White Plains, NY, 1988.

Moder, Joseph J., Cecil R. Phillips, and Edward W. Davis, *Project Management with CPM, PERT and Precedence Diagramming*, 3ed, Van Nostrand Reinhold, New York, 1983.

Moder, Joseph J. and E. G. Rodgers, "Judgment Estimates of the Moments of PERT Type Distributions," *Management Science*, Vol. 15, 1968, pp. B76-B83.

Moffat, Donald W., *Handbook of Manufacturing and Production Management Formulas, Charts, and Tables*, Prentice-Hall, Englewood Cliffs, NJ, 1987.

Mohring, Rolf H., "Minimizing Costs of Resource Requirements in Project Networks Subject to Fixed Completion Time," *Operations Research*, Vol. 32, No. 1, 1984, pp. 89-120.

Monden, Yasuhiro, R. Shibakawa, S. Takayanagi, and T. Nagao, *Innovations in Management: The Japanese Corporation*, Industrial Engineering and Management Press, Norcross, GA, 1985.

Moodie, C. L. and H. H. Young, "A Heuristic Method of Assembly Line Balancing for Assumptions of Constant or Variable Work Element Times," *Journal of Industrial Engineering*, Vol. 26, No. 1, 1965, pp. 23-29.

Moore, Laurence J., B. W. Taylor III, E. R. Clayton, and Sang M. Lee, "Analysis of a Multi-Criteria Project Crashing Model," *AIIE Transactions*, June 1978, pp. 163-169.

Mueller, Frederick W., *Integrated Cost and Schedule Control for Construction Projects*, Van Nostrand Reinhold, New York, 1986.

Mukherjee, S. P. and A. K. Chattopadhyay, "A Stochastic Analysis of a Staffing Problem," *Journal of Operational Research Society*, Vol. 40, No. 5, 1989, pp. 489-494.

Mustafa, Mohammad A. and Jamal F. Al-Bahar, "Project Risk Assessment Using the Analytic Hierarchy Process," *IEEE Transactions on Engineering Management*, Vol. 38, No. 1, 1991, pp. 46-52.

Mustafa, Mohammed A. and E. Lile Murphree, "A Multicriteria Decision Support Approach for Project Compression," *Project Management Journal*, Vol. 20, No. 2, June 1989, pp. 29-34.

Nanda, Ravinder, "Using Learning Curves in Integration of Production Resources," *Proceedings of 1979 IIE Fall Conference*, 1979, pp. 376-380.

Navon, Ronie, "Financial Planning in a Project-Oriented Industry," *Project Management Journal*, Vol. 21, No. 1, 1990, pp. 43-48.

Nelson, C. A., "A Scoring Model for Flexible Manufacturing Systems Project Selection," *European Journal of Operations Research*, Vol. 24, No. 3, 1986, pp. 346-359.

Nelson, Charles R., *Applied Times Series Analysis for Mangerial Forecasting*, Holden-Day, Inc., San Francisco, 1973.

Newman, William H., E. K. Warren, and A. R. McGill, *The Process of Management: Strategy, Action, Results*, Prentice-Hall, Englewood Cliffs, NJ, 1987.

Newnan, Donald G., *Engineering Economic Analysis*, 4ed, Engineering Press, Inc., San Jose, CA, 1991.

Noori, Hamid, *Managing the Dynamics of New Technology: Issues in Manufacturing Management*, Prentice-Hall, Englewood Cliffs, NJ, 1990.

Noori, Hamid and R. W. Radford, *Readings and Cases in the Management of New Technology: An Operations Perspective*, Prentice-Hall, Englewood Cliffs, NJ, 1990.

O'Brien, James J., *CPM in Construction Management*, 3ed, McGraw-Hill, New York, 1984.

Obradovitch, M. M. and S. E. Stephanou, *Project Management: Risks and Productivity*, Daniel Spencer Publishers, Malibu, CA, 1990.

Oral, M., O. Kettani, and P. Lang, "A Methodology for Collective Evaluation and Selection of Industrial RandD Projects," *Management Science*, Vol. 37, No. 7, 1991, pp. 871-885.

Orczyk, Joseph J. and Luh-Maan Chang, "Parametric Regression Model for Project Scheduling," *Project Management Journal*, Vol. 22, No. 4, 1991, pp. 41-47.

Ostle, Bernard and George P. Steck, "Correlation Between Sample Means and Sample Ranges," *Journal of American Statistical Association*, Vol. 54, 1959, pp. 465-471.

Ostwald, Phillip F., *Cost Estimating for Engineering and Management*, Prentice-Hall, Englewood Cliffs, NJ, 1974.

Ozden, Mufit, "A Dynamic Planning Technique for Continuous Activities Under Multiple Resource Constraints," *Management Science*, Vol. 33, No. 10, 1987, pp. 1333-1347.

Park, Chan S. and Gunter P. Sharp-Bette, *Advanced Engineering Economics*, John Wiley & Sons, NY, 1990.

Park, Chan S. and Young K. Son, "An Economic Evaluation Model for Advanced Manufacturing Systems," *The Engineering Economist*, Vol. 34, No. 1, Fall 1988, pp. 1-26.

Patterson, J. H., "Comparison of Exact Approaches for Solving Multiconstrained Resource Project Scheduling," *Management Science*, Vol. 30, No. 7, 1984, pp. 854-867.

Patterson, J. H. and W. D. Huber, "A Horizon-varying, Zero-one Approach to Project Scheduling," *Management Science*, Vol. 20, No. 6, 1974, pp. 990-998.

Patterson, James H., "Project Scheduling: The Effects of Problem Structure on Heuristic Performance," *Naval Research Logistics Quarterly*, Vol. 23, No. 1, 1976, pp. 95-123.

Patterson, James H., F. Brian Talbot, Roman Slowinski, and Jan Weglarz, "Computational Experience with a Backtracking Algorithm for Solving a General Class of Precedence and Resource-Constrained Scheduling Problems," *European Journal of Operational Research*, Vol. 49, 1990, pp. 68-79.

Patterson, James H. and G. W. Roth, "Scheduling a Project Under Multiple Resource Constraints: A Zero-One Programming Approach," *AIIE Transactions*, Vol. 8, No. 4, December 1976, pp. 449-455.

Pegels, Carl C., "Start Up or Learning Curves - Some New Approaches," *Decision Sciences*, Vol. 7, No. 4, Oct. 1976, pp. 705-713.

Pegels, Carl C., "On Startup or Learning Curves: An Expanded View," *AIIE Transactions*, Vol. 1, No. 3, September 1969, pp. 216-222.

Phillips, Don T. and A. Garcia-Diaz, *Fundamentals of Network Analysis*, Prentice-Hall, Englewood Cliffs, NJ, 1981.

Phillips, Don T. and G. L. Hogg, "Stochastic Network Analysis with Resource Constraints, Cost Parameters and Queueing Capabilities Using GERTS Methodologies," *Computers and Industrial Engineering*, Vol. 1, 1976, pp. 13-25.

Pienar, A. et al., "An Evaluation Model for Quantifying System Value," *IIE Transactions*, Vol. 18, No. 1, March 1986, pp. 10-15.

Pitts, Carl E., "For Project Managers: An Inquiry into the Delicate Art and Science of Influencing Others," *Project Management Journal*, Vol. 21, No. 1, 1990, pp. 21-23, 42.

Pritsker, A. B., L. J. Walters, and P. M. Wolfe, "Multi-Project Scheduling with Limited Resources: A Zero-One Programming Approach," *Management Science*, Vol. 16, Septemeber 1969.

Quinn, James Brian, "Managing Innovation: Controlled Chaos," *Harvard Business Review*, May-June, 1985, pp. 73-84.

Ravindran, A., Don T. Phillips, and James J. Solberg, *Operations Research: Principles and Practice*, 2ed, John Wiley & Sons, New York, 1987.

Reinfeld, N. V. and W. R. Vogel, *Mathematical Programming*, Prentice-Hall, Englewood Cliffs, N.J., 1958.

Render, Barry and Ralph M. Stair, Jr., *Quantitative Analysis for Management*, 3ed, Allyn and Bacon, Inc., Needham, MA, 1988.

Richardson, Wallace J., "Use of Learning Curves to Set Goals and Monitor Progress in Cost Reduction Programs," *Proceedings of 1978 IIE Spring Conference*, 1978, pp. 235-239.

Riggs, James L. and Thomas M. West, *Engineering Economics*, 3ed, McGraw-Hill, New York, 1986.

Roman, Daniel D., *Managing Projects: A Systems Approach*, Elsevier Science Publishing Co., Inc., New York, 1986.

Ronen, David, "Allocation of Trips to Trucks Operating from a Single Terminal," *Computers and Operations Research*, Vol. 19, No. 5, 1992, pp. 445-451.

Rosenau, M. D., Jr., *Successful Project Management*, Lifetime Learning Publications, Belmont, CA, 1981.

Rosenau, Milton D., Jr., *Project Management for Engineers*, Lifetime Learning Publications, Belmon, CA, 1984.

Rothkopf, Michael H., "Scheduling with Random Service Times," *Management Science*, Vol. 12, No. 9, 1966, pp. 707-713.

Ruefli, T., "A Generalized Goal Decomposition Model," *Management Science*, Vol. 17, April 1971, pp. B505-B518.

Ruskin, Arnold M. and W. Eugene Estes, *What Every Engineer Should Know About Project Management*, Marcel Dekker, New York, 1982.

Russell, Edward J., "Extension of Dantzig's Algorithm to Finding an Initial Near-Optimal Basis for the Transportation Problem," *Operations Research*, Vol. 17, 1969, pp. 187-191.

Russell, Robert A., "A Comparison of Heuristics for Scheduling Projects with Cash Flows and Resource Restrictions," *Management Science*, Vol. 32, No. 10, Oct. 1986, pp. 1291-1300.

Saaty, Thomas L., *The Analytic Hierarchy Process*, McGraw-Hill, New York, 1980.

Saaty, Thomas L., "A Scaling Method for Priorities in Hierarchical Structures," *Journal of Mathematical Psychology*, Vol. 15, June 1977, pp. 235-281.

Samaras, Thomas T. and Kim Yensuang, *Computerized Project Management Techniques for Manufacturing and Construction Industries*, Prentice-Hall, NJ, 1979.

Sasieni, M. W., "A Note on PERT Times," *Management Science*, Vol. 32, No. 12, 1986, pp. 1652-1653.

Sathi, Arvind, T. E. Morton, and Steven F. Roth, "Callisto: An Intelligent Project Management System," *AI Magazine*, Winter 1986, pp. 34-52.

Scheer, A. W., *Enterprise-Wide Data Modelling: Information Systems in Industry*, Springer-Verlag, New York, 1989.

Schneider, Kenneth C. and C. R. Byers, *Quantitative Management: A Self-Teaching Guide*, John Wiley & Sons, New York, 1979.

Schultz, R. L., D. P. Slevin, and J. K. Pinto, "Strategy and Tactics in a Process Model of Project Implementation," *Interfaces*, May-June, 1987.

Schwartz, S. L. and I. Vertinsky, "Multi-Attribute Investment Decisions: A Study of RandD Project Selection," *Management Science*, Vol. 24, 1977, pp. 285-301.

Sharda, Ramesh, "Linear Programming Software for Personal Computers: 1992 Survey," *OR/MS Today*, Vol. 19, No. 3, June 1992, pp. 44-60.

Shtub, A., "Scheduling of Programs with Repetitive Projects," *Project Management Journal*, Vol. 22, No. 4, 1991, pp. 49-53.

Silver, Edward A. and Rein Peterson, *Decision Systems for Inventory Management and Production Planning*, 2ed, John Wiley & Sons, New York, 1985.

Silverman, Melvin, *Project Management: A Short Course for Professionals*, 2ed, John Wiley & Sons, New York, 1988.

Silverman, Melvin, *The Art of Managing Technical Projects*, Prentice-Hall, NJ, 1987.

Simon, H. A., *The New Science of Management Decision*, rev. ed., Prentice-Hall, Englewood Cliffs, NJ, 1977.

Slowinski, R., "Two Approaches to Problems of Resource Allocation Among Project Activities: A Comparative Study," *Journal of the Operational Research Society*, Vol. 31, August 1980, pp. 711-723.

Smith, David E., *Quantitative Business Analysis*, John Wiley & Sons, New York, 1977.

Smith, Jason, *Learning Curve for Cost Control*, Industrial Engineering and Management Press, Norcross, GA, 1989.

Smith-Daniels, D. E. and N. J. Aquilano, "Constrained Resource Project Scheduling Subject to Material Constraints," *Journal of Operations Management*, Vol. 4, No. 4, 1980, pp. 369-388.

Smunt, Timothy L., "A Comparison of Learning Curve Analysis and Moving Average Ratio Analysis for Detailed Operational Planning," *Decision Sciences*, Vol. 17, 1986.

Somansundaram, S. and Adedeji B. Badiru, "Project Management for Successful Implementation of Continuous Quality Improvement," *International Journal of Project Management*, Vol. 10, No. 2, May 1992, pp. 89-101

Spinner, M., *Elements of Project Management: Plan, Schedule, and Control*, Prentice-Hall, Englewood Cliffs, NJ, 1981.

Sprague, J. C. and J. D. Whittaker, *Economic Analysis for Engineers and Managers*, Prentice-Hall, Englewood Cliffs, NJ, 1986.

Stark, Robert M. and Robery H. Mayer, Jr., *Quantitative Construction Management: Uses of Linear Optimization*, John Wiley & Sons, New York, 1983.

Steiner, Henry M., *Engineering Economic Principles*, McGraw-Hill, New York, 1992.

Steiner, Henry M., *Basic Engineering Economy*, Books Associates, Glen Echo, MD, 1988.

Stephanou, S. E. and M. M. Obradovitch, *Project Management: System Developments and Productivity*, Daniel Spencer Publishers, Malibu, CA, 1985.

Stevens, G. T., Jr., *Economic and Financial Analysis of Capital Investments*, John Wiley & Sons, New York, 1979.

Stinson, J. P., E. W. Davis, and B. M. Khumawala, "Multiple Resource-Constrained Scheduling Using Branch and Bound," *AIIE Transactions* Vol. 10, No. 3, September 1978, pp. 252-259.

Stuckenbruck, Linn C., "The Matrix Organization," *Project Management Quarterly*, September 1979.

Stuckenbruck, Linn C., ed., *The Implementation of Project Management: The Professional's Handbook*, Addison-Wesley Publishing Co., New York, 1981.

Sule, D. R., "The Effect of Alternate Periods of Learning and Forgetting on Economic Manufacturing Quantity," *AIIE Transactions*, Vol. 10, No. 3, 1978, pp. 338-343.

Swalm, Ralph O. and J. L. Lopez-Leautaud, *Engineering Economic Analysis: A Future Wealth Approach*, John Wiley & Sons, New York, 1984.

Taguchi, Genichi, *Introduction to Quality Engineering: Designing Quality into Products and Processes*, Quality Resources, White Plains, NY, 1986.

Taha, Hamdy A., *Operations Research: An Introduction*, 3ed, Macmillan, New York, 1982.

Talbot, F. B., "Project Scheduling with Resource-Duration Interactions: The Nonpreemptive Case," *Management Science*, Vol. 28, No. 10, 1982, pp. 1197-1210.

Talbot, F. B., "Resource-Constrained Project Scheduling with Time-Resource Tradeoffs: The Nonpreemptive Case," *Management Science*, Vol. 28, No. 10, October 1982, pp. 1197-1209.

Talbot, F. B. and J. H. Patterson, "An Efficient Integer Programming Algorithm with Network Cuts for Solving Resource-Constrained Scheduling Problems," *Management Science*, Vol. 28, No. 11, July 1978, pp. 1163-1174.

Taylor, Frederick, W., *Scientific Management*, Harper and Row Publishers, Inc., New York, 1911.

Thesen, Arne, *Computer Methods in Operations Research*, Academic Press, New York, 1978.

Thesen, Arne, "Heuristic Scheduling of Activities Under Resource and Precedence Restrictions," *Management Science*, Vol. 23, No. 4, December 1976, pp. 412-422.

Thierauf, R. J., *An Introductory Approach to Operations Research*, John Wiley & Sons, New York, 1978.

Tingley, Kim M. and Judith S. Liebman, "A Goal Programming Example in Public Health Resource Allocation," *Management Science*, Vol. 30, No. 3, March 1984, pp. 279-289.

Toelle, Richard A. and J. Witherspoon, "From 'Managing the Critical Path' to 'Managing Critical Activities'," *Project Management Journal*, Vol. 21, No. 4, 1990, pp. 33-36.

Towill, D. R. and U. Kaloo, "Productivity Drift in Extended Learning Curves," *Omega*, Vol. 6, No. 4, 1978, pp. 295-304.

Traylor, Robert C., R. C. Stinson, J. L. Madsen, R. S. Bell, and K. R. Brown, "Project Management Under Uncertainty," *Project Management Journal*, March 1984, pp. 66-75.

Troutt, Marvin D., "On the Generality of the PERT Average Time Formula," *Decision Sciences*, Summer 1989, No. 3, pp. 410-412.

Troxler, Joel W. and Leland Blank, "A Comprehensive Methodology for Manufacturing System Evaluation and Comparison," *Journal of Manufacturing Systems*, Vol. 8, No. 3, 1989, pp. 176-183.

Tsubakitani, Shigeru and Richard F. Deckro, "A Heuristic for Multi-Project Scheduling with Limited Resources in the Housing Industry," *European Journal of Operational Research*, Vol. 49, 1990, pp. 80-91.

Tushman, Michael L. and W. L. Moore, eds., *Readings in the Management of Innovation*, Ballinger Publishing Co., Cambridge, MA, 1988.

Van Slyke, Richard M., "Monte Carlo Methods and the PERT Problem," *Operations Research*, 11, 1963, pp. 839-860.

Verma, H. L. and C. W. Gross, *Introduction to Quantitative Methods: A Managerial Approach*, John Wiley & Sons, New York, 1978.

Villeda, R. and B. V. Dean, "On the Optimal Safe Allocation and Scheduling of a Work Force in a Toxic Substance Environment," *IEEE Transactions on Engineering Management*, Vol. 37, No. 2, 1990, pp. 95-101.

Wagner, Harvey M., *Principles of Operations Research*, Prentice-Hall, Englewood Cliffs, NJ, 1969.

Waller, Eugene W. and Thomas J. Dwyer, "Alternative Techniques for Use in Parametric Cost Analysis," *Concepts - Journal of Defense Systems Acquisition Management*, Vol. 4, No. 2, Spring 1981, pp. 48-59.

Weglarz, J., J. Blazewicz, W. Cellary, and R. Slowinski, "An Automatic Revised Simplex Method for Constrained Resource Network Scheduling," *ACM Transactions on Mathematical Software*, Vol. 3, No. 3, 1977, pp. 295-300.

Weglarz, Jan, "Project Scheduling with Continuously-Divisible, Doubly Constrained Resources," *Management Science*, Vol. 27, No. 9, September 1981, pp. 1040-1053.

Welsh, D. J., "Errors Introduced by a PERT Assumption," *Operational Research*, Vol. 13, 1965, pp. 141-143.

White, John A., Marvin H. Agee, and Kenneth E. Case, *Principles of Engineering Economic Analysis*, 3cd, John Wiley & Sons, NY, 1989.

Whitehouse, G. E. and J. R. Brown, "GENRES: An Extension of Brooks' Algorithm for Project Scheduling With Resource Constraints," *Computers and Industrial Engineering*, Vol. 3, No. 4, December 1979, pp. 261-268.

Whitehouse, Gary E., "A Comparison of Computer Search Heuristics to Analyze Activity/Networks with Limited Resources," *Project Management Journal*, June 1983, pp. 35-39.

Whitehouse, Gary E., *Systems Analysis and Design Using Network Techniques*, Prentice-Hall, Englewood Cliffs, NJ, 1973.

Whitehouse, Gary E. and Ben L. Wechler, *Applied Operations Research: A Survey*, John Wiley & Sons, New York, 1976.

Wiest, J. D, "Some Properties of Schedules for Large Projects with Limited Resources," *Operations Research*, Vol. 3, 1964, pp. 395-418.

Wiest, Jerome D., "Precedence Diagramming Methods: Some Unusual Characteristics and Their Implications for Project Managers," *Journal of Operations Management*, Vol. 1, No. 3, February 1981, pp. 121-130.

Wiest, Jerome D., "A Heuristic Model for Scheduling Large Projects with Limited Resources," *Management Science*, Vol. 13, February 1967, pp. B-359-B377.

Wiest, Jerome D. and F. K. Levy, *A Management Guide to PERT/CPM With GERT/PDM/DCPM and Other Networks*, 2ed, Prentice-Hall, Englewood Cliffs, NJ, 1977.

Willborn, Walter, *Quality Management System: A Planning and Auditing Guide*, Industrial Press, Inc., New York, 1989.

Wit, Jan De and Willy Herroelen, "An Evaluation of Microcomputer-Based Software Packages for Project Management," *European Journal of Operational Research*, Vol. 49, 1990, pp. 102-139.

Womer, Norman K., "Estimating Learning Curves from Aggregate Monthly Data," *Management Science*, Vol. 30, No. 8, 1984, pp. 982-992.

Womer, Norman K., "Learning Curves, Production Rate, and Program Costs," *Management Science*, Vol. 25, No. 4, 1979, pp. 312-319.

Woodworth, B. M. and C. T. Willie, "A Heuristic Algorithm for Resource Leveling in Multi-Project, Multi-Resource Scheduling," *Decision Sciences*, Vol. 6, 1975, pp. 525-540.

Wright, T. P., "Factors Affecting the Cost of Airplanes," *Journal of Aeronautical Science*, Vol. 3, No. 2, February 1936, pp. 122-128.

Wu, Nesa and Richard Coppins, *Linear Programming and Extensions*, McGraw-Hill, New York, 1981.

Yelle, Louis E., "Adding Life Cycles to Learning Curves," *Long Range Planning*, Vol. 16, No. 6, December 1983, pp. 82-87.

Yelle, Louis E., "The Learning Curve: Historical Review and Comprehensive Survey," *Decision Sciences*, Vol. 10, No. 2, April 1979, pp. 302-328.

Yelle, Louis E., "Estimating Learning Curves for Potential Products," *Industrial Marketing Management*, Vol. 5, No. 2/3, June 1976, pp. 147-154.

Yunus, Nordin B., D. L. Babcock, and C. O. Benjamin, "Development of a Knowledge-Based Schedule Planning System," *Project Management Journal*, Vol. 21, No. 4, 1990, pp. 39-45.

Zaloom, Victor, "On the Resource Constrained Project Scheduling Problem," *AIIE Transactions*, Vol. 3, No. 4, December 1971, pp. 302-305.

INDEX

About the Author

ADEDEJI BADUNDE BADIRU is an associate professor of industrial engineering at the University of Oklahoma. He received his BS degree in Industrial Engineering, MS in Mathematics, and MS in Industrial Engineering from Tennessee Tech University. He received his Ph.D. degree in Industrial Engineering from the University of Central Florida. He has authored several technical papers and books including *Project Management in Manufacturing and High Technology Operations* (1988), *Computer Tools, Models, and Techniques for Project Management* (1989), *Project Management Tools for Engineering and Management Professionals* (1991), and *Expert Systems Applications in Engineering and Manufacturing* (1992). He is a member of IIE, SME, TIMS, ORSA, PMI, and AAAI. He has conducted project management training programs for several organizations including AT&T, Sony, Institute of Industrial Engineers, Tinker Air Force Base, and China Productivity Center.